CPAG's

CW00474217

Child Supp

The Legislation

Ninth edition

2009/2010

Supplement

Commentary by
Edward Jacobs *Barrister and Upper Tribunal Judge*

Statutory instruments up to date to **6 April 2010**

Published by CPAG, 94 White Lion Street, London N1 9PF

CPAG promotes action for the prevention and relief of poverty among children and families with children. To achieve this, CPAG aims to raise awareness of the causes, extent, nature and impact of poverty, and strategies for its eradication and prevention; bring about positive policy changes for families with children in poverty; and enable those eligible for income maintenance to have access to their full entitlement. If you are not already supporting us, please consider making a donation, or ask for details of our membership schemes, training courses and publications.

Published by Child Poverty Action Group
94 White Lion Street, London N1 9PF
Tel: 020 7837 7979
staff@cpag.org.uk
www.cpag.org.uk

© Child Poverty Action Group 2010

A CIP record for this book is available from the British Library

Main work: ISBN 978 1 906076 25 2
Supplement: ISBN 978 1 906076 48 1

Child Poverty Action Group is a charity registered in England and Wales (registration number 294841) and in Scotland (registration number SC039339), and is a company limited by guarantee, registered in England (registration number 1993854). VAT number: 690 808117

Design by Devious Designs
Cover photograph by David Mansell/reportdigital.co.uk
Typeset by David Lewis XML Associates Limited
Printed in the UK by CPI William Clowes

Preface

It is always wise to do three things. To do fewer suggests lack of effort. To do more suggests over exertion. With that in mind, I have set three objectives for this supplement.

The first objective is to update the commentaries. In that regard, I am grateful to those who have drawn my attention to those things that I have done or left undone. Helen Robinson, one of the registrars to the Administrative Appeals Chamber, deserves a special mention. She took the unusual approach of not only pointing out what was wrong, but telling me how to correct it. That is a model to follow.

The second objective is to include new legislation. That includes the inevitably amendments, provisions now brought into force, and the Child Support (Management of Payments and Arrears) Regulations 2009, with commentary.

The third objective is to include the Child Support (Maintenance Assessments and Special Cases) Regulations 1992 that were omitted from the main volume. The text of the legislation has been brought up to date, as have the commentaries.

The Noter-up section takes account of developments known to me at the beginning of July 2010. Since then, the Court of Appeal has given its judgment in *R (Cart) v the Upper Tribunal, the Secretary of State for Justice, the Child Maintenance and Enforcement Commission, Cart and the Public Law Project* [2010] EWCA Civ 859. This deals with the scope of judicial review of decisions of the Upper Tribunal. The Court dismissed the appeal against the decision of the Divisional Court, which is included in the commentary to section 13(8) of the Tribunals, Courts and Enforcement Act 2007. However, it defined the scope of judicial review slightly differently. An appeal against the Scottish decision of *Eba*, mentioned in the same commentary, has been heard but not yet decided.

One further development that came to my attention too late to include concerns the scope of 'decision' in section 11 of the 2007 Act. The commentary lists the cases that have been decided so far. A three-judge panel is currently considering that issue and, hopefully, its decision will replace the case-by-case approach that has been taken so far.

Thanks are due to Nicola Johnston for editing and managing the production of this book and to Susan Mitchell for keeping track of the legislation. Thanks also to Richard Gillard at David Lewis XML.

The next main edition is planned for 2011. Online subscribers will be able to access updated legislation and commentary throughout the year as well as having access to CPAG's *Child Support Handbook* – for more information see www.cpag.org.uk/publications.

Edward Jacobs

Contents

Preface   iii
Table of cases   v
Table of Upper Tribunal decisions   vi
Table of commissioners' decisions   vii
How to use this supplement   viii

Part 1: Noter Up   1
Introduction and Overview   1
Child Support Act 1991   2
Social Security Act 1998   13
Human Rights Act 1998   14
Child Maintenance and Other Payments Act 2008   15
Child Support (Arrears, Interest and Adjustment of Maintenace Assessments) Regulations 1992   17
Child Support (Collection and Enforcement) Regulation 1992   17
Social Security and Child Support (Decisions and Appeals) Regulations 1999   18
Child Support (Maintenance Calculations and Special Cases) Regulations 2000   19
Child Support (Variations) Regulations 2000   20
Child Support (Transitional Provisions) Regulations 2000   22
Child Support (Maintenance Calculation Procedure) Regulations 2000   23
Child Support Information Regulations 2008   24
Tribunals, Courts and Enforcement Act 2007   27
Tribunal Procedure (First-tier Tribunal) (Social Entitlement Chamber) Rules 2008 38
Tribunal Procedure (Upper Tribunal) Rules 2008   43

Part 2: New regulations   45
Child Support (Management of Payments and Arrears) Regulations 2009   45

Part 3: Other legislation   52
Child Support (Maintenance Assessments and Special Cases) Regulations 1992   52

Table of cases

B v R [2010] 1 FLR 563... **4**

Baker v Willoughby [1969] 3 All ER 1528... **99**

Bird v Secretary of State for Work and Pensions [2009] 2 FLR 660... **8**

Brookes v Secretary of State for Work and Pensions and the Child Maintenance and Enforcement Commission [2010] EWCA Civ 420... **2, 6, 9, 14, 31**

Child Maintenance and Enforcement Commission v Beesley and Whyman [2010] EWHC 485 (Ch)... **7**

Child Maintenance and Enforcement Commission v Forrest [2010] EWHC 1264 (Admin)... **3, 4**

Child Maintenance and Enforcement Commission v Mitchell and Clements [2010] EWCA Civ 333... **9, 17**

Child Maintenance and Enforcement Commission v Smith in the Sherrifdom of Tayside, Central and Fife at Kirkcaldy (reference B92/09)... **8**

Cooke v Secretary of State for Social Security [2002] 3 All ER 279... **29**

Department of Social Security v Butler [1995] 1 WLR 1528... **6**

Dunne v Department of Health and Social Security, unreported, Court of Appeal in Northern Ireland, January 22 1992... **104**

Farley v Child Support Agency [2006] 1 WLR 1817... **8**

H v C [2009] 2 FLR 1540... **3**

HW v Secretary of State for Work and Pensions [2009] CSIH 21... **19**

Inland Revenue Commissioners v Reid's Trustees [1949] AC 361... **19**

Ishak v Thowfeek [1968] 1 WLR 1718... **2, 15**

McGinley and Egan v United Kingdom (1998) 27 EHRR 1... **20**

McLoughlin v O'Brian [1983] 1 AC 410... **99**

Pabari v Secretary of State for Work and Pensions [2005] 1 All ER 287... **106**

Parsons v Hogg [1985] 2 All ER 897... **99**

Paulin v Paulin [2009] 2 FLR 354... **42**

Petition of Eba [2010] ScotCS CSOH 45... **iii, 29**

Petition of Sharon Currie [2009] CSOH 145... **36**

R (Cart, U and XC) v the Upper Tribunal, the Special Immigration Appeal Commission, the Secretary of State for Justice, the Secretary of State for the Home Department, the Public Law Project, the Child Maintenance and Enforcement Commission and Wendy Cart [2010] 1 All ER 908...**iii, 29**

R v Bristol CC ex p Jacobs (1999) 32 HLR 841... **104**

R v Doncaster BC ex p Boulton [1992] 25 HLR 195, QBD... **99**

R v Hertfordshire County Council ex p Green Environmental Industries Ltd [2000] 2 AC 412... **3**

R v North Cornwall District Council ex p Singer, The Times, January 12, 1994... **104**

Re B (Residence: Second Appeal) [2009] 2 FLR 632... **28**

Re C (A Minor) (Child Support Agency: Disclosure) [1995] 1 FLR 201... **26**

Re N (A Child) v A [2010] 1 FLR 454... **29**

Re P-J (Abduction: Habitual residence: Consent) [2009] 2 FLR 1051... **10**

Re W (Children) (Care proceedings: evidence) [2010] 1 WLR 701... **40**

Re Z (Abduction) [2009] 2 FLR 298... **10**

Riniker v University College London [2001] 1 WLR 13... **29**

Secretary of State for Work and Pensions v Menary-Smith [2006] EWCA Civ 1751... **47**

Secretary of State for Work and Pensions v Roach [2006] EWCA Civ 1746... **18**

Smith v Child Maintenance and Enforcement Commission [2009] EWHC 3358 (Admin)... **15**

Smith v Smith and Secretary of State for Work and Pensions [2004] EWCA Civ 1318... **19**

Terrapin International Ltd v Inland Revenue Commissioners [1976] 2 All ER 461... **111**

Table of Upper Tribunal decisions

AC v CMEC [2009] UKUT 152 (AAC)… **93**

AM v Secretary of State for Work and Pensions [2009] UKUT 224 (AAC)… **39**

AR v Bradford MBC [2008] UKUT 30 (AAC), reported as R(H) 6/09… **19**

AW v Essex County Council (SEN) [2010] UKUT 74 (AAC)… **27, 39**

Bank Mellat v Her Majesty's Treasury [2010] EWCA Civ 483… **40**

BK v Secretary of State for Work and Pensions [2009] UKUT 258 (AAC)… **38**

CF v Child Maintenance and Enforcement Commission (CSM) UKUT 39 (AAC)… **11**

CH v Child Maintenance and Enforcement Commission (CSM) [2010] UKUT 140 (AAC)… **4, 10, 23**

Child Maintenance and Enforcement Commission v NC [2009] UKUT 106 (AAC)… **1**

Child Maintenance and Enforcement Commission v NC [2009] UKUT 106 (AAC)… **20**

CS v Child Maintenance and Enforcement Commission [2010] UKUT 182 (AAC)… **20**

DA v Secretary of State for Work and Pensions CE/1033/2010… **39**

Dorset Healthcare NHS Foundation Trust v MH [2009] UKUT 4 (AAC)… **27**

DY v Child Maintenance and Enforcement Commission [2010] UKUT 19 (AAC)… **1, 19, 23**

EF v Secretary of State for Work and Pensions [2009] UKUT 92 (AAC)… **36**

FL v First-tier Tribunal and CICA [2010] UKUT 158 (AAC)… **39**

GB v London Borough of Hillingdon [2010] UKUT 11 (AAC)… **3**

Goldman Sachs v Commissioners for Her Majesty's Revenue and Customs [2009] UKUT 290 (TCC)… **27**

KC v London Borough of Newham (SEN) [2010] UKUT 96 (AAC)… **27**

KF v Birmingham and Solihull Mental Health NHS Foundation Trust [2010] UKUT 185 (AAC)… **41**

LC v Secretary of State for Work and Pensions [2009] UKUT 153 (AAC)… **38**

LM v London Borough of Lewisham [2009] UKUT 204 (AAC)… **27**

MC v Secretary of State for Defence [2009] UKUT 173 (AAC)… **3, 42**

MD v Secretary of State for Work and Pensions (Enforcement Reference) [2010] UKUT 202 (AAC)… **39**

MG v Child Maintenance and Enforcement Commission (CSM) [2010] UKUT 83 (AAC)… **19, 20**

MP v Secretary of State for Work and Pensions (DLA) [2010] UKUT 103 (AAC)… **27, 42**

MR v Child Maintenance and Enforcement Commission (No.1) [2009] UKUT 285 (AAC)… **39**

NH v Child Maintenance and Enforcement Commission [2009] UKUT 183 (AAC)… **18**

PB v Child Maintenance and Enforcement Commission [2009] UKUT 262 (AAC)… **20**

R (RB) v First-tier Tribunal (Review) [2010] UKUT 160 (AAC)… **28, 42**

RB v CMEC and ED [2009] UKUT 53 (AAC) reported as R(CS) 5/09… **4**

RF v Child Maintenance and Enforcement Commission (CSM) [2010] UKUT 41 (AAC)… **38**

RM v St Andrew's Healthcare [2010] UKUT 119 (AAC)… **27, 40**

SL v Child Maintenance and Enforcement Commission [2009] UKUT 270 (AAC)… **11**

SSWP v RH [2008] UKUT 19 (AAC), R(CS) 3/09… **19**

SW v Secretary of State for Work and Pensions (IB) UKUT 73 (AAC)… **38**

Synergy Child Services Ltd v Ofsted [2009] UKUT 125 (AAC)… **27**

TW v Secretary of State for Work and Pensions [2009] UKUT 91 (AAC)… **18**

VH v Suffolk County Council [2010] UKUT 203 (AAC)… **28, 42**

Table of commissioners' decisions

CCS 12/1994... **103, 105**
CCS 15/1994... **91**
CCS 9/1995... **103, 106**
CCS 12/1995... **103**
CCS 2750/1995... **106**
CCS 4923/1995... **99**
CCS 8189/1995... **71, 94**
CCS 12769/1996... **73**
CCS 13698/1996... **71, 91, 94, 107**
CCS 13923/1996... **91, 94**
CCS 16518/1996... **111**
CCS 349/1997... **104, 105**
CCS 1039/1997... **91**
CCS 1318/1997... **94**
CCS 1321/1997... **106**
CCS 1554/1997... **111**
CCS 316/1998... **111**
CCS 318/1998... **92, 94**
CCS 4912/1998... **92, 93**
CCS 3675/2004... **92**
CCS 185/2005... **93, 99**
CCS 2678/2007... **93**
CCS 1992/2008... **99**
CCS 3144/2009... **12**
CH 4262/2007... **38, 39**
CIS 17/1988... **105**
CIS 702/1991... **99**
CIS 616/1992... **105**
CIS 636/1992... **103**
CIS 141/1993... **106**
CIS 264/1993... **104, 105**
CIS 453/1993... **105**
CIS 392/1994... **104, 105**
CIS 11482/1995... **92**
CIS 14483/1996... **103, 104**
CIS 2285/1999... **99**
CSB 420/1985... **105**
CSB 265/1987... **105**
CSB 598/1989... **93**
CSC 2/1996... **104**

CSC 3/1996... **104**
CSCS 8/1995... **71, 94**
CSCS 3/1996... **105**
CSCS 1/1998... **111**
CSCS 2/1998... **111**
CSIS 4/90... **104**
R 1/94 (CSC)... **104**
R 2/96 (CSC)... **91**
R(AF) 1/09... **4**
R(CS) 3/96... **104**
R(CS) 6/98... **103, 104**
R(CS) 9/98... **92, 103**
R(CS) 10/98... **106**
R(CS) 11/98... **104**
R(CS) 12/98... **107**
R(CS) 14/98... **107**
R(CS) 15/98... **5**
R(CS) 8/99... **11**
R(CS) 9/99... **111**
R(CS) 2/00... **91, 99**
R(CS) 3/00... **91**
R(CS) 4/02... **69**
R(CS) 3/05... **103**
R(CS) 4/07... **18**
R(CS) 2/09... **3**
R(FC) 2/92... **19**
R(I) 7/94... **39**
R(IS) 3/91... **103, 104**
R(IS) 4/91... **103, 104**
R(IS) 4/92... **104, 105**
R(IS) 14/93... **38**
R(IS) 19/93... **104, 105**
R(IS) 4/94... **99**
R(IS) 6/94... **103**
R(IS) 3/09... **4**
R(SB) 5/81... **3, 42**
R(SB) 38/85... **92**
R(SB) 40/85... **93**
R(SB) 3/87... **104, 105**
R(SB) 2/89... **93, 99**

How to use this supplement

This Supplement to the ninth edition of *Child Support: The Legislation* has been compiled according to the structure of the main volume.

The tables of caselaw, commissioners' decisions and Upper Tribunal decisions at the start of the book are those cited in the Supplement only.

Use the Noter-up to find out about changes to the main volume. The page numbers refer to pages in the main volume.

Part I: Noter-up

Part 1
INTRODUCTION AND OVERVIEW

pp4-5   **Precedent**

[Add new paragraph:]

Decisions of the First-tier Tribunal are of no precedent value in later cases (*DY v Child Maintenance and Enforcement Commission* [2010] UKUT 19 (AAC) at paras 46-52).

p6   **Relationship between EC law and the ECHR**

[Add to end of point (4):]

For an attempt to rely on the European Convention on Human Rights in conjunction with freedom of movement, see *Child Maintenance and Enforcement Commission v NC* [2009] UKUT 106 (AAC).

Part II
STATUES

Child Support Act 1991

section 2   Welfare of children: the general principle

[p12: General Note, add:]

This section was considered in *Brookes v Secretary of State for Work and Pensions and the Child Maintenance and Enforcement Commission* [2010] EWCA Civ 420. The court decided that the section applies to the enforcement powers under this Act (para 16). It confirmed that the welfare test is not the first or paramount consideration (para 13(1)) and that it applies to other children of the non-resident parent as it does to the qualifying child (para 12). The court also decided that this section does not require the CMEC to achieve any particular result. There is no duty to promote a child's welfare, only to take it into account. Nor does the section require the CMEC to refrain from making a decision that will impact adversely on a child's welfare. Nor, conversely, does the duty to make maintenance payments always override welfare considerations. See paras 13(i) and (ii) and 14. As Hughes LJ explained:

> '14. . . . The correct position is clearly that all the circumstances of each case must be considered. What section 2 requires is that any impact on children's welfare be taken into account as a factor in deciding whether or not to do something discretionary under the Act. Clearly, the greater the likely negative impact on welfare, the greater the case against making the decision. But the welfare considerations must still be balanced against all other relevant considerations. Those will include, but are not limited to: the welfare of other children with different interests, the duty of the paying parent to support his/her children, the general public interest in a parent meeting that duty and the particular interest of the public, *qua* taxpayer, in that duty being enforced rather than the support of the children being left to fall on the State.'

See also *Ishak v Thowfeek* [1968] 1 WLR 1718 at 1725.

The duty under this section may require the CMEC to make inquiries about the children who may be affected by a decision. The issue did not arise for decision in *Brookes*, but Hughes LJ commented:

> '15. . . . On the face of it, the duty to have regard to welfare can only arise in relation to those children of whose existence the Commission knows, or of whom it has been put on notice, and in relation to circumstances of theirs which it knows about or ought to be able to infer from information in its hands. If, however, the information known to the Commission is such as to suggest that there is or may be a child of particular sensitivity or vulnerability, or there is otherwise a particular reason to think that an unusual impact on welfare might be the result of a discretionary decision, then on ordinary principles one would expect a decision maker to make such enquiries as are reasonable. That is to say no more than that anyone charged with making a discretionary decision ought to behave reasonably.'

The prohibition of disclosure to a party in the interests of the child's welfare would now be dealt with under rule 14(2) Tribunal Procedure (First-tier Tribunal) (Social Entitlement Chamber) Rules 2008.

section 6   Applications by those claiming or receiving benefit

[p24, General Note, add:]

When it comes to enforcement, there is no conflict of interest between the CMEC and the Secretary of State on account of the money owing being paid to the taxpayer; the latter is entitled to payment as any other creditor (*Brookes v Secretary of State for Work and Pensions and the Child Maintenance and Enforcement Commission* [2010] EWCA Civ 420 at para 7(ii)).

In the housing benefit case of *GB v London Borough of Hillingdon* [2010] UKUT 11 (AAC) at para 35, the judge distinguished *R(CS) 2/09* as applying to the specific context of this section.

section 8   Role of the courts with respect to maintenance for children

[p30: General Note, add:]

Subsection 8(6)

For an example of the operation of this subsection in a complex case involving a consent order, a subsequent maintenance assessment and a later application for additional maintenance, see *H v C* [2009] 2 FLR 1540.

section 11   Maintenance calculations

[p37: General Note, add:]

Some decisions turn on the state of mind of the CMEC; they may depend on suspicion or opinion. On appeal, the tribunal may substitute its view for that of the CMEC (*R(SB) 5/81*, para 8; *MC v Secretary of State for Defence* [2009] UKUT 173 (AAC), paras 10-16).

section 14   Information required by the Commission

[p40: General Note, add at the end of the paragrapgh on Subsection (3):]

The Child Support (Management of Payment and Arrears) Regulations 2009 are made in part under this subsection.

section 14A Information – offences

[p40: subs (3A) subsituted by art 2(3) of the Welfare Reform Act 2009 (Commencement No.1) Order 2010 SI No.45 from 14 January 2010:]

"(3A)   In the case of regulations under section 14 which require a person liable to make payments of child support maintenance to notify–
(a)   a change of address, or
(b)   any other change of circumstances,
a person who fails to comply with the requirement is guilty of an offence."

[p41: new subs (6) to (8) inserted by art 2(3) of the Welfare Reform Act 2009 (Commencement No.1) Order 2010 SI No.45 from 14 January 2010:]

"(6)   In England and Wales, an information relating to an offence under subsection (2) may be tried by a magistrates' court if it is laid within the period of 12 months beginning with the commission of the offence.
(7)   In Scotland, summary proceedings for an offence under subsection (2) may be commenced within the period of 12 months beginning with the commission of the offence.
(8)   Section 136(3) of the Criminal Procedure (Scotland) Act 1995 (c. 46) (date when proceedings deemed to be commenced) applies for the purposes of subsection (7) as it applies for the purposes of that section."

[p41: General Note, Subsection (4), replace text with:]

This subsection provides a defence to subss (3) and (3A). There is no definition or indication of what may constitute a reasonable excuse. The burden of proof is on the defendant. Self-incrimination and protecting others from criminal charges is not a reasonable excuse for failing to comply. In *Child Maintenance and Enforcement Commission v Forrest* [2010] EWHC 1264 (Admin), the Divisional Court gave three reasons for this conclusion. First, as such a defence was provided by s15(7), its absence in this section was significant (para 14). Second, following *R v Hertfordshire County Council ex p Green Environmental Industries Ltd* [2000] 2 AC 412, such a defence applied in any criminal proceedings but not to the requirement to provide the information (para 17). Third, public policy required compliance. Elias LJ explained:

'18. . . . There is plainly a powerful public interest here in ensuring that fathers pay the appropriate maintenance to their spouse or partner and their children. That is the purpose behind the requirement of this information, to enable the Child Support Agency to ensure that the appropriate sums are provided in accordance with the legislation.'

section 15   Powers of inspectors

[p42: General Note, add:]

Subsection (7)

The defence under this subsection only applies if the question is put under this section. It is not available if the question is asked under another section, such as s14 (*Child Maintenance and Enforcement Commission v Forrest* [2010] EWHC 1264 (Admin), para 12).

section 16   Revisions of decisions

[p44: General Note, Subsection (1), add:]

A decision refusing to revise is not appealable under s20. The original decision is appealable as revised. See *RB v CMEC and ED* [2009] UKUT 53 (AAC) reported as *R(CS) 5/09*.

section 20   Appeals to the First-tier Tribunal

[p47: General Note, add:]

If an application is withdrawn before it is decided, no decision can be given on an appeal, not even a decision to refuse the application. This applies both to the 1993 scheme (*CCS 2910/2001*) and to the 2003 scheme (*CH v Child Maintenance and Enforcement Commission (CSM)* [2010] UKUT 140 (AAC), para 52). It follows that the First-tier Tribunal has no jurisdiction to hear a dispute about whether an application has been withdrawn.

The core duties of the First-tier Tribunal were set out in *R(IS) 3/09*:

'10. Tribunals must act within their statutory jurisdiction, because that defines the limits of their power. They must act judicially, because that is their nature. They must decide the issues that arise for resolution, because that is their function. And they must make decisions that are clear, sufficiently complete and capable of being implemented, because the discharge of their duty to decide the issues judicially must be effective.'

[p48: General Note, Jurisdiction, add:]

The tribunal is under a duty to ensure that it has jurisdiction to make its proposed decision, but not to seek out other bases on which it might have jurisdiction (*B v R* [2010] 1 FLR 563, paras 33 and 37).

The tribunal may also refuse to accept jurisdiction if an appeal has been wrongly admitted after an absolute time limit (*R(AF) 1/09*).

[p49: General Note, Revision and refusal to revise:]

The decision in *RB* is reported as *R(CS) 5/09*.

[p49: General Note, Subsection (7)(a), add:]

A tribunal is entitled to limit itself to issues raised by a competent representative (*Jeleniewicz v Secretary of State for Work and Pensions*, a decision of the Court of Appeal reported as part of *R(IS) 3/09*).

section 24   Appeals to Upper Tribunal

[p52: replace the text of s24 with:]

[¹ Appeals to Upper Tribunal]

24.–[²(1)   Each of the following may appeal [¹to the Upper Tribunal under section 11 of the Tribunals, Courts and Enforcement Act 2007 from any decision of the First-tier Tribunal under section 20 of this Act]–

(a)   the Commission,

(b)   the Secretary of State, and

(c)   any person who is aggrieved by the decision of an appeal tribunal.]

[¹(2)   Where a question which would otherwise fall to be determined by the Commission or the Secretary of State under this Act first arises in the course of an appeal to the Upper Tribunal, that tribunal may, if it thinks fit, determine the question even though it has not been considered by the Commission or the Secretary of State.]

Amendments

1.   Transfer of Tribunal Functions Order 2008 (SI 2008 No.2833) art 9 and Sch 3 para 85 (November 3, 2008, subject to the transitional provisions in Sch 4 of SI 2008 No.2833).

2.   Child Maintenance and Other Payments Act 2008 (2008 c.6) s13 and Sch 3, para 16 (November 1, 2008); Child Maintenance and Other Payments Act 2008 (Commencement No.4 and Transitional Provision) Order 2008 (SI 2008 No.2675) art 3.

[p52: General Note, add:]

Subsection (1)

The CMEC may appeal to the Upper Tribunal. Section 13(2)(a) of the 2008 Act does not transfer to the CMEC the Secretary of State's function in respect of appeals. That Act amended this section to confer a right of appeal on both the Secretary of State and the CMEC (Sch 3, para 16(2)). When the Upper Tribunal came into existence, the new version of s24 expressly referred to the Secretary of State, but not to the CMEC. However, the CMEC may come within s24 as a person aggrieved. It is a person by virtue of s1(1) of the 2008 Act and it may be aggrieved in the sense discussed below. Accordingly, the effect of s13(2)(a) of the 2008 Act is to preserve the right of the Secretary of State without restricting the rights of the CMEC.

The meaning of "person . . . aggrieved" has been considered in various statutory contexts. It is difficult to distill any general principles from those decisions, as so much depends on the context. These words may limit the scope of the right of appeal in two ways. They may limit its personal scope by preventing someone who is not a person with care, a non-resident parent or (in Scotland) a qualifying child from appealing. It is difficult to envisage who else might be included, although it is possible that a grandparent or someone else with a close personal connection to a child might wish to lodge an appeal in the interests of a child. The words may also limit the material scope of the right of appeal by restricting the circumstances in which a person may appeal. The CMEC might wish to appeal in the interests of one of the other parties if it thought that the First-tier Tribunal had made an error of law. Its role as decision maker and its other responsibilities under the 2008 Act might give it sufficient interest to be aggrieved. The issue was considered by the commissioner in *R(CS) 15/98*, para 14. The case concerned a reduced benefit direction. The parent had not taken any part in the procedures leading to the making of the direction. Nonetheless, the commissioner treated the parent as personally aggrieved and said that she might also be vicariously aggrieved on behalf of her child. This leaves open the possibility for, say, a grandparent to appeal in the interests of a child. This limitation on the right of appeal has not been used to exclude appeals that raise points of principle without any effect on the outcome. Even if permission has been given, the Upper Tribunal has sufficient other powers to deal expeditiously with those cases.

(i)   It may refuse to hear the appeal on the ground that the issue is of abstract interest only.

(ii)   It may strike out the proceedings under rule 8(3)(c) of the Tribunal Procedure (Upper Tribunal) Rules 2008.

(iii)   It may exercise its discretion under s12(2)(a) of the Tribunals, Courts and Enforcement Act 2007 not to set aside a First-tier Tribunal's decision even if it contained an error of law.

section 28 Power of Secretary of State to initiate or defend actions of declarator: Scotland

[p58: in the section heading, change 'Secretary of State' to '[⁹ Commission]'.]

section 28J Voluntary payments

[p75: General Note, add:]

Subsection (3)

The Child Support (Management of Payment and Arrears) Regulations 2009 are made in part under this subsection.

Collection and enforcement

[p75: add a General Note before s29:]

General Note

According to the Court of Appeal in *Department of Social Security v Butler* [1995] 1 WLR 1528, the child support legislation provides a complete code for the collection of payments due under maintenance assessments and the enforcement of liability orders made. The duty to pay a maintenance assessment is not expressed as a civil debt and cannot be directly enforced by action in any civil court or by any means other than as provided in the Act. Consequently, the CMEC is not entitled to be granted a *Mareva* injunction to prevent a liable person from disposing of assets before a liability order can be obtained. However, once a liability order has been made under s33, the country court has jurisdiction to grant a *Mareva* injunction under reg 3(3)(a) and (c) County Court Remedies Regulations 1991.

Section 2 of the Act may apply to discretionary decisions on enforcement. As Hughes LJ explained in *Brookes v Secretary of State for Work and Pensions and the Child Maintenance and Enforcement Commission* [2010] EWCA Civ 420:

'16. ... Some discretionary decisions related to potential enforcement may not of themselves have any potential for impact on children, whether supported children or those in the payer's present household. An example will ordinarily be a decision to seek a liability order under s33, which of itself accomplishes no enforcement but only establishes the sum owing and opens a gateway to particular kinds of possible subsequent enforcement. It might be possible to postulate an unusual situation in which a child was so vulnerable that even the possible knowledge that a parent would have to attend court could have a dramatic adverse effect, but absent such a circumstance, the seeking of a liability order must be followed by other discretionary enforcement decisions before there can be any question of impact on welfare. However, the decision under s35 to seek distraint via bailiffs is capable of having some impact on the welfare of both supported children, if any recovered sum may benefit them, and children in the payer's present household since chattels may be removed from that household. Similarly, a decision to seek committal of the non-payer by the magistrates could have an impact on both groups of children. That section 2 is applicable to both kinds of decision has not been in question before us.'

A decision to take discretionary enforcement action has a limited duration. It lasts for a reasonable time to allow it to be put into effect, but after that time it must be remade before it can be acted on. In *Brookes* (para 38), the Court of Appeal decided that an enforcement decision would have lapsed after two years. This does not mean that an enforcement decision is effective for two years; only that it is not effective thereafter.

The effect of a non-resident parent's personal insolvency was considered in *Child Maintenance and Enforcement Commission v Beesley and Whyman* [2010] EWHC 485 (Ch). The non-resident parent agreed with his other creditors to pay 27 pence in the pound over five years. The bulk of his debts were arrears of child support maintenance. The CMEC's main argument was that it was not a creditor for the purposes of an individual voluntary arrangement (IVA) and so was not bound by the arrangement. The judge reviewed the three regimes that governed personal insolvency.

(i)   Bankruptcy would not usually discharge arrears of child support maintenance. The arrears would be a bankruptcy debt, but would not be provable in the bankruptcy. Discharge from the bankruptcy would not discharge those arrears unless the court so ordered.

(ii)   A debt relief order would not have any effect on arrears, as they are an excluded debt.

(iii)   An IVA could apply, as the arrears were a bankruptcy debt. Accordingly, the judge rejected the CMEC's main argument. Alternatively, it argued that the court should revoke the approval given to the IVA on the ground that it was unfairly prejudicial. The judge accepted this argument on the ground that the arrangement deprived the CMEC of the chance to enforce the arrears even if the non-resident parent were declared bankrupt.

section 32   Regulations about deduction from earnings orders

[p82: General Note, Subsection (2), note that:]

The relevant provisions of the Arrears, Interest and Adjustment of Maintenance Assessments Regulations have been revoked by the Child Support (Management of Payment and Arrears) Regulations 2009.

section 32L Orders preventing avoidance

[p90: new s32L inserted by s24 Child Maintenance and Other Payments Act 2008 (2008 c.6) from 6 April 2010:]

Orders preventing avoidance

32L.–(1)   The Commission may apply to the court, on the grounds that a person–

(a)   has failed to pay an amount of child support maintenance, and

(b)   with the intention of avoiding payment of child support maintenance, is about to make a disposition or to transfer out of the jurisdiction or otherwise deal with any property,

for an order restraining or, in Scotland, interdicting the person from doing so.

(2)   The Commission may apply to the court, on the grounds that a person–

(a)   has failed to pay an amount of child support maintenance, and

(b)   with the intention of avoiding payment of child support maintenance, has at any time made a reviewable disposition,

for an order setting aside or, in Scotland, reducing the disposition.

(3)   If the court is satisfied of the grounds mentioned in subsection (1) or (2) it may make an order under that subsection.

(4)   Where the court makes an order under subsection (1) or (2) it may make such consequential provision by order or directions as it thinks fit for giving effect to the order (including provision requiring the making of any payments or the disposal of any property).

(5)   Any disposition is a reviewable disposition for the purposes of subsection (2), unless it was made for valuable or, in Scotland, adequate consideration (other than marriage) to a person who, at the time of the disposition, acted in relation to it in good faith and without notice of an intention to avoid payment of child support maintenance.

(6)   Subsection (7) applies where an application is made under this section with respect to–

(a)   a disposition or other dealing with property which is about to take place, or

(b) a disposition which took place after the making of the application on which the maintenance calculation concerned was made.

(7) If the court is satisfied–

(a) in a case falling within subsection (1), that the disposition or other dealing would (apart from this section) have the consequence of making ineffective a step that has been or may be taken to recover the amount outstanding, or

(b) in a case falling within subsection (2), that the disposition has had that consequence,

it is to be presumed, unless the contrary is shown, that the person who disposed of or is about to dispose of or deal with the property did so or, as the case may be, is about to do so, with the intention of avoiding payment of child support maintenance.

(8) In this section "disposition" does not include any provision contained in a will or codicil but, with that exception, includes any conveyance, assurance or gift of property of any description, whether made by an instrument or otherwise.

(9) This section does not apply to a disposition made before the coming into force of section 24 of the Child Maintenance and Other Payments Act 2008.

(10) In this section "the court" means–

(a) in relation to England and Wales, the High Court;

(b) in relation to Scotland, the Court of Session or the sheriff.

(11) An order under this section interdicting a person–

(a) is effective for such period (including an indefinite period) as the order may specify;

(b) may, on application to the court, be varied or recalled.

section 33   Liabilty orders

[p92: General Note, Subsection 1, add:]

The Information Regulations contain powers to allow the CMEC to discover the liable person's gross earnings and the deductions from those earnings, which will inform the decision whether to apply for a liability order.

In *Child Maintenance and Enforcement Commission v Smith* in the Sherrifdom of Tayside, Central and Fife at Kirkcaldy (reference B92/09), the Sheriff held that it was not permissible to inquire whether it was appropriate to make a deduction from earnings order under subs(1)(b)(i). He applied *Farley v Child Support Agency* [2006] 1 WLR 1817 as authority for the proposition that the court had to grant the liability order sought 'without investigating [the CMEC's] deliberative procedures.' *Farley* decided that the court could not question the underlying maintenance calculation. *Smith* extends that reasoning. Although subs(1) sets out conditions that must be satisfied before an order can be made, it is sufficient if it appears to the CMEC that a deduction from earnings order is inappropriate. As the Sheriff noted, the court was not acting in an appellate capacity under s33.

[p92, General Note, Subsection 3:]

The reference to *Parley* is wrong. The correct citation is: *Farley v Child Support Agency* [2006] 1 WLR 1817.

[p92, General Note, add:]

Subsection 6
This subsection does not apply if the liable person has paid the child support to the person specified but by a different method from that specified (*Bird v Secretary of State for Work and Pensions* [2009] 2 FLR 660).

section 35   Enforcement of liability orders by distress

[p94: General Note, add:]

It may be reasonable for the CMEC to decide on enforcing immediate payment and the use of a bailiff to do so is not necessarily contrary to s2 of the Act. The Court of Appeal rejected arguments to the contrary in *Brookes v Secretary of State for Work and Pensions and the Child Maintenance and Enforcement Commission* [2010] EWCA Civ 420, paras 24 and 28.

section 39A Commitment to prison and disqualification from driving

[p97: General Note, add a second paragraph:]

This section was considered by the Court of Appeal in *Child Maintenance and Enforcement Commission v Mitchell and Clements* [2010] EWCA Civ 333. The CMEC was attempting to recover arrears of child support maintenance for the period from 1996 to 2001. It applied for an order disqualifying the non-resident parent from driving. The magistrates made the order for 12 months, suspended on condition that he pays £5 a week towards the arrears. This decision was reversed on appeal by the circuit judge, who decided that the proceedings were barred under s9 Limitation Act 1980. The Court of Appeal allowed the appeal, deciding that the proceedings were not statute barred as they were not an 'action to recover any sum recoverable by virtue of any enactment'. They were not a money claim, but an application for a committal order or a disqualification order, even if they might indirectly lead to the recovery of money. Aikens LJ noted (paras 41 and 53) that the court's powers were discretionary. He left open (para 53) whether an application brought under this section more than six years after the date of the liability order might be an abuse of process.

section 41 Arrears of child support maintenance

[p102: General Note, third paragraph, note:]

Regulation 10(1)(a) Arrears, Interest and Adjustment of Maintenance Assessments Regulations has been replaced by reg 8(1) Child Support (Management of Payment and Arrears) Regulations 2009.

section 41B Repayment of overpaid child support maintenance

[p104: General Note, replace the first paragraph:]

This section deals with overpayments by the non-resident parent. The CMEC may apply the overpayment first to reduce arrears under previous maintenance calculations and then to adjust the amount payable under the current calculation. See reg 8 Child Support (Management of Payments and Arrears) Regulations 2009 on p45 of this Supplement. The CMEC may in turn recover the amount from the person who benefited from it: see regs 10A and 10B Arrears, Interest and Adjustment of Maintenance Assessments Regulations.

section 41C Power to treat liability as satisfied

[p104: new s41C inserted by s31 Child Maintenance and Other Payments Act 2008 (2008 c.6) from 26 November 2009 for making regulations and 25 January 2010 for all other purposes:]

Power to treat liability as satisfied

41C.–(1)   The Secretary of State may by regulations–

(a)   make provision enabling the Commission in prescribed circumstances to set off liabilities to pay child support maintenance to which this section applies;

(b)   make provision enabling the Commission in prescribed circumstances to set off against a person's liability to pay child support maintenance to which this section applies a payment made by the person which is of a prescribed description.

(2)   Liability to pay child support maintenance shall be treated as satisfied to the extent that it is the subject of setting off under regulations under subsection (1).

(3)   In subsection (1), the references to child support maintenance to which this section applies are to child support maintenance for the collection of which the Commission is authorised to make arrangements.

Definition

"Commission": see s54.

General Note

Part 2 of the Child Support (Management of Payments and Arrears) Regulations 2009 are made under this section.

section 43A Recovery of arrears from deceased's estate

[p106: new s43A inserted by s38 Child Maintenance and Other Payments Act 2008 (2008 c.6) from 26 November 2009:]

Recovery of arrears from deceased's estate

43A.–(1)   The Secretary of State may by regulations make provision for the recovery from the estate of a deceased person of arrears of child support maintenance for which the deceased person was liable immediately before death.

(2)   Regulations under subsection (1) may, in particular–

(a)   make provision for arrears of child support maintenance for which a deceased person was so liable to be a debt payable by the deceased's executor or administrator out of the deceased's estate to the Commission;

(b)   make provision for establishing the amount of any such arrears;

(c)   make provision about procedure in relation to claims under the regulations.

(3)   Regulations under subsection (1) may include provision for proceedings (whether by appeal or otherwise) to be instituted, continued or withdrawn by the deceased's executor or administrator.

Definition

"Commission": see s54.

General Note

Part 4 of the Child Support (Management of Payments and Arrears) Regulations 2009 are made in part under this section.

section 44   Jurisdiction

[p109: General Note, head (vi), add:]

Residence for a short period or conditional on future events may be sufficient to establish habitual residence (*Re P-J (Abduction: Habitual residence: Consent)* [2009] 2 FLR 1051, para 26(4)).

[p111: General Note, insert a new head (xiv):]

Fraud or mistake may prevent habitual residence being acquired or retained, although the person may nonetheless become habitually resident. Everything depends on the facts of the case (*Re Z (Abduction)* [2009] 2 FLR 298, para 13).

In *CH v Child Maintenance and Enforcement Commission (CSM)* [2010] UKUT 140 (AAC), the judge dealt with the possibility that a non-resident parent might avoid the child support scheme by moving abroad:

'84. . . . In such cases, as the Commission has no jurisdiction, the courts may still have jurisdiction to make a child maintenance order. I also acknowledge that cross-border enforcement of such a civil order in practice under the Maintenance Orders (Reciprocal Enforcement) Act 1972 may not be easy. However, the

Official Solicitor has a special unit devoted to the Reciprocal Enforcement of Maintenance Orders (see further www.officialsolicitor.gov.uk/os/remo.htm).'

section 50   Unauthorised disclosure of information

[p119: General Note, add:]

Subsections (1A) and (1C)

Regulation 14(1) and (2) of the Information Regulations is made under these subsections.

section 51   Supplementary powers to make regulations

[p120: General Note, add:]

Subsection (2)

The Child Support (Management of Payment and Arrears) Regulations 2009 are made in part under paras (d), (e) and (f).

section 55   Meaning of "child"

[p126: General Note, head (iv), add:]

The approval of a child's education by an officer of the local education authority is not the approval of a Secretary of State (*CF v Child Maintenance and Enforcement Commission (CSM)* UKUT 39 (AAC), paras 45-50).

[p127: General Note, add to table:]

Cessation dates (inclusive)	Period ends
January 7, 2008 to March 30, 2008	April 6, 2008
March 31, 2008 to August 31, 2008	June 22, 2008
September 1, 2008 to January 4, 2009	January 4, 2009
January 5, 2009 to April 19, 2009	April 5, 2009
April 20, 2009 to September 6, 2009	July 19, 2009
September 7, 2009 to January 3, 2010	January 3, 2010
January 4, 2010 to April 11, 2010	April 4, 2010
April 12, 2010 to September 5, 2010	July 4, 2010
September 6, 2010 to January 2, 2011	January 2, 2011

section 57   Application to Crown

[p129: General Note, Subsection 1, add:]

Regulation 4(2)(h) and (3) of the Information Regulations is made under this subsection.

[p129: General Note, add:]

Subsection 2

Regulation 11 of the Information Regulations is made under this subsection.

Schedule 1   Calculation of weekly amount of child support maintenance

[p132: para 10B, in the opening words delete '[¹ Commission]' and replace with 'Secretary of State'. At the end of head (a), delete 'Secretary of State' and replace with '[¹ Commission]'.]

[p141: General Note, add:]

Paragraph 16(1)(b) and (d)

The authorities on these provisions were reviewed in *SL v Child Maintenance and Enforcement Commission* [2009] UKUT 270 (AAC). The judge disagreed with *R(CS) 8/99* and decided (at para 32): 'the correct analysis is that paragraph 16(1)(b) is indeed about there no longer being a qualifying "child", rather than being about the particular child no longer "qualifying".' The issue has arisen again and an oral hearing is being held in *CCS 3144/2009*.

Paragraph 16(10)

Regulation 10 of the Information Regulations is made under this subparagraph.

Social Security Act 1998

section 3   Use of information

[p165: section 3 amended by 2010/697 art 2(b) and Sch 7 para 3 of 2008 Act from 6 April 2010:]

3.–(1)   The Social Security Act 1998 is amended as follows.

(2)   In section 3 (use of information held by the Secretary of State or the Northern Ireland Department which relates to certain matters), in subsection (1A) (which lists the matters concerned)–

   (a)   in paragraph (a), the words '', child support'' are omitted;

   (b)   after that paragraph insert–

     ''(aa) child support in Northern Ireland;''.

   (3)   *[Omitted]*

Human Rights Act 1998

Schedule 1   Article 8 – right to respect for private and family life

[p193: General Note, Paragraph (1), add:]

If this article is engaged, any enforcement decision must be proportionate. Hughes LJ explained what this entailed in *Brookes v Secretary of State for Work and Pensions and the Child Maintenance and Enforcement Commission* [2010] EWCA Civ 420:

> '41. The test of proportionality is not identical to the question whether an action in *Wednesbury* unreasonable, albeit that in many cases both tests may on the facts yield the same answer. Whereas the *Wednesbury* test involves asking whether the decision was within the range of those reasonably or rationally available to the decision maker, where proportionality is in question, the court must apply anxious scrutiny to ensure that the decision maker has struck the balance fairly between the conflicting interests of the claimant's right to respect for family life on the one hand and the public or competing interests within Article 8(2) on the other. In doing so, however, the court does not simply substitute its own decision. Its function is supervisory. It recognises and allows to the public body's decision maker a discretionary area of judgment. It will often be appropriate to adopt the two-stage process of asking first whether the intended objective can be achieved by means less interfering with the Article 8 right and second whether, if not, yet still the effect is excessive or disproportionate. For those various propositions see amongst other cases *R (Daly) v SSHD* [2001] 2 AC 532 and *Samaroo v SSHD* [2001] EWCA Civ 1139.'

The Court of Appeal decided that, in the circumstances of the case, it was neither disproportionate nor excessive to ask magistrates to use their powers if the non-resident parent's conduct justified it (para 42).

Child Maintenance and Other Payments Act 2008

section 1 The Child Maintenance and Enforcement Commission

[p203: add:]

General Note

As its name indicates, the CMEC is not exclusively concerned with child support maintenance, but with child maintenance generally. It has, though, taken over most of the functions previously exercised by the Secretary of State through the Child Support Agency. For exceptions, see s13.

section 2 Objectives of the Commission

[p204: add:]

General Note

This section sets out the main and subsidiary objectives of the CMEC. They are not the functions that it must undertake; those are set out in s3. Rather, they are objectives that it must aim to pursue and have regard to when exercising those functions. As the Privy Council said in *Ishak v Thowfeek* [1968] 1 WLR 1718 at 1725: 'The requirement that the board shall "have regard" to certain matters tends in itself to show that the board's duty in respect of these matters is limited to having regard to them. They must take them into account and consider them and give due weight to them, but they have an ultimate discretion . . . ' Presumably, they must also be taken into account when the CMEC is deciding whether or not to exercise a function, such as that to promote child maintenance under s4.

Subsection (2)

In *Smith v Child Maintenance and Enforcement Commission* [2009] EWHC 3358 (Admin), a non-resident parent argued that the CMEC had acted contrary to this section in continuing to enforce arrears. The court held that it had not. In particular, it held (at paras 25-26) that an agreement about arrears is not a voluntary maintenance arrangement within para (a), but payment of arrears is a parental obligation under para (b).

section 3 Functions of the Commission: general

[p204: add:]

General Note

The child support functions are transferred to the CMEC by s13. The additional functions are those that deal with aspects of child maintenance outside the statutory child support scheme.

section 4 Promotion of child maintenance

[p204: add:]

General Note

This section gives the CMEC a power to exercise an educative function in respect of parents and their responsibility for maintaining their children. The power is unlimited, but must be exercised in the light of the objectives in s2. An application for child support maintenance may, but need not, be an appropriate arrangement. This is a subsidiary objective for the CMEC under s2(2)(b). The CMEC's work under this section can be found on its website at www.childmaintenance.org.

section 5 Provision of information and guidance

[p204: add:]

General Note

Subsection (1) imposes a duty on the CMEC but only to provide such information and guidance as it thinks appropriate to help secure effective maintenance arrangements. Subs (2) confers an ancillary power to provide information for other purposes at the same time. The information provided by the CMEC under this section can be found on its website at www.childmaintenance.org.

section 6   Fees

[p205: add:]

General Note

No regulations have been made under this section.

section 10   Directions and guidance

[p207: add:]

General Note

The Secretary of State may give the CMEC written guidance or directions. The directions are binding and must be laid before Parliament. The guidance is not binding, but the CMEC is under a duty to have regard to it. For the meaning of "have regard to", see the General Note to s2. Guidance does not have to be laid before Parliament.

section 13   Transfer of child support functions

[p208: add:]

General Note

This section transfers all functions under the Act to the CMEC, with some exceptions. The most interesting of the exceptions are the powers to agree to a redetermination (s23A of the Act) and the right of appeal (s24 of the Act), in both cases in respect of decisions of the First-tier Tribunal. Effectively, these exceptions give the Secretary of State some of the powers of a party to the proceedings without actually being a party.

Section 25 of the Act has been repealed. It dealt with appeals from the commissioners to the Court of Appeal. The equivalent appeal from the Upper Tribunal is now governed by s13 Tribunals, Courts and Enforcement Act 2007.

section 24   Orders preventing avoidance

[p211: this is in force from 6 April 2010 by art 2(a) of SI 2010 No.697.]

section 31   Power to treat liability as satisfied

[p222: this is in force from 26 November 2009 for making regulations and 5 January 2010 for all other purposes by art 2(1) of SI 2009 No.3072.]

section 38   Recovery of arrears from deceased's estate

[p225: this is in force from 26 November 2009 by art 2(2) of SI 2009 No.3072.]

Schedule 7   Social Security Act 1998 (c.14)

[p243: paragraph 3 is in force from 6 April 2010 by art 2(b) of SI 2010 No.697.]

PART III
REGULATIONS

Child Support (Arrears, Interest and Adjustment of Maintenance Assessments) Regulations 1992

pp299-312

Regulations 2 to 7, 9, 10 and 11 to 17 are revoked by reg 14 and Sch Child Support (Management of Payments and Arrears) Regulations 2009 No.3151 from 25 January 2010.

Child Support (Collection and Enforcement) Regulations 1992

Reg 22   Appeals against deduction from earnings order

[p330: General Note, Paragraph (4), add:]

Overpayments of child support may be reimbursed under s41B of the Act, or by reduction of arrears or of payments under the current calculation: see reg 8 Child Support (Management of Payments and Arrears) Regulations 2009.

Reg 28   Application for a liability order

[p345: General Note, Paragraph (2), add:]

It seems that the current text of this paragraph may not have been drawn to the attention of the Court of Appeal in *Child Maintenance and Enforcement Commission v Mitchell and Clements* [2010] EWCA Civ 333. See the comments of Aikens LJ at paras 51-52.

Sch 2   Charges connected with distress

[p350: paragraph 2(1)(b), at the end replace 'and per cent. on any additional sum;' with 'and 1/4 per cent. on any additional sum;']

Social Security and Child Support (Decisions and Appeals) Regulations 1999

reg 2   Service of notices or documents

[p428: General Note, head (b):]

Roach is reported as *R(CS) 4/07*.

reg 6A   Supersession of child support decisions

[p436: General Note, add:]

Paragraph (2)(c)

Neither the CMEC nor a tribunal may correct a mistake made in error of law by a previous tribunal. If the decision was not changed on appeal, it stands (*NH v Child Maintenance and Enforcement Commission* [2009] UKUT 183 (AAC)).

[p436: General Note, Paragragh (6), add:]

A decision on a variation under s28G of the Act can only be made on supersession under this paragraph, not under any other paragraph such as para (2)(b) (*TW v Secretary of State for Work and Pensions* [2009] UKUT 91 (AAC)).

reg 30A   Appeals to the First-tier Tribunal in child support cases

[p449: regulation 30A is revoked by reg 14 and Sch Child Support (Management of Payments and Arrears) Regulations 2009 No.151 from 25 January 2010, subject to the savings provisions in reg 15(2) of SI 2009 No.3151).]

[p449: replace the General Note:]

This regulation extends the scope of s20 of the Act, which governs appeals to the First-tier Tribunal. That tribunal has jurisdiction over decisions relating to adjustments in respect of overpayments and voluntary payments. It is revoked under reg 14 Child Support (Management of Payments and Arrears) Regulations 2009, but subject to the saving in reg 15(2) in respect of certain appeals.

reg 34   Death of a party to an appeal

[p453: after the definition, add:]

General Note

In the case of a deceased non-resident parent, reg 12(2) Child Support (Management of Payments and Arrears) Regulations 2009 substitutes a different provision for paras (1) and (2).

Child Support (Maintenance Calculations and Special Cases) Regulations 2000

reg 1   Citation, commencement and interpretation

[p509: General Note, Self-employed earner:]

The reference to *R(PC) 2/92* is wrong. The correct citation is *R(FC) 2/92*.

[p509: General Note, Self-employed earner, add:]

The test of whether a person is a self-employed earner is that provided by the Social Security Contributions and Benefits Act 1992, not the test used for tax purposes (*MG v Child Maintenance and Enforcement Commission (CSM)* [2010] UKUT 83 (AAC), para 22).

[p510: General Note, Student, after the second paragraph add:]

There is no particular number of hours that amount to full-time and the 12-hour rule that is used for the purposes of s55 of the Act does not apply (*DY v Child Maintenance and Enforcement Commission* [2010] UKUT 19 (AAC), paras 28-29).

    The definition of sandwich course referred to in head (b) is now out of date (*DY v Child Maintenance and Enforcement Commission* [2010] UKUT 19 (AAC), para 45).

reg 11   Non-resident parent liable to pay maintenance under a maintenance order

[p520: General Note, add a new first paragraph:]

This regulation only applies if maintenance is being paid under a maintenance order. It does not apply if maintenance is being paid under an agreement. This is not discriminatory. A non-resident parent who pays under an agreement is able, unlike a non-resident parent who pays under a court order, to apply for a maintenance calculation under s4 of the Act (*HW v Secretary of State for Work and Pensions* [2009] CSIH 21).

Schedule   Net weekly income

[p529: General Note, third paragraph:]

For the reference to *Brumby* substitute *Inland Revenue Commissioners v Reid's Trustees* [1949] AC 361 at 371-372.

[p529: General Note, Income, add:]

The classification of drawings from a partnership was considered in *AR v Bradford MBC* [2008] UKUT 30 (AAC), reported as *R(H) 6/09*. The judge decided that they were not income. As partners are self-employed, their income was the gross receipts of the partnership less deductions. Taking drawings into account could lead to double counting of income or effectively override the legislative test. The judge considered whether the drawings were in fact by way of a loan from one partner to the other. If they had been, they would have been income. However, there was no evidence to show a loan in this case.

[p530: General Note, "expenses", second paragraph:]

The separate references to paras 3(4)(b)(iii) and 3(4)(b)(v) are out of date, as they refer to earlier provisions that have now been revoked.

[p538: General Note, Paragraph 7(1), add:]

This amended provision reverses the effect of the decision of the House of Lords in *Smith v Smith and Secretary of State for Work and Pensions* [2004] EWCA Civ 1318. Its purpose is to restore the link with the position in tax law (*MG v Child Maintenance and Enforcement Commission (CSM)* [2010] UKUT 83 (AAC), para 31).

[p539: General Note, Paragraph 8(3)(b)(vii):]

This provision has been revoked.

[p539: General Note, Paragraph 13A:]

The decision in *RH* is reported as *SSWP v RH* [2008] UKUT 19 (AAC), *R(CS) 3/09*.

Child Support (Variations) Regulations 2000

reg 9   Procedure in relation to the determination of an application

[p547: General Note, Paragraph (2)(b), head (vii):]

The reference for *McGinley* is (1998) 27 EHRR 1.

reg 10   Special expenses – contact costs

[p549: General Note, Paragraph (3), add:]

There must be a set pattern, but it need not be a rigid pattern that never varies. The issue has to be decided 'with a degree of realism and common sense, bearing in mind the practicalities of the lives of separated families' (*PB v Child Maintenance and Enforcement Commission* [2009] UKUT 262 (AAC), para 11).

No variation can be made if the child with whom contact is being maintained is resident abroad. This is not inconsistent with the non-resident parent's freedom of movement in EC law when read in conjunction with the European Convention on Human Rights (*Child Maintenance and Enforcement Commission v NC* [2009] UKUT 106 (AAC)).

reg 18   Assets

[p561: General Note, Head (a), add:]

In *CS v Child Maintenance and Enforcement Commission* [2010] UKUT 182 (AAC), the judge decided that property that is subject to a court order for transfer as part of financial provision on divorce is not within the control of the beneficiary until it has been transferred. He explained:
> '9. . . . the ability to request a third party [the court in this case] to do something with the asset negates the concept that one has the ability to control it. The ability to control imports the notion of independent control of it to sell it or otherwise deal with it.'

CCS 8/2000 deals with the identification or classification of an asset. Once an asset has been identified or classified as consisting of one or more particular items, this regulation must be applied to that asset individually (*MG v Child Maintenance and Enforcement Commission (CSM)* [2010] UKUT 83 (AAC), para 40).

[p562: General Note, Head (d), add:]

Assets used in the course of a trade or business are excluded only if income from them was taken into account as self-employed income under the Schedule to the Maintenance Calculations and Special Cases Regulations. This limitation was analysed in *MG v Child Maintenance and Enforcement Commission (CSM)* [2010] UKUT 83 (AAC). Having classified the non-resident parent as a self-employed earner under the definition in the Maintenance Calculations and Special Cases Regulations, the judge decided that the treatment of the income under the Schedule to those Regulations was determined by the way that Her Majesty's Revenue and Customs dealt with the income. This seems inconsistent, as it appears to involve switching over from the definition of self-employed earner that applies for child support purposes to the one used for tax approach. The judge rejected the argument that the words added in 2002 were merely a declaratory clarification to distinguish between business and investment properties:
> '34. The submission for CMEC and for the father was that the intention of the amendment was merely to reinforce and clarify the existing position, that only assets used in a business were taken out of account by regulation 18(3)(d), not assets held merely as investments or in a way which did not amount to the carrying on of a business. Mr Ellis and Mr Scoon both accepted that on the basis put forward for CMEC the amendment made no difference to the legal outcome, but submitted that it still had a point in providing clarification. But, if so, as Ms Spicer submitted for the mother, why did the Explanatory Notes to the Child Support (Miscellaneous Amendments) Regulations 2002 (SI 2002 No 1204) say that the new provision was that land or property held as a business or trade asset

was excluded from the definition of asset "in certain circumstances"? And why was an allegedly merely clarifying amendment put in such an obscure form? I need not go too deeply into all that, because the answer lies in the assumption, that I have found to have been soundly based, that the income from such assets, even when used for business or trade purposes, could not in law go into the calculation of net weekly income under Part III or any other Part of the Schedule to the MCSC Regulations.'

The judge applied head (d) to each property separately:

'40. ... It seems to me that the key is that in principle sub-paragraphs (b) to (d) of regulation 18(3), through the reference to "any asset", must be applied to each separate asset individually. It is the total value of assets referred to in regulation 18(2), thus excluding assets disregarded by virtue of the other parts of regulation 18(3), that is to be tested against the £65,000 limit in sub-paragraph (a). There will no doubt be scope for legitimate differences of approach to when a parcel of rights is to be regarded as one asset, as discussed in Commissioner's decision *CCS/8/2000*. What was in issue there was some farm land and a farm house, either of which it appears could have been sold off separately. Mr Commissioner Jacobs was plainly right to hold that the appeal tribunal there had been entitled to treat the items individually or collectively, depending on the particular circumstances. But that does not in any way undermine the basic principle. In the case of a holding of a portfolio of let properties as part of a business, it must be asked of each property (without needing here to determine whether a house or block in which several flats were let is one asset or several) whether it is used in the course of a trade or business and whether the exception applies. The test in the exception is not whether the business in which the asset is used produces income, or even less "an income". The test is in terms of whether the asset produces income. It seems to me that it will often be impossible to know whether the expenses related to each particular asset exceed the rental income, at least not without more detailed investigation than is required for income tax purposes or is sensible to expect in the child support context. Mortgage interest will be easy to identify, but normal accounting procedures would not require more general expenses of the business to be apportioned among different properties. Therefore, in my judgment the test can only be whether the property asset produces gross income receipts, regardless of the overall profitability or otherwise of the business.

'41. But how then can one ask whether such income forms part of the parent's net weekly income as calculated under Part III of the MCSC Regulations? The difficulty is much lessened by my conclusion as to the treatment of ordinary rental income under Part III. Since that conclusion is that any profit from a property business that is not required for income tax purposes to be reported on the self-employment pages of the self-assessment tax return cannot go into the calculation under Part III, the income produced by each property asset can never form part of the parent's net weekly income. Therefore, the exception to regulation 18(3)(d) applies. That comes to much the same thing as asking whether the income is of a type that can go into the calculation under Part III. Indeed, it seems to me that the relevant part of regulation 18(3)(d) can legitimately be read as if it said "except where the asset is of a type specified in paragraph (2)(b) which does not produce income that formspart of the net weekly income of the non-resident parent" as calculated under Part III.'

Child Support (Transitional Provisions) Regulations 2000

reg 3   **Decision and notice of decision**

[p475: subparas (4) and (5) are missing, add:]

(4)   Where at the calculation date there is an interim maintenance assessment in force and there is insufficient information held by the Secretary of State to make a maintenance assessment, or a decision in accordance with paragraph (1), the Secretary of State shall–

    (a)   supersede the interim maintenance assessment to make a default maintenance decision; and

    (b)   notify the non-resident parent, the person with care and, where the maintenance assessment was made in response to an application under section 7, the child, in writing, in accordance with regulation 15C(2) of the Decisions and Appeals Regulations.

(5)   In a case to which paragraph (1)(c) or (4) applies, where after the calculation date information is made available to the Secretary of State to enable him to make a maintenance assessment he may–

    (a)   where the decision was made under paragraph (1)(c), revise the interim maintenance assessment in accordance with the Assessment Procedure Regulations, and supersede the conversion decision in accordance with the Decisions and Appeals Regulations;

    (b)   where the decision was made under paragraph (4), revise the interim maintenance assessment in accordance with the Assessment Procedure Regulations, and revise the default maintenance decision in accordance with the Decisions and Appeals Regulations.

Child Support (Maintenance Calculation Procedure) Regulations 2000

reg 5   Notice of an application for a maintenance calculation

[p583: General Note, add:]

Paragraph (2)

The notification requirement applies even if notice is effected by the parent with care (*CH v Child Maintenance and Enforcement Commission (CSM)* [2010] UKUT 140 (AAC), para 73).

reg 25   Effective dates of maintenance calculations

[p589: General Note, Paragraph (3), add:]

The notification may be effective even if it is effected by the parent with care, although it must comply with the notice requirements in reg 5(2) (*CH v Child Maintenance and Enforcement Commission (CSM)* [2010] UKUT 140 (AAC), paras 36 and 73).

Schedule   Meaning of "child" for the purpose of the Act

[p596: after the definition, add:]

General Note

For commentary on the provisions of this Schedule, see the General Note to s55 of the Act. The definition in para 3 applies only for the purposes of that section and does not apply to the definition of student in the Maintenance Calculations and Special Cases Regulations (*DY v Child Maintenance and Enforcement Commission* [2010] UKUT 19 (AAC), paras 27-28).

Child Support Information Regulation 2008

reg 2   Interpretation

[p622: add:]

General Note

Paragraph (2)

The regulations are worded in terms of the 2003 scheme. They also apply, with appropriate modifications, to the 1993 scheme. The principal effect is that references to non-resident parents and maintenance calculations must be read to apply to absent parents and maintenance assessments.

Paragraph (4)

This provides for an extended meaning of non-resident parent. It includes a parent who is the non-resident parent for the purposes of an application, even if paternity is challenged. See, however, reg 5. It covers both non-resident parents of current maintenance calculations and those who were non-resident parents under calculations that are no longer in force. It extends to those who are treated as non-resident parents by virtue of a special case under s42 of the Act.

reg 3   Information from the applicant

[p622: add:]

General Note

This regulation is made under ss4(4) and 7(5) of the Act. It imposes a duty on an applicant to provide all the information required to identify and trace the non-resident parent, calculate that parent's liability to child support maintenance, and enforce that liability. In the case of a child applicant in Scotland, there is no duty to provide information about that parent's identity.

The duty is subject to two qualifications. First, it is qualified by reasonableness. Sections 4(4) and 7(5) apply only to the extent that the applicant reasonably can comply: see the general note to s4(4). Regulation 7(1) provides that there is no duty to acquire information unless it is reasonable to expect this to be done. And reg 10 provides that a person with care is only under a duty to provide information that the CMEC reasonably requires. Second, the scope of the duty is limited, by both the regulation itself and ss4(4) and 7(5), to information that the CMEC requires. If the CMEC can obtain the information elsewhere, it is not required of the applicant.

The duty is not limited to the time of the application. It continues to apply thereafter, but it only arises on request. There is a limited continuing duty for a person with care, but not a child, to provide information without a request in reg 10.

reg 4   Information from other persons

[p623: add:]

General Note

Most of this regulation is made under s14(1) of the Act, although paras 2(h) and (3) are made under s57(1). It imposes duties on persons (other than the applicant) and organisations to provide information. As with reg 3, the duty does not arise unless the information is required.

The duty is not limited to the time of the application. It applies both then and thereafter, but it only arises on request. There is a limited continuing duty for a non-resident parent to provide information without a request in reg 9.

reg 5   Information from persons denying parentage

[p623: add:]

General Note

This regulation limits the duties owed if an alleged non-resident parent (i) denies parentage and (ii) is not within any of the cases in s26 of the Act. The only duties that arise in respect of such a person are to provide information about (a) the person's identity and (b) the CMEC's jurisdiction under s44.

reg 6   Information from a court

[p623: add:]

General Note

This regulation is made under s14(1) of the Act and imposes a duty on the listed court officers to provide information and evidence. The duty arises if there is, or has ever been, a relevant court order made or if there are, or ever have been, proceedings.

reg 7   Duty of persons from whom information requested

[p623: add:]

General Note

Paragraph (1)

This paragraph provides for the extent of the duties to provide information or evidence. They only arise if the person possesses it or can reasonably be expected to acquire it. For the latter, the ease with which it can be obtained and any cost involved will be relevant considerations.

Paragraph (2)

This paragraph provides for the time within which the evidence or information must be provided. Inevitably, it is not specific.

reg 8   Commission to warn of consequences of failing to provide information or providing false information

[624: add:]

General Note

The CMEC must set out the consequences of failing to provide, or providing false, information, including offences under s14A of the Act. In view of the powers under that section, tribunals may prefer to obtain information through the CMEC rather than under their own powers.

reg 9   Duty to notify change of address

[p624: add:]

General Note

This is one of two continuing duties to provide information without a request by the CMEC. For the other, see reg 10. Both are limited. This one applies to non-resident parents and is limited to a change of address.

reg 10   Continuing duty of person with care

[p624: add:]

General Note

This is one of two continuing duties to provide information without a request by the CMEC. For the other, see reg 9. Both are limited. This one applies to persons with care and is limited to circumstances in which a maintenance calculation ceases to exist. It is made under Sch 1 para 16(10) to the Act. It arises if the CMEC loses jurisdiction, the qualifying child ceases to be a child, and the circumstances in Sch 1 para 16 to the Act apply. It is more curtailed than the duty under reg 3. It only applies if the person believes that the calculation has ceased, not may have ceased.

On the wording, the belief must concern the effect on the maintenance calculation, not merely the facts that give rise to that effect.

reg 11 Powers of inspection in relation to Crown premises

[p624: add:]

General Note

This regulation is made under s57(2) of the Act.

reg 12 Disclosure of information to a court or tribunal

[p624: add:]

General Note

This regulation is made under s14(3) of the Act. It permits disclosure in connection with legal proceedings, principally to courts, tribunals and parties to appeals and references before tribunals. The persons who have a right of appeal to the First-tier Tribunal are set out in s20(2) of the Act. There is no power to disclose information in connection with any other proceedings than those covered by this regulation (*Re C (A Minor) (Child Support Agency: Disclosure)* [1995] 1 FLR 201).

reg 13 Disclosure of information to other parties

[p625: add:]

General Note

This regulation is made under s14(3) of the Act. It permits disclosure, for limited purposes only, to other parties to a maintenance calculation. This strikes a balance between transparency of decision-making and respecting confidentiality. In contrast to other regulations, it arises only when disclosure is essential for one of the stated purposes. This is a stringent condition that suggests that disclosure must be indispensable to achieve the stated purpose.

reg 14 Employment to which section 50 of the 1991 Act applies

[p626: add:]

General Note

This substituted regulation is made under s50(1A) and (1C) of the Act. It prescribes employments to which the offence in s50(1) applies.

reg 15 Revocation and saving

[p626: add:]

General Note

These regulations operate with effect from 27 October 2008. The Child Support (Information, Evidence and Disclosure) Regulations 1992 continue to apply prior to that date.

reg 16 Transitional provisions in relation to transfer of child support functions

[p626: add:]

General Note

Section 13 of the 2008 Act came into force on 1 November 2008.

Part IV
PROCEDURAL RULES

Tribunals, Courts and Enforcment Act 2007

section 11   Right to appeal to Upper Tribunal

[p634: General Note, add:]

So far, the Administrative Appeals Chamber has decided or accepted that the following decisions are appealable under this section:

- a direction for disclosure of documents (*Dorset Healthcare NHS Foundation Trust v MH* [2009] UKUT 4 (AAC));
- order for production of privileged material (*LM v London Borough of Lewisham* [2009] UKUT 204 (AAC));
- a direction prohibiting disclosure of documents (*RM v St Andrew's Healthcare* [2010] UKUT 119 (AAC));
- a refusal to set aside a decision (*MP v Secretary of State for Work and Pensions* (DLA) [2010] UKUT 103 (AAC));
- a decision striking out a case that could not be reinstated (*AW v Essex County Council* (SEN) [2010] UKUT 74 (AAC));
- a refusal to reinstate a case (*Synergy Child Services Ltd v Ofsted* [2009] UKUT 125 (AAC));
- a decision to strike out an appeal (*KC v London Borough of Newham* (SEN) [2010] UKUT 96 (AAC)).

The Tax and Chancery Chamber has accepted an appeal against a decision whether to direct a preliminary issue (*Goldman Sachs v Commissioners for Her Majesty's Revenue and Customs* [2009] UKUT 290 (TCC)).

Although case management decisions are, on the authorities, within this section, judges enjoy a wide discretion and the decisions should not be questioned unless there is point of substance that requires an urgent challenge and speedy resolution (*Re P and P (Care Proceedings: Appointment of Experts)* [2009] 2 FLR 1370, para 17). *RM v St Andrew's Healthcare* [2010] UKUT 119 (AAC) was an example of such a case. It concerned an order prohibiting disclosure of information that was central to the patient's case. The judge analysed why case management decisions are usually supported on appeal and the circumstances in which they would be susceptible to challenge.

'7. The non-disclosure order was a case management decision. Appellate courts are supportive of these decisions and discourage appeals against them. They often have to be made with little time for analysis or reflection. Appeals can disrupt the proceedings, produce inefficiency and increase costs. They are capable of being used for tactical purposes. Ultimately, the judge dealing with the case is probably best placed to make a judgment on how best to proceed in the context of the proceedings. Challenges are best considered at the end of the proceedings, when it is possible to judge whether the decision adversely affected the outcome.

8. This does not mean that case management decisions are immune from scrutiny. The decision may have been given after a hearing and with time for analysis. If it is made ahead of the final hearing, it may be possible to deal with an appeal quickly to avoid disrupting the First-tier Tribunal's timetable. There may be no question of seeking a tactical advantage. The issue may be severable from the more routine management of the proceedings. And it may be possible to anticipate the likely effect.

9. On the spectrum of case management decisions, the non-disclosure order is more susceptible to scrutiny than most. The judge held a hearing and took time before issuing her reasons. The issue is severable from the routine management of the case. It is important and its effects can be anticipated: the patient's solicitors argue that they are unable to obtain his instructions on the real case for his continued detention. There is no question of tactical advantage being sought and it has been possible to deal with the appeal quickly.'

Judicial review

Those decisions of the First-tier Tribunal that are not appealable under this section may be subject to judicial review. In the case of a review decision, there is such a substantial element of judgment or discretion that an application for judicial review will seldom succeed (*R (RB) v First-tier Tribunal (Review)* [2010] UKUT 160 (AAC), para 30).

The tribunal is the respondent to a judicial review application. It is permissible for the tribunal to make submissions, but it is doubtful whether it is appropriate for the tribunal to support the decision on its merits, especially where there is another party with an interest to oppose the application (*R (RB) v First-tier Tribunal*, para 14).

section 12   Proceedings on appeal to Upper Tribunal

[p635: General Note, add after first paragraph:]

Additional evidence

In *VH v Suffolk County Council* [2010] UKUT 203 (AAC), the judge explained when additional evidence would be admitted by the Upper Tribunal. He first defined 'additional evidence':

> '2. By 'additional evidence', I mean evidence produced to show: (i) the circumstances as they were at the time of the hearing before the First-tier Tribunal; (ii) that those circumstances have changed; (iii) how the local education authority has, or has not, implemented the statement. Parties regularly produce, respond to and complain about the introduction of evidence on these matters. Such evidence is potentially relevant, but only for limited purposes. Its relevance depends on the Upper Tribunal's powers in the particular case.
>
> 3. Parties may also produce evidence of what happened at the hearing. That evidence is in a different category and does not arise in this case.'

He then explained:

> '7. The first question for the Upper Tribunal under this section is: did the making of the First-tier Tribunal's decision involve the making of an error on a point of law? The Upper Tribunal must answer this question on the evidence that was before the First-tier Tribunal. A tribunal cannot go wrong in law by failing to take account of evidence that was not before it. See the decisions of the Social Security Commissioner in *R(S) 1/88* at [3] and of Underhill J in *R (S) v Hertfordshire County Council* [2006] EWHC 328 (Admin) at [25]. If the answer to this question is 'no', the Upper Tribunal's only power is to dismiss the appeal. If the answer is 'yes', a second question arises.
>
> 8. The second question is: how should the tribunal dispose of the case? There are three options: (a) leave the First-tier Tribunal's decision in place; (b) remit the case to the First-tier Tribunal; (c) re-make the decision. The tribunal may take account of additional evidence in order to decide which form of disposal is appropriate. If it decides to re-make the decision, evidence will also be needed of current circumstances.
>
> 9. In practice, it can be difficult for parties to know when additional may be relevant. For example, an oral hearing of an application may also consider the appeal and disposal. The Upper Tribunal, and representatives for other parties, need to be flexible in receiving evidence whose ultimate relevance will depend on how the case proceeds. Forcing a party to produce the additional evidence only if and when it is required could lead to inefficiency and delay.'

section 13   Right of appeal to Court of Appeal etc

[p642: General Note, add:]

The fact that the decision under appeal was arguably plainly wrong is not a compelling reason for giving permission to appeal. Nor is the fact that the decisions, at different levels, were in conflict. It is, though, possible that the impact of a decision on the welfare of a child could provide a compelling reason. See *Re B (Residence: Second Appeal)* [2009] 2 FLR 632, paras 10-12 and 14.

The appeals from the Upper Tribunal to the Court of Appeal Order 2008 was made under the authority of s13(6) of the Tribunals, Courts and Enforcement Act 2007. That subsection only applies to applications for permission to appeal against a decision given under s11. That section only applies to cases that came before the Upper Tribunal on appeal. It does not apply to cases that come before the Upper Tribunal on referral under s9(5)(b). Accordingly, the order does not apply if a party applies for permission to appeal against a decision made by the Upper Tribunal on a referral. An appeal to the Court of Appeal in those circumstances would not be a second appeal. In *Cooke v Secretary of State for Social Security* [2002] 3 All ER 279, Hale LJ applied the s55(1) criteria to applications for permission to appeal against decisions of the commissioners. It is possible that the reasoning in that case would apply to a case that was referred to the Upper Tribunal, as there has, in substance (though not in form), been two judicial appeals.

It is not sufficient for an appellant simply to identify the parts of the tribunal's decision with which the party disagrees without identifying the issues or the reasons why the decision is said to be wrong (*Re N (A Child) v A* [2010] 1 FLR 454, paras 69-72).

Subsection (8)

The Court of Appeal has no inherent power that would allow it to bypass the prohibition in para (c) on appeals against refusals of permission to appeal (*Riniker v University College London* [2001] 1 WLR 13).

Judicial review

Those decisions of the Upper Tribunal that are not appealable under this section may be subject to judicial review. Different answers have been given in England and Wales and in Scotland.

In England and Wales, the issue is governed by the decision of the Divisional Court in *R (Cart, U and XC) v the Upper Tribunal, the Special Immigration Appeal Commission, the Secretary of State for Justice, the Secretary of State for the Home Department, the Public Law Project, the Child Maintenance and Enforcement Commission and Wendy Cart* [2010] 1 All ER 908. The court held that, given the status of the Upper Tribunal, it was only susceptible to judicial review if it acted outside its jurisdiction or there was a wholly exceptional collapse of fair procedure. This decision is under appeal to the Court of Appeal. Argument has been heard and the decision is awaited.

In Scotland, the issue is governed by the decision of the Outer House of the Court of Session in the petition of *Eba* [2010] ScotCS CSOH 45. Lord Glennie decided that the issue was not determined by the status of the Upper Tribunal. Instead, it had to be decided by the application of a variety of principles to the type of case. Decisions refusing permission to appeal to the Upper Tribunal in social security matters would only be subject to judicial review in exceptional circumstances. As child support decisions are analogous to social security decisions, the same approach should apply to both.

See also the General Note to s11.

ss15-21   Judicial review

[p644: add sections 15-21 with commentary:]

"Judicial review"

Upper Tribunal's "judicial review" jurisdiction

15.–(1)   The Upper Tribunal has power, in cases arising under the law of England and Wales or under the law of Northern Ireland, to grant the following kinds of relief–

(a)   a mandatory order;

(b)   a prohibiting order;

(c)   a quashing order;

(d)   a declaration;

(e)   an injunction.

(2)   The power under subsection (1) may be exercised by the Upper Tribunal if–

(a)   certain conditions are met (see section 18), or

(b)   the tribunal is authorised to proceed even though not all of those conditions are met (see section 19(3) and (4)).

(3)   Relief under subsection (1) granted by the Upper Tribunal–

(a)   has the same effect as the corresponding relief granted by the High Court on an application for judicial review, and

(b)   is enforceable as if it were relief granted by the High Court on an application for judicial review.

(4)   In deciding whether to grant relief under subsection (1)(a), (b) or (c), the Upper Tribunal must apply the principles that the High Court would apply in deciding whether to grant that relief on an application for judicial review.

(5)   In deciding whether to grant relief under subsection (1)(d) or (e), the Upper Tribunal must–

(a)   in cases arising under the law of England and Wales apply the principles that the High Court would apply in deciding whether to grant that relief under section 31(2) of the Supreme Court Act 1981 (c. 54) on an application for judicial review, and

(b)   in cases arising under the law of Northern Ireland apply the principles that the High Court would apply in deciding whether to grant that relief on an application for judicial review.

(6)   For the purposes of the application of subsection (3)(a) in relation to cases arising under the law of Northern Ireland–

(a)   a mandatory order under subsection (1)(a) shall be taken to correspond to an order of mandamus,

(b)   a prohibiting order under subsection (1)(b) shall be taken to correspond to an order of prohibition, and

(c)   a quashing order under subsection (1)(c) shall be taken to correspond to an order of certiorari.

General Note

This section confers judicial review powers on the Upper Tribunal equivalent to the High Court.

Application for relief under section 15(1)

16.–(1)   This section applies in relation to an application to the Upper Tribunal for relief under section 15(1).

(2)   The application may be made only if permission (or, in a case arising under the law of Northern Ireland, leave) to make it has been obtained from the tribunal.

(3)   The tribunal may not grant permission (or leave) to make the application unless it considers that the applicant has a sufficient interest in the matter to which the application relates.

(4)   Subsection (5) applies where the tribunal considers–

(a)   that there has been undue delay in making the application, and

(b)   that granting the relief sought on the application would be likely to cause substantial hardship to, or substantially prejudice the rights of, any person or would be detrimental to good administration.

(5)   The tribunal may–

(a)   refuse to grant permission (or leave) for the making of the application;

(b)   refuse to grant any relief sought on the application.

(6)   The tribunal may award to the applicant damages, restitution or the recovery of a sum due if–

(a)   the application includes a claim for such an award arising from any matter to which the application relates, and

(b)   the tribunal is satisfied that such an award would have been made by the High Court if the claim had been made in an action begun in the High Court by the applicant at the time of making the application.

(7)   An award under subsection (6) may be enforced as if it were an award of the High Court.

(8)   Where–

(a)   the tribunal refuses to grant permission (or leave) to apply for relief under section 15(1),

(b)   the applicant appeals against that refusal, and

  (c)   the Court of Appeal grants the permission (or leave), the Court of Appeal may
        go on to decide the application for relief under section 15(1).
  (9)   Subsections (4) and (5) do not prevent Tribunal Procedure Rules from limiting
the time within which applications may be made.

General Note

Subsection (1)

An application must identify the decision that is the subject of the application and the errors of law
on which it is based. Particularity is necessary. It is not acceptable to present a claim as a narrative
or as unfocussed complaints or as general reflections on the law. See *Brookes v Secretary of State
for Work and Pensions and the Child Maintenance and Enforcement Commission* [2010] EWCA
Civ 420 at para 4.

Subsection (2)

As in the High Court, the applicant must first apply for permission to make an application for judicial
review. Only with permission may the application for judicial review itself be made.

Subsection (3)

As in the High Court, the applicant must have sufficient interest in the matter. This is unlikely to
present a problem in the child support cases that may come before the Upper Tribunal.

Subsection (4)

This deals with delay. The Upper Tribunal may refuse permission or relief if two conditions are
satisfied. The first condition is that there must have been undue delay. Rule 28(2) of the Tribunal
Procedure (Upper Tribunal) Rules 2008 provides that an application must be received within three
months of the decision, action or omission, although this may be extended under rule 5(3)(a). The
second condition is that giving relief would involve substantial hardship or substantial prejudice or
would be detrimental to good administration.
    It may be that the decision that is the subject of the application is a continuing one. However,
this must be distinguished from a decision that remains in effect. See *Brookes* at para 7(i).

Quashing orders under section 15(1): supplementary provision

  17.–(1)   If the Upper Tribunal makes a quashing order under section 15(1)(c) in
respect of a decision, it may in addition–
  (a)   remit the matter concerned to the court, tribunal or authority that made the
        decision, with a direction to reconsider the matter and reach a decision in
        accordance with the findings of the Upper Tribunal, or
  (b)   substitute its own decision for the decision in question.
  (2)   The power conferred by subsection (1)(b) is exercisable only if–
  (a)   the decision in question was made by a court or tribunal,
  (b)   the decision is quashed on the ground that there has been an error of law, and
  (c)   without the error, there would have been only one decision that the court or
        tribunal could have reached.
  (3)   Unless the Upper Tribunal otherwise directs, a decision substituted by it under
subsection (1)(b) has effect as if it were a decision of the relevant court or tribunal.

General Note

If the Upper Tribunal quashes a decision, it has power to substitute its own decision rather than
direct that the decision be remade. This is subject to the three conditions in subs (3). It only applies
to decisions of courts or tribunals. The decision must have been quashed for error of law. And there
must be only one decision that the court or tribunal could properly make.

Limits of jurisdiction under section 15(1)

  18.–(1)   This section applies where an application made to the Upper Tribunal seeks
(whether or not alone)–
  (a)   relief under section 15(1), or

(b)   permission (or, in a case arising under the law of Northern Ireland, leave) to apply for relief under section 15(1).

(2)   If Conditions 1 to 4 are met, the tribunal has the function of deciding the application.

(3)   If the tribunal does not have the function of deciding the application, it must by order transfer the application to the High Court.

(4)   Condition 1 is that the application does not seek anything other than–

(a)   relief under section 15(1);

(b)   permission (or, in a case arising under the law of Northern Ireland, leave) to apply for relief under section 15(1);

(c)   an award under section 16(6);

(d)   interest;

(e)   costs.

(5)   Condition 2 is that the application does not call into question anything done by the Crown Court.

(6)   Condition 3 is that the application falls within a class specified for the purposes of this subsection in a direction given in accordance with Part 1 of Schedule 2 to the Constitutional Reform Act 2005 (c. 4).

(7)   The power to give directions under subsection (6) includes–

(a)   power to vary or revoke directions made in exercise of the power, and

(b)   power to make different provision for different purposes.

(8)   Condition 4 is that the judge presiding at the hearing of the application is either–

(a)   a judge of the High Court or the Court of Appeal in England and Wales or Northern Ireland, or a judge of the Court of Session, or

(b)   such other persons as may be agreed from time to time between the Lord Chief Justice, the Lord President, or the Lord Chief Justice of Northern Ireland, as the case may be, and the Senior President of Tribunals.

(9)   Where the application is transferred to the High Court under subsection (3)–

(a)   the application is to be treated for all purposes as if it–

    (i)   had been made to the High Court, and

    (ii)   sought things corresponding to those sought from the tribunal, and

(b)   any steps taken, permission (or leave) given or orders made by the tribunal in relation to the application are to be treated as taken, given or made by the High Court.

(10)   Rules of court may make provision for the purpose of supplementing subsection (9).

(11)   The provision that may be made by Tribunal Procedure Rules about amendment of an application for relief under section 15(1) includes, in particular, provision about amendments that would cause the application to become transferrable under subsection (3).

(12)   For the purposes of subsection (9)(a)(ii), in relation to an application transferred to the High Court in Northern Ireland–

(a)   an order of mandamus shall be taken to correspond to a mandatory order under section 15(1)(a),

(b)   an order of prohibition shall be taken to correspond to a prohibiting order under section 15(1)(b), and

an order of certiorari shall be taken to correspond to a quashing order under section 15(1)(c).

General Note

This section identifies the cases over which the Upper Tribunal has exclusive jurisdiction. They must satisfy four conditions. The Upper Tribunal also has, at the discretion of the High Court, a shared jurisdiction with that Court over cases that satisfy all but the third condition: see s19.

Subsection (4) – Condition 1

This limits the cases over which the Upper Tribunal has jurisdiction to those that deal exclusively with judicial review and ancillary matters. If the application is linked with any other claim, it is outside the Upper Tribunal's jurisdiction.

Subsection (5) – Condition 2

This restricts judicial review affecting the Crown Court to the High Court.

Subsection (6) – Condition 3

The Lord Chief Justice for England and Wales has given a *Direction – Classes of cases specified under section 18(6) of the Tribunals, Courts and Enforcement Act 2007* [2009] 1 WLR 327:

'It is ordered as follows
1. The following direction takes effect in relation to an application made to the High Court or Upper Tribunal on or after 3 November 2008 that seeks relief of a kind mentioned in section 15(1) of the Tribunals, Courts and Enforcement Act 2007 ("the 2007 Act").
2. The Lord Chief Justice hereby directs that the following classes of case are specified for the purposes of section 18(6) of the 2007 Act–
   a. Any decision of the First-tier Tribunal on an appeal made in the exercise of a right conferred by the Criminal Injuries Compensation Scheme in compliance with section 5(1) of the Criminal Injuries Compensation Act 1995 (appeals against decisions on review); and
   b. Any decision of the First-tier Tribunal made under Tribunal Procedure Rules or section 9 of the 2007 Act where there is no right of appeal to the Upper Tribunal and that decision is not an excluded decision within paragraph (b), (c), or (f) of section 11(5) of the 2007 Act.
3. This Direction does not have effect where an application seeks (whether or not alone) a declaration of incompatibility under section 4 of the Human Rights Act 1998.
4. This Direction is made by the Lord Chief Justice with the agreement of the Lord Chancellor. It is made in the exercise of powers conferred by section 18(6) of the 2007 Act and in accordance with Part 1 of Schedule 2 to the Constitutional Reform Act 2005.'

The significance of these provisions depends on how wide an interpretation is given to 'decision' in s11. The wider that interpretation, the less the scope for judicial review.

Subsection (8) – Condition 4

This limits the judges who may hear judicial review cases in the Upper Tribunal. All the salaried judges dealing with child support cases who are based in England and Wales are authorised under para (b).

Transfer of judicial review applications from High Court
19.–(1)   In the Supreme Court Act 1981 (c. 54), after section 31 insert–

"31A   Transfer of judicial review applications to Upper Tribunal
(1)   This section applies where an application is made to the High Court–
(a)   for judicial review, or
(b)   for permission to apply for judicial review.
(2)   If Conditions 1, 2, 3 and 4 are met, the High Court must by order transfer the application to the Upper Tribunal.
(3)   If Conditions 1, 2 and 4 are met, but Condition 3 is not, the High Court may by order transfer the application to the Upper Tribunal if it appears to the High Court to be just and convenient to do so.
(4)   Condition 1 is that the application does not seek anything other than–
(a)   relief under section 31(1)(a) and (b);
(b)   permission to apply for relief under section 31(1)(a) and (b);
(c)   an award under section 31(4);

(d) interest;

(e) costs.

(5) Condition 2 is that the application does not call into question anything done by the Crown Court.

(6) Condition 3 is that the application falls within a class specified under section 18(6) of the Tribunals, Courts and Enforcement Act 2007.

(7) Condition 4 is that the application does not call into question any decision made under–

(a) the Immigration Acts,

(b) the British Nationality Act 1981 (c. 61),

(c) any instrument having effect under an enactment within paragraph (a) or (b), or

(d) any other provision of law for the time being in force which determines British citizenship, British overseas territories citizenship, the status of a British National (Overseas) or British Overseas citizenship.''

(2) In the Judicature (Northern Ireland) Act 1978 (c. 23), after section 25 insert–

"25A Transfer of judicial review applications to Upper Tribunal

(1) This section applies where an application is made to the High Court–

(a) for judicial review, or

(b) for leave to apply for judicial review.

(2) If Conditions 1, 2, 3 and 4 are met, the High Court must by order transfer the application to the Upper Tribunal.

(3) If Conditions 1, 2 and 4 are met, but Condition 3 is not, the High Court may by order transfer the application to the Upper Tribunal if it appears to the High Court to be just and convenient to do so.

(4) Condition 1 is that the application does not seek anything other than–

(a) relief under section 18(1)(a) to (e);

(b) leave to apply for relief under section 18(1)(a) to (e);

(c) an award under section 20;

(d) interest;

(e) costs.

(5) Condition 2 is that the application does not call into question anything done by the Crown Court.

(6) Condition 3 is that the application falls within a class specified under section 18(6) of the Tribunals, Courts and Enforcement Act 2007.

(7) Condition 4 is that the application does not call into question any decision made under–

(a) the Immigration Acts,

(b) the British Nationality Act 1981,

(c) any instrument having effect under an enactment within paragraph (a) or (b), or

(d) any other provision of law for the time being in force which determines British citizenship, British overseas territories citizenship, the status of a British National (Overseas) or British Overseas citizenship.''

(3) Where an application is transferred to the Upper Tribunal under 31A of the Supreme Court Act 1981 (c. 54) or section 25A of the Judicature (Northern Ireland) Act 1978 (transfer from the High Court of judicial review applications)–

(a) the application is to be treated for all purposes as if it–

   (i) had been made to the tribunal, and

   (ii) sought things corresponding to those sought from the High Court,

(b) the tribunal has the function of deciding the application, even if it does not fall within a class specified under section 18(6), and

(c) any steps taken, permission given, leave given or orders made by the High Court in relation to the application are to be treated as taken, given or made by the tribunal.

(4) Where–

(a)   an application for permission is transferred to the Upper Tribunal under section 31A of the Supreme Court Act 1981 (c. 54) and the tribunal grants permission, or

(b)   an application for leave is transferred to the Upper Tribunal under section 25A of the Judicature (Northern Ireland) Act 1978 (c. 23) and the tribunal grants leave,

the tribunal has the function of deciding any subsequent application brought under the permission or leave, even if the subsequent application does not fall within a class specified under section 18(6).

(5)   Tribunal Procedure Rules may make further provision for the purposes of supplementing subsections (3) and (4).

(6)   For the purposes of subsection (3)(a)(ii), in relation to an application transferred to the Upper Tribunal under section 25A of the Judicature (Northern Ireland) Act 1978–

(a)   a mandatory order under section 15(1)(a) shall be taken to correspond to an order of mandamus,

(b)   a prohibiting order under section 15(1)(b) shall be taken to correspond to an order of prohibition, and

(c)   a quashing order under section 15(1)(c) shall be taken to correspond to an order of certiorari.

General Note

The amendments made by this section deal with judicial review cases that are commenced in the High Court. If they are cases that satisfy the four conditions in s18, they *must* be transferred to the Upper Tribunal. If they are cases that satisfy all but the third condition, the High Court *may* transfer them to the Upper Tribunal. This allows the High Court to transfer to the Upper Tribunal any case involving child support in which the judges' expertise in the law may be helpful.

Transfer of judicial review applications from the Court of Session

20.–(1)   Where an application is made to the supervisory jurisdiction of the Court of Session, the Court–

(a)   must, if Conditions 1, 2 and 4 are met, and

(b)   may, if Conditions 1, 3 and 4 are met, but Condition 2 is not, by order transfer the application to the Upper Tribunal.

(2)   Condition 1 is that the application does not seek anything other than an exercise of the supervisory jurisdiction of the Court of Session.

(3)   Condition 2 is that the application falls within a class specified for the purposes of this subsection by act of sederunt made with the consent of the Lord Chancellor.

(4)   Condition 3 is that the subject matter of the application is not a devolved Scottish matter.

(5)   Condition 4 is that the application does not call into question any decision made under–

(a)   the Immigration Acts,

(b)   the British Nationality Act 1981 (c. 61),

(c)   any instrument having effect under an enactment within paragraph (a) or (b), or

(d)   any other provision of law for the time being in force which determines British citizenship, British overseas territories citizenship, the status of a British National (Overseas) or British Overseas citizenship.

(6)   There may not be specified under subsection (3) any class of application which includes an application the subject matter of which is a devolved Scottish matter.

(7)   For the purposes of this section, the subject matter of an application is a devolved Scottish matter if it–

(a)   concerns the exercise of functions in or as regards Scotland, and

(b)   does not relate to a reserved matter within the meaning of the Scotland Act 1998 (c. 46).

(8)   In subsection (2), the reference to the exercise of the supervisory jurisdiction of the Court of Session includes a reference to the making of any order in connection with or in consequence of the exercise of that jurisdiction.

General Note
Subsection (1)

All applications to the supervisory jurisdiction of the Court of Session must be made to that Court. They cannot be made to the Upper Tribunal: *EF v Secretary of State for Work and Pensions* [2009] UKUT 92 (AAC). The Court has a duty and a power to transfer the case to the Upper Tribunal, depending on which of the following conditions are satisfied.

Subsection (2) – Condition 1

This limits the cases over which the Upper Tribunal has jurisdiction to those that deal exclusively with supervisory jurisdiction, as read with subs (8).

Subsection (3) – Condition 2

This deals with those cases that the Court of Session must transfer to the Upper Tribunal under subs (1)(a). They may not include a devolved matter: subs (6). Paragraph 3 of the Act of Sederunt (Transfer of Judicial Review Applications from the Court of Session) 2008 specifies those cases that must be transferred:
> 'The class of application is an application which challenges a procedural decision or a procedural ruling of the First-tier Tribunal, established under section 3(1) of the Tribunals, Courts and Enforcement Act 2007.'

Despite its wording, this extends to procedural errors in substantive decisions. In the *Petition of Sharon Currie* [2009] CSOH 145, Lord Hodge said (at para 6) that it includes 'decisions which are vitiated by procedural errors . . . In other words, I interpret procedural decisions and procedural rulings as extending to procedural omissions or oversights giving rise to unfairness.' In that case, the basis of the application was an error of law that was not of a procedural nature. As such, it was outside the scope of mandatory transfers. It is possible to read Lord Hodge's reasons to mean that a challenge to a procedural decision for an error of law that is not of a procedural nature (such as a lack of jurisdiction) would be outside the scope of mandatory transfers. In other words, the Act of Sederunt applies only to challenges on procedural grounds rather than to challenges of procedural decisions. A discretionary transfer was not possible, as the case involved a devolved matter – criminal injuries compensation.

The Court has power under subs (1)(b), but not a duty, to transfer other cases, provided that the other three conditions are met.

Subsection (4) – Condition 3

This excludes devolved matters from the Upper Tribunal's jurisdiction. This is defined in subs (7). Child support is not a devolved matter.

Subsection (5) – Condition 4

This excludes immigration and nationality decisions from the Upper Tribunal's jurisdiction.

Upper Tribunal's "judicial review" jurisdiction: Scotland

21.–(1)   The Upper Tribunal has the function of deciding applications transferred to it from the Court of Session under section 20(1).

(2)   The powers of review of the Upper Tribunal in relation to such applications are the same as the powers of review of the Court of Session in an application to the supervisory jurisdiction of that Court.

(3)   In deciding an application by virtue of subsection (1), the Upper Tribunal must apply principles that the Court of Session would apply in deciding an application to the supervisory jurisdiction of that Court.

(4)   An order of the Upper Tribunal by virtue of subsection (1)–

(a)   has the same effect as the corresponding order granted by the Court of Session on an application to the supervisory jurisdiction of that Court, and

(b)   is enforceable as if it were an order so granted by that Court.

(5)   Where an application is transferred to the Upper Tribunal by virtue of section 20(1), any steps taken or orders made by the Court of Session in relation to the application

(other than the order to transfer the application under section 20(1)) are to be treated as taken or made by the tribunal.

(6)   Tribunal Procedure Rules may make further provision for the purposes of supplementing subsection (5).

General Note

This equates the Upper Tribunal with the Court of Session in respect of those judicial review cases that are within its jurisdiction.

section 25   Supplementary powers of Upper Tribunal

[p645: add:]

General Note

This section confers on the Upper Tribunal the powers of enforcement of the High Court and the Court of Session. The First-tier Tribunal may refer cases to the Upper Tribunal for enforcement. See the General Note to rule 7(3) Tribunal Procedure (First-tier Tribunal) (Social Entitlement Chamber) Rules 2008.

Tribunal Procedure (First-tier Tribunal) (Social Entitlement Chamber) Rules 2008

rule 1   Citation, commencement, application and interpretation

[p651: rule 1 amended by rule 3 of The Tribunal Procedure (Amendment) Rules 2010 No.43 from 18 January 2010:]

3.   In rule 1(3) of the Tribunal Procedure (First-tier Tribunal)(Social Entitlement Chamber) Rules 2008 (citation, commencement, application and interpretation) in the definition of "legal representative", for "an authorised advocate or authorised litigator as defined by section 119(1) of the Courts and Legal Services Act 1990" substitute "a person who, for the purposes of the Legal Services Act 2007, is an authorised person in relation to an activity which constitutes the exercise of a right of audience or the conduct of litigation within the meaning of that Act".

rule 2   Overriding objective and parties' obligation to co-operate with the Tribunal

[p654: General Note, Natural justice and analogous case, add:]

Bias arising from a series of connections between a fee-paid judge's former firm and the claimant was discussed in *SW v Secretary of State for Work and Pensions (IB)* UKUT 73 (AAC), paras 51-52.

[p655: General Note, Natural justice and analogous case, add:]

Insensitivity on the part of the tribunal is unlikely to deprive a party of a fair hearing (*BK v Secretary of State for Work and Pensions* [2009] UKUT 258 (AAC), paras 28-31).

[p656: General Note, Rule 2(2)(c), add a second paragraph:]

Taken together with the duty to co-operate, this provision covers the proper preparation of a bundle in a form that is useable by the other parties (*CH 4262/2007*, paras 39-40).

[p658: General Note, The inquisitorial approach, add:]

Concessions may be withdrawn, either before the same tribunal (*R(IS) 14/93*, para 7) or on appeal (*LC v Secretary of State for Work and Pensions* [2009] UKUT 153 (AAC), para 11). It is unlikely that concessions by a presenting officer at a hearing will create a legitimate expectation, as they will seldom amount to a clear and unambiguous representation that the CMEC would not exercise its statutory powers (*LC v Secretary of State for Work and Pensions*, para 12).

In furtherance of the inquisitorial approach, the tribunal may have to investigate an issue that is not raised by any of the parties. This is not indicative of bias (*BK v Secretary of State for Work and Pensions* [2009] UKUT 258 (AAC), paras 13-14).

rule 5   Case management powers

[p660: General Note, Rule 5(2), add:]

The power to give directions includes power to direct the CMEC to arrange for a presenting officer to attend the hearing (*RF v Child Maintenance and Enforcement Commission (CSM)* [2010] UKUT 41 (AAC), para 12).

[p660: General Note, Rule 5(3)(b), add:]

A decision to treat a case as a lead case must be made by the Chamber President: para 10 of the Senior President's Practice Statement on *Composition of Tribunals in Social Security and Child Support Cases in the Social Entitlement Chamber on or after 3 November 2008*.

[p660: General Note, Rule 5(3)(c), add:]

This includes power to direct the CMEC to arrange for a presenting officer to attend the hearing (*RF v Child Maintenance and Enforcement Commission (CSM)* [2010] UKUT 41 (AAC), para 12).

[p661: General Note, Rule 5(3)(f), add:]

In *DA v Secretary of State for Work and Pensions* CE/1033/2010, the judge applied this principle as a basic requirement of natural justice and a fair hearing. He set aside the tribunal's decision on the ground that the appeal had been heard within the time allowed by the pre-listing Enquiry Form for the production of the further evidence that was being obtained by the claimant's representative.

[p663: General Note, add:]

Rule 5(3)(i)

The bundle produced must be useable by the tribunal and the other parties (*CH 4262/2007*, paras 39-40).

rule 7   Failure to comply with rules etc.

[p664: General Note, add:]

In *AM v Secretary of State for Work and Pensions* [2009] UKUT 224 (AAC), the judge decided that a purported review was a nullity. The judge did not explain how he had jurisdiction to do so given the decision in *R(I) 7/94*.

Rule 7(3)

A number of procedural issues relating to enforcement references were considered by the three-judge panel in *MD v Secretary of State for Work and Pensions (Enforcement Reference)* [2010] UKUT 202 (AAC).

(i)   Enforcement potentially affected the liberty of the subject. Accordingly, although procedural irregularities could be waived, it was particularly important that procedural safeguards should be complied with. See para 12.

(ii)   Rule 6(4) required notice to be served on any person affected by a direction. Service would be effected under s7 Interpretation Act 1978. See para 13.

(iii)   A direction that a professional attend a hearing before the First-tier Tribunal should only be made if there is a compelling reason to do so. See para 15.

(iv)   A decision to refer a case to the Upper Tribunal must be made by the Chamber President: para 10 Senior President's Practice Statement on *Composition of Tribunals in Social Security and Child Support Cases in the Social Entitlement Chamber on or after 3 November 2008*. See para 17.

(v)   The tribunal must make clear to the person concerned what has to be done and the consequences of not doing it. See para 19.

(vi)   In *MR v Child Maintenance and Enforcement Commission (No.1)* [2009] UKUT 285 (AAC), a three-judge panel decided to reissue the directions given by the First-tier Tribunal. That is not a requirement of the section, although it may be appropriate in individual cases. See para 20.

(vii) The panel left open the extent to which the parties against whom enforcement was not sought were entitled to be involved in the enforcement proceedings. See paras 21-23.

There has also been a reference in a special educational needs case.

rule 8   Striking out a party's case

[p665: General Note, add:]

For the meaning of jurisdiction, see the General Note to s20 of the Act. Jurisdiction must be distinguished from cases where the tribunal has power to deal with the issue, but can properly come to only one decision (*AW v Essex County Council* (SEN) [2010] UKUT 74 (AAC), paras 12-16; *FL v First-tier Tribunal and CICA* [2010] UKUT 158 (AAC), para 17).

rule 14   Use of documents and information

[p669: General Note, add:]

The tribunal must not use its power to prohibit disclosure in a way that prevents a party knowing sufficient of another party's case to give proper instructions to a representative and, in so far as this is possible, to refute that case (*RM v St Andrew's Healthcare* [2010] UKUT 119 (AAC); *Bank Mellat v Her Majesty's Treasury* [2010] EWCA Civ 483, paras 18 and 21).

rule 15   Evidence and submissions

[p673: General Note, Children as witnesses, add:]

The Supreme Court considered the calling of children as witnesses in *Re W (children) (care proceedings: evidence)* [2010] 1 WLR 701. The case concerned care proceedings, but the general principles apply to child support proceedings. They were set out by Lady Hale:

'22. . . . The existing law erects a presumption against a child giving evidence which requires to be rebutted by anyone seeking to put questions to the child. That cannot be reconciled with the approach of the European Court of Human Rights, which always aims to strike a fair balance between competing Convention rights. Article 6 requires that the proceedings overall be fair and this normally entails an opportunity to challenge the evidence presented by the other side. . . .

23. The object of the proceedings is to achieve a fair trial in the determination of the rights of all the people involved. . . . The court cannot ignore relevant evidence just because other evidence might have been better. It will have to do the best it can on what it has.

24. When the court is considering whether a particular child should be called as a witness, the court will have to weigh two considerations: the advantages that that will bring to the determination of the truth and the damage it may do to the welfare of this or any other child. A fair trial is a trial which is fair in the light of the issues which have to be decided. Mr Geekie accepts that the welfare of the child is also a relevant consideration, albeit not the paramount consideration in this respect. He is right to do so, because the object of the proceedings is to promote the welfare of this and other children. The hearing cannot be fair to them unless their interests are given great weight.

25. In weighing the advantages that calling the child to give evidence may bring to the fair and accurate determination of the case, the court will have to look at several factors. One will be the issues it has to decide in order properly to determine the case. Sometimes it may be possible to decide the case without making findings on particular allegations. Another will be the quality of the evidence it already has. Sometimes there may be enough evidence to make the findings needed whether or not the child is cross-examined. Sometimes there will be nothing useful to be gained from the child's oral evidence. The case is built upon a web of behaviour, drawings, stray remarks, injuries and the like, and not upon concrete allegations voiced by the child. The quality of any ABE interview will also be an important factor, as will be the nature of any challenge which the party may wish to make. The court is unlikely to be helped by generalised accusations of lying, or by a fishing expedition in which the child is taken slowly through the story yet again in the hope that something will turn up, or by a cross-examination which is designed to intimidate the child and pave the way for accusations of inconsistency in a future criminal trial. On the other hand, focussed questions which put forward a different explanation for certain events may help the court to do justice between the parties. Also relevant will be the age and maturity of the child and the length of time since the events in question, for these will have a bearing on whether an account now can be as reliable as a near-contemporaneous account, especially if given in a well-conducted ABE interview.

26. The age and maturity of the child, along with the length of time since the events in question, will also be relevant to the second part of the inquiry, which is the risk of harm to the child. Further specific factors may be the support which the child has from family or other sources, or the lack of it, the child's own wishes and feelings about giving evidence, and the views of the child's guardian and, where appropriate, those with parental responsibility. We endorse the view that an unwilling child should rarely, if ever, be obliged to give evidence. The risk of further delay to the proceedings is also a factor: there is a general principle that

delay in determining any question about a child's upbringing is likely to prejudice his welfare: see the Children Act 1989, section 1(2). There may also be specific risks of harm to this particular child. Where there are parallel criminal proceedings, the likelihood of the child having to give evidence twice may increase the risk of harm. The parent may be seeking to put his child through this ordeal in order to strengthen his hand in the criminal proceedings rather than to enable the family court to get at the truth. On the other hand, as the family court has to give less weight to the evidence of a child because she has not been called, then that may be damaging too. However, the court is entitled to have regard to the general evidence of the harm which giving evidence may do to children, as well as to any features which are particular to this child and this case. That risk of harm is an ever-present feature to which, on the present evidence, the court must give great weight. The risk, and therefore the weight, may vary from case to case, but the court must always take it into account and does not need expert evidence in order to do so.

27. But on both sides of the equation, the court must factor in what steps can be taken to improve the quality of the child's evidence and at the same time to decrease the risk of harm to the child. These two aims are not in opposition to one another. The whole premise of "Achieving Best Evidence" and the special measures in criminal cases is that this will improve rather than diminish the quality of the evidence to the court. It does not assume that the most reliable account of any incident is one made from recollection months or years later in the stressful conditions of a courtroom. Nor does it assume that an "Old Bailey style" cross-examination is the best way of testing that evidence. It may be the best way of casting doubt upon it in the eyes of a jury but that is another matter. A family court would have to be astute both to protect the child from the harmful and destructive effects of questioning and also to evaluate the answers in the light of the child's stage of development.

28. The family court will have to be realistic in evaluating how effective it can be in maximising the advantage while minimising the harm. There are things that the court can do but they are not things that it is used to doing at present. It is not limited by the usual courtroom procedures or to applying the special measures by analogy. The important thing is that the questions which challenge the child's account are fairly put to the child so that she can answer them, not that counsel should be able to question her directly . . . '

rule 17   Withdrawal

[p682: General Note, add:]

Rule 17(2)

The tribunal should refuse permission to withdraw if the application is a tactical ploy, but the power to refuse is not so limited and depends on the circumstances of the case (*KF v Birmingham and Solihull Mental Health NHS Foundation Trust* [2010] UKUT 185 (AAC), paras 36-37).

rule 24   Responses and replies

[p686: General Note, add:]

Rule 24(6) and (7)

These provisions allow the other parties one month in which to make further submissions or supply more documents to the tribunal. There is a breach of natural justice if the tribunal holds a hearing within that time and thereby deprives a party of a chance to do so (*MP v Secretary of State for Work and Pensions* (DLA) [2010] UKUT 103 (AAC), para 26).

Chapter 3   Decisions

[p692: General Note to Chapter 3, Appeal by way of rehearing, add:]

The rehearing covers matters of fact, law and opinion. The tribunal is entitled to substitute its opinion for that of the CMEC, even if the application of the legislation expressly depends on the CMEC's opinion (*R(SB) 5/81*, para 8; *MC v Secretary of State for Defence* [2009] UKUT 173 (AAC), paras 10-16).

rule 36   Clerical mistakes and accidential slips or omissions

[p700: General Note, add:]

For a discussion of control over a decision before promulgation, see the decision of the Court of Appeal in *Paulin v Paulin* [2009] 2 FLR 354.

rule 40   Review of a decision

[p704: add:]

General Note

The exercise of the power to review was considered on judicial review by a three-judge panel of the Upper Tribunal in *R (RB) v First-tier Tribunal (Review)* [2010] UKUT 160 (AAC), paras 22-29. On the panel's analysis, review provides an alternative remedy to an appeal to allow corrective action without delay. It must not, though, usurp the Upper Tribunal's function of deciding contentious issues of law. It should only be used to set aside decisions in clear cases. This approach must be applied flexibly. For example, some cases may benefit from a further fact-finding hearing before being considered by the Upper Tribunal. There is no need for reasons in a review decision to be of the length or in the style appropriate for a self-contained decision of the Upper Tribunal (para 32).

If the tribunal does not identify an error of law, it cannot review its decision. It follows that it cannot exercise the powers given by s9(4) Tribunals, Courts and Enforcement Act 2007, because they only arise on a review. In *VH v Suffolk County Council* [2010] UKUT 203 (AAC), the judge decided that an amendment to the tribunal's reasons (permissible under s9(4)(b)) was not valid as the tribunal had not identified an error of law in its decision.

rule 41   Power to treat an application as a different type of application

[p704: General Note, add:]

The argument in the text does not hold if the power given by this rule is inherent in the rules (specifically, rules 2 and 5-7), as the three-judge panel said in *R (RB) v First-tier Tribunal (Review)* [2010] UKUT 160 (AAC), para 10. On the other hand, if the panel is correct that the power is inherent in the other rules, it will also apply to the Upper Tribunal, which has no equivalent to this rule.

Tribunal Procedure (Upper Tribunal) Rules 2008

The amendments below conern child support. Amendments that do not apply to child support have been omitted.

rule 1   Citation, commencement, application and interpretation

[p708: rule 1(3) amended by rule 4 Tribunal Procedure (Upper Tribunal) (Amendment) Rules 2010 No.747 from 6 April 2010:]

4.   In rule 1(3) (interpretation)–

(a)   for the definition of ''applicant'' substitute–

''''applicant'' means–

    (a)   a person who applies for permission to bring, or does bring, judicial review proceedings before the Upper Tribunal and, in judicial review proceedings transferred to the Upper Tribunal from a court, includes a person who was a claimant or petitioner in the proceedings immediately before they were transferred; or

    (b)   a person who refers a financial services case to the Upper Tribunal;'';

(b)   *[Omitted]*

(c)   in the definition of ''interested party''–

    (i)   in sub-paragraph (a) for ''(substitution and addition of parties)'' substitute ''(addition, substitution and removal of parties)'';

    (ii)   after sub-paragraph (a) omit ''and''; and

    (iii)   *[Omitted]*

(d)   in the definition of ''party'' after ''question'' insert ''or matter'';

(e)   *[Omitted]*

(f)   *[Omitted]*

rule 11   Representatives

[p714: rule 11 amended by rule 8 Tribunal Procedure (Amendment) Rules 2010 No.43 from 18 January 2010:]

8.   In rule 11(9) (representatives) for ''an authorised advocate or authorised litigator as defined by section 119(1) of the Courts and Legal Services Act 1990'' substitute ''a person who, for the purposes of the Legal Services Act 2007, is an authorised person in relation to an activity which constitutes the exercise of a right of audience or the conduct of litigation within the meaning of that Act''.

rule 13   Sending and delivering of documents

[p715: rule 13 amended by rule 10 Tribunal Procedure (Amendment No.2) Rules 2010 No.44 from 15 February 2010:]

10.   In rule 13 (sending and delivery of documents) after paragraph (5) insert–

''(6)   Subject to paragraph (7), if a document submitted to the Upper Tribunal is not written in English, it must be accompanied by an English translation.

(7)   In proceedings that are in Wales or have a connection with Wales, a document or translation may be submitted to the Tribunal in Welsh.''

rule 23   Notice of appeal

[p722: rule 23(3)(a) amended by rule 8 Tribunal Procedure (Upper Tribunal) (Amendment) Rules 2010 No.747 from 6 April 2010:]

8.   In rule 23(1)(a) (notice of appeal) after ''26A'' insert ''or 26B''.

rule 24   Response to the notice of appeal

[p723: rule 24(2) amended by rule 9 Tribunal Procedure (Amendment) Rules 2010 No.43 from 18 January 2010:]

(9)　In rule 24(2) (response to the notice of appeal) for ''(1)'' substitute ''(1A)''.

[p723: rule 24(2) amended by rule 15 Tribunal Procedure (Amendment No.2) Rules 2010 No.44 from 15 February 2010:]

15.　In rule 24(2) (response to the notice of appeal)–
(a)　for paragraph (a) substitute–
　　''(a)　if an application for permission to appeal stands as the notice of appeal, no later than one month after the date on which the respondent was sent notice that permission to appeal had been granted;'';
(b)　after paragraph (a) omit ''or''; and
(c)　insert–
　　''(aa)　in a fast-track case, one day before the hearing of the appeal; or''.

rule 44　　**Application for permission to appeal**

[p731: rule 44 amended by rule 10 Tribunal Procedure (Upper Tribunal) (Amendment) Rules 2010 No.747 from 6 April 2010:]

10.　In rule 44 (application for permission to appeal)–
(a)　*[Omitted]*
(b)　in paragraph (4) for ''or (3A)'' substitute '', (3A) or (3D)''; and
(c)　in paragraph (6) after ''(3A)'' insert '', (3D)''.

The Child Support (Management of Payments and Arrears) Regulations 2009
(2009 No.3151)

Made	*30th November 2009*
Laid before Parliament	*4th December 2009*
Coming into force	*25th January 2010*

PART 1
General

1.   Citation and commencement
2.   Interpretation
3.   Arrears notices
4.   Attribution of payments

PART 2
Set Off

5.   Set off of liabilities to pay child support maintenance
6.   Set off of payments against child support maintenance liability
7.   Application of set off

PART 3
Overpayments and Voluntary Payments

8.   Application of overpayments
9.   Application of voluntary payments

PART 4
Recovery from Estates

10.   Application and interpretation
11.   Recovery of arrears from a deceased person's estate
12.   Appeals and other proceedings
13.   Disclosure of information

PART 5
Revocations and Savings

14.   Revocations
15.   Savings

SCHEDULE

Revocations

PART 1
General

Citation and commencement
1.   These Regulations may be cited as the Child Support (Management of Payments and Arrears) Regulations 2009 and come into force on 25th January 2010.

Interpretation
2.–(1)   In these Regulations–

"the 1991 Act" means the Child Support Act 1991;

"a 1993 scheme case" means a case in respect of which the provisions of the Child Support, Pensions and Social Security Act 2000 have not been brought into force in accordance with article 3 of the Child Support, Pensions and Social Security Act 2000 (Commencement No. 12) Order 2003;

"the AIMA Regulations" means the Child Support (Arrears, Interest and Adjustment of Maintenance Assessments) Regulations 1992;

"the Decisions and Appeals Regulations" means the Social Security and Child Support (Decisions and Appeals) Regulations 1999;

"non-resident parent" includes a person treated as a non-resident parent by virtue of regulations made under section 42 of the 1991 Act;

"relevant person" means–

(a)   a person with care;

(b)   a non-resident parent;

(c)   where the application for a maintenance calculation is made by a child under section 7 of the 1991 Act, that child,

in respect of whom a maintenance calculation is or has been in force.

(2)   In the application of these Regulations to a 1993 scheme case, any reference to expressions in the 1991 Act (including "non-resident parent" and "maintenance calculation") or to regulations made under that Act are to be read with the necessary modifications.

General Note

Subsection (2)

The regulations are worded in terms of the 2003 scheme. They also apply, with appropriate modifications, to the 1993 scheme. The principal effect is that references to non-resident parents and maintenance calculations must be read to apply to absent parents and maintenance assessments.

Arrears notices

3.–(1)   This regulation applies to a case where–

(a)   the Commission is arranging for the collection of child support maintenance under section 29 of the 1991 Act; and

(b)   the non-resident parent has failed to make one or more payments of child support maintenance due.

(2)   Where the Commission is considering taking action with regard to a case falling within paragraph (1) it must serve a notice on the non-resident parent.

(3)   The notice must–

(a)   itemize the payments of child support maintenance due and not paid;

(b)   set out in general terms the provisions as to arrears contained in this regulation and regulation 8 of the AIMA Regulations; and

(c)   request the non-resident parent make payment of all outstanding arrears.

(4)   Where a notice has been served under paragraph (2), no duty to serve a further notice under that paragraph arises in relation to further arrears unless those further arrears have arisen after an intervening continuous period of not less than 12 weeks during the course of which all payments of child support maintenance due from the non-resident parent have been paid on time in accordance with regulations made under section 29 of the 1991 Act.

Definitions

"the 1991 Act": see reg 2(1).

"the AIMA Regulations": see reg 2(1).

"non-resident parent": see reg 2(1).

General Note

This regulation imposes a duty on the CMEC to give notice to a non-resident parent who is in arrears if it is arranging for the collection of maintenance and it is considering taking action. The terms of the notice are specified in para (3). The notice covers future arrears unless and until the non-resident parent has discharged current liability on time for a continuous period of 12 weeks or more.

Attribution of payments

4.   Where a maintenance calculation is or has been in force and there are arrears of child support maintenance, the Commission may attribute any payment of child support maintenance made by a non-resident parent to child support maintenance due as it thinks fit.

Definition
> "non-resident parent": see reg 2(1).

General Note
> This regulation allows the CMEC to attribute any payments made by a non-resident parent who is in arrears as it thinks fit. This allows it to attribute the payments either to current liability or in discharge of arrears or part and part.
>
> An attribution under this regulation can be effective for the purposes of income support (*Secretary of State for Work and Pensions v Menary-Smith* [2006] EWCA Civ 1751, para 40).

PART 2
Set Off

General Note
> The regulations in this Part are made under s41C(3) of the Act.

Set off of liabilities to pay child support maintenance

5.–(1)   The circumstances prescribed for the purposes of section 41C(1)(a) of the 1991 Act, in which the Commission may set off liabilities to pay child support maintenance, are set out in paragraph (2).

(2)   The Commission may set off the liability to pay child support maintenance of one person ("A") against the liability to pay child support maintenance of another person ("B") where–

    (a)   A is liable to pay child support maintenance under a maintenance calculation, whether that calculation is current or no longer in force, in relation to which B is the person with care; and

    (b)   B is liable to pay child support maintenance under a maintenance calculation, whether that calculation is current or no longer in force, in relation to which A is the person with care.

(3)   There shall be no set off in relation to any amount which if paid could be retained under section 41 of the 1991 Act.

Definition
> "the 1991 Act": see reg 2(1).

General Note
> This regulation applies when A is the non-resident parent and B the person with care in respect of one maintenance calculation and their roles are reversed in respect of another calculation. It gives the CMEC power of set off in order to avoid money passing in a circle from A to B and back again. The power does not apply to any amount that could be retained under s41 of the Act on account of benefits that the parent with care received while arrears were owing.

Set off of payments against child support maintenance liability

6.–(1)   The circumstances prescribed for the purposes of section 41C(1)(b) of the 1991 Act, in which the Commission may set off a payment against a person's liability to pay child support maintenance, are set out in paragraph (2).

(2)   The Commission may set off a payment against a non-resident parent's liability to pay child support maintenance where–

    (a)   the payment falls within paragraph (3); and

    (b)   the person with care agreed to the making of the payment.

(3)   A payment is of a prescribed description for the purposes of section 41C(1)(b) of the 1991 Act if it was made by the non-resident parent in respect of–

    (a)   a mortgage or loan taken out on the security of the property which is the qualifying child's home where that mortgage or loan was taken out to facilitate the purchase of, or to pay for essential repairs or improvements to, that property;

    (b)   rent on the property which is the qualifying child's home;

(c)   mains-supplied gas, water or electricity charges at the qualifying child's home;
(d)   council tax payable by the person with care in relation to the qualifying child's home;
(e)   essential repairs to the heating system in the qualifying child's home; or
(f)   repairs which are essential to maintain the fabric of the qualifying child's home.

Definitions
"the 1991 Act": see reg 2(1).
"non-resident parent": see reg 2(1).

General Note
This regulation applies when the non-resident parent makes payments for the benefit of the qualifying child with the person with care's agreement. The CMEC then has power to set those payments off against liability for child support maintenance.

   Three issues potentially arise. Did the non-resident parent make the payments? There is likely to be documentary evidence of payment for most, if not all, of the types of payment covered by para (3). There may be dispute if the payment was from a joint account and the non-resident parent was not the only person paying into that account. Were the conditions in para (3) satisfied? This is only likely to occur in relation to subparas (e) and (f), where there is scope to argue about whether work amounted to repairs and whether it was essential. Did the person with care agree? There can be no dispute if there is a written agreement. This will not always be so. If the non-resident parent continued to pay bills following a separation, will the person with care's acquiescence count as an agreement?

Application of set off
7.–(1)   In setting off a person's liability for child support maintenance under this Part, the Commission may apply the amount to be set off to reduce any arrears of child support maintenance due under any current maintenance calculation, or any previous maintenance calculation made in respect of the same relevant persons.

   (2)   Where there are no arrears of child support maintenance due, or an amount remains to be set off after the application of paragraph (1), the Commission may adjust the amount payable in relation to the current maintenance calculation by such amount as it considers appropriate in all the circumstances of the case, having regard in particular to–
(a)   the circumstances of the relevant persons; and
(b)   the amount to be set off and the period over which it would be reasonable to adjust the amount payable to set off that amount.

   (3)   An adjustment of the amount payable in relation to the current maintenance calculation under paragraph (2) may reduce the amount payable to nil.

Definition
"relevant person": see reg 2(1).

General Note
The CMEC may apply an amount to be set off to reduce arrears. If there are no (longer) arrears, the CMEC may adjust the amount payable, even to nil.

PART 3
Overpayments and Voluntary Payments

Application of overpayments
8.–(1)   Where for any reason, including the retrospective effect of a maintenance calculation, there has been an overpayment of child support maintenance, the Commission may apply the amount overpaid to reduce any arrears of child support maintenance due under any previous maintenance calculation in respect of the same relevant persons.

   (2)   Where there is no previous maintenance calculation, or an amount of the overpayment remains after the application of paragraph (1), the Commission may adjust the amount payable in relation to the current maintenance calculation by such amount as it considers appropriate in all the circumstances of the case, having regard in particular to–

(a)   the circumstances of the relevant persons; and

(b)   the amount of the overpayment and the period over which it would be reasonable to adjust the amount payable for the overpayment to be rectified.

(3)   An adjustment of the amount payable in relation to the current maintenance calculation under paragraph (2) may reduce the amount payable to nil.

Definition

"relevant person": see reg 2(1).

General Note

This regulation is made under s51(2)(d), (e) and (f) of the Act. The CMEC may attribute an overpayment to reduce arrears under a previous maintenance calculation in respect of the same persons. Otherwise, the CMEC may adjust the amount payable under the current calculation, even to nil. The adjustment reduces the payment, not the liability, which is unaffected.

If an adjustment is not made, the CMEC may reimburse the non-resident parent under s41B of the Act.

Application of voluntary payments

9.–(1)   Where there has been a voluntary payment the Commission may apply the amount of the voluntary payment to reduce any arrears of child support maintenance due under any previous maintenance calculation in respect of the same relevant persons.

(2)   Where there is no previous maintenance calculation, or an amount of the voluntary payment remains after the application of paragraph (1), the Commission may adjust the amount payable in relation to the current maintenance calculation by such amount as it considers appropriate in all the circumstances of the case, having regard in particular to–

(a)   the circumstances of the relevant persons; and

(b)   the amount of the voluntary payment and the period over which it would be reasonable to adjust the amount payable for the voluntary payment to be taken into account.

(3)   An adjustment of the amount payable in relation to the current maintenance calculation under paragraph (2) may reduce the amount payable to nil.

Definition

"relevant person": see reg 2(1).

General Note

This regulation is made under s28J(3) of the Act. It makes provision for voluntary payments equivalent to that for overpayments under reg 8. See the general note to that regulation.

PART 4
Recovery from Estates

General Note

The regulations in this Part are made under ss14(3) and 43A of the Act.

Application and interpretation

10.–(1)   This Part applies in relation to the estate of a person who dies on or after the day on which these Regulations come into force.

(2)   In this Part, "child support maintenance" means child support maintenance for the collection of which the Commission is authorised to make arrangements.

Recovery of arrears from a deceased person's estate

11.   Arrears of child support maintenance for which a deceased person was liable immediately before death are a debt payable by the deceased's executor or administrator out of the deceased's estate to the Commission.

Definition

"child support maintenance": see reg 10(2).

General Note
Arrears owing at death are recoverable from the estate of the non-resident parent.

Appeals and other proceedings

12.–(1) The deceased's executor or administrator has the same rights, subject to the same procedures and time limits, as the deceased person had immediately before death to institute, continue or withdraw any proceedings under the 1991 Act, whether by appeal or otherwise.

(2) Regulation 34 of the Decisions and Appeals Regulations shall apply to a case where the non-resident parent is the deceased party to the proceedings as if for paragraphs (1) and (2) there were substituted the following paragraph–

"(1) In any proceedings, on the death of a non-resident parent, the Commission must appoint the deceased's executor or administrator to proceed with the appeal in place of the deceased, unless there is no such person in which circumstances it may appoint such person as it thinks fit to proceed with the appeal.".

Definitions
"the 1991 Act": see reg 2(1).
"the Decisions and Appeals Regulations": see reg 2(1).

General Note
This regulation allows the necessary procedural safeguards in respect of the right of recovery under reg 11. Procedural rights transfer to the non-resident parent's executor or administrator, who is appointed to proceed with any appeal (but not a referral) if the non-resident parent was a party.

Disclosure of information

13.–(1) The Commission may disclose information held for the purposes of the 1991 Act to the deceased's executor or administrator where, in the opinion of the Commission, such information is essential to enable the executor or administrator to administer the deceased's estate, including, where necessary, to institute, continue or withdraw proceedings under the 1991 Act.

(2) Any application for information under this regulation shall be made to the Commission in writing setting out the reasons for the application.

(3) Except where a person gives written permission to the Commission that the information mentioned in sub-paragraphs (a) and (b) in relation to that person may be disclosed to other persons, any information disclosed under paragraph (1) must not contain–

(a) the address of any person, except that of the recipient of the information in question and the office of the officer concerned who is exercising functions of the Commission under the 1991 Act, or any other information the use of which could reasonably be expected to lead to any such person being located;

(b) any other information the use of which could reasonably be expected to lead to any person, other than a party to the maintenance calculation, being identified.

Definition
"the 1991 Act": see reg 2(1).

General Note
This regulation allows the CMEC to disclose information to the non-resident parent's executor or administrator, subject to the usual confidentiality provision.

PART 5
Revocations and Savings

Revocations

14. The Regulations specified in the Schedule are revoked to the extent specified.

Savings

15.–(1)   Where before these Regulations come into force, an adjustment has been made under regulation 10(1) of the AIMA Regulations in a 1993 scheme case, regulations 10(2) and (3) and 11 to 17 of those Regulations continue to apply to that case for the purposes of–

(a)   making and determining any appeal against the adjustment;

(b)   making and determining any application for a revision of the adjustment;

(c)   determining any application for a supersession made before these regulations come into force.

(2)   Where before these Regulations come into force, an adjustment has been made under regulation 10(1) or (3A) of the AIMA Regulations in a case other than a 1993 scheme case, regulation 30A of the Decisions and Appeals Regulations continues to apply to that case for the purposes of making and determining any appeal against the adjustment.

Definitions
"a 1993 scheme case": see reg 2(1).
"the AIMA Regulations": see reg 2(1).
"the Decisions and Appeals Regulations": see reg 2(1).

SCHEDULE
Revocations
Regulation 14

Regulations revoked	References	Extent of revocation
Child Support (Arrears, Interest and Adjustment of Maintenance Assessments) Regulations 1992	S.I. 1992/1816	Regulations 2 to 7, 9, 10 and 11 to 17.
Child Support (Miscellaneous Amendments) Regulations 1993	S.I. 1993/913	Regulations 35 to 40.
Child Support and Income Support (Amendment) Regulations 1995	S.I. 1995/1045	Regulations 7 to 11.
Social Security and Child Support (Decisions and Appeals) Regulations 1999	S.I. 1999/991	Regulation 30A.
Child Support (Decisions and Appeals) (Amendment) Regulations 2000	S.I. 2000/3185	Regulation 10, insofar as it inserts regulation 15D in S.I. 1999/991.Regulation 12.
Child Support (Collection and Enforcement and Miscellaneous Amendments) Regulations 2000	S.I. 2001/162	Regulation 5(3)(b), (c) and (e) and (4)(d).
Child Support (Miscellaneous Amendments) Regulations 2009	S.I. 2009/396	Regulations 3 and 4(15).

The Child Support (Maintenance Assessments and Special Cases) Regulations 1992
(1992 No.1815)

General Note

The Child Support (Maintenance Assessments and Special Cases) Regulations 1992 have been revoked for particular cases by reg 15 Child Support (Maintenance Calculations and Special Cases) Regulations 2000 (SI 2001 No.155) (this revocation came into force in relation to a particular case on the date on which the amendments to Part I of Schedule 1 of the Child Support Act 1991 made by the Child Support, Pensions and Social Security Act, 2000 came into force in relation to that type of case – which is 3 March 2000 for the types of cases detailed in art 3 Child Support, Pensions and Social Security Act 2000 (Commencement No.12) Order 2003 (SI 2003 No.192)). See reg 15 of SI 2001 No.155 for savings provisions. For those for whom this revocation does not apply, the Child Support (Maintenance Assessments and Special Cases) Regulations 1992 are reproduced below.

PART I
General
1.   Citation, commencment and interpretation

PART II
Calculation or estimation of child support maintenance
2.   Calculation or estimation of amounts
3.   Calculation of AG
4.   Basic rate of child benefit
5.   The general rule
6.   The additional element
7.   Net income: calculation or estimation of N
8.   Net income: calculation or estimation of M
9.   Exempt income: calculation or estimation of E
10.   Exempt income: calculation or estimation of F
10A.   Assessment income: working tax credit paid to or in respect of a parent with care or an absent parent
10B.   Assessable income: state pension credit paid to or in respect of a parent with care or an absent parent
11.   Protected income
12.   Disposable income
13.   The minimum amount
14.   Eligible housing costs
15.   Amount of housing costs
16.   Weekly amount of housing costs
18.   Excessive housing costs

PART III
Special cases
19.   Both parents are absent
20.   Persons treated as absent parents
21.   One parent is absent and the other is treated as absent
22.   Multiple applications relating to an absent parent
23.   Person caring for children of more than one absent parent
24.   Persons with part-time care-not including a person treated as an absent parent
25.   Care provided in part by local authority
26.   Cases where child support maintenance is not to be payable
27.   Child who is a boarder or an in-patient

27A.   Child who is allowed to live with his parent under section 23(5) of the Children Act 1989
28.   Amount payable where absent parent is in receipt of income support or other prescribed benefit

SCHEDULE 1 – Calculation of N and M
SCHEDULE 2 – Amounts to be disregarded when calculating or estimating N and M
SCHEDULE 3 – Eligible housing costs
SCHEDULE 3A – Amount to be allowed in respect of transfers of property
SCHEDULE 3B – Amount to be allowed in respect of travelling costs
SCHEDULE 4 – Cases where child support maintenance is not to be payable
SCHEDULE 5 – Provisions applying to cases to which section 43 of the Act and regulation 28 apply

PART I
GENERAL

Citation, commencement and interpretation
   1.–(1) These Regulations may be cited as the Child Support (Maintenance Assessments and Special Cases) Regulations 1992 and shall come into force on 5th April 1993.
   (2)   In these Regulations unless the context otherwise requires–
"the Act" means the Child Support Act 1991;
[¹⁵"care home" has the meaning assigned to it by section 3 of the Care Standards Act 2000;
"care home service" has the meaning assigned to it by section 2(3) of the Regulation of Care (Scotland) Act 2001;]
[⁵"Child Benefit Rates Regulations" means the Child Benefit and Social Security (Fixing and Adjustment of Rates) Regulations 1996;]
[¹⁴"child tax credit" means a child tax credit under section 8 of the Tax Credits Act 2002;]
"claimant" means a claimant for income support;
"Contributions and Benefits Act" means the Social Security Contributions and Benefits Act 1992;
[⁸"Contributions and Benefits (Northern Ireland) Act" means the Social Security Contributions and Benefits (Northern Ireland) Act 1992;]
"council tax benefit" has the same meaning as in the Local Government Finance Act 1992;
[¹[¹⁶"couple" means–
   (a)   a man and woman who are married to each other and are members of the same household;
   (b)   a man and woman who are not married to each other but are living together as husband and wife;
   (c)   two people of the same sex who are civil partners of each other and are members of the same household; or
   (d)   two people of the same sex who are not civil partners of each other but are living together as if they were civil partners,
and for the purposes of paragraph (d), two people of the same sex are to be regarded as living together as if they were civil partners if, but only if, they would be regarded as living together as husband and wife were they instead two people of the opposite sex;]]
"course of advanced education" means–
   (a)   a full-time course leading to a postgraduate degree or comparable qualification, a first degree or comparable qualification, a Diploma of Higher Education, a higher national diploma, a higher national diploma or higher national certificate of the Business and [¹Technology] Education Council or the Scottish Vocation Education Council or a teaching qualification; or

    (b)   any other full-time course which is a course of a standard above that of an ordinary national diploma, a national diploma or national certificate of the Business and [¹Technology] Education Council or the Scottish Vocational Education Council, the advanced level of the General Certificate of Education, Scottish certificate of education (higher level) or a Scottish certificate of sixth year studies;

"covenant income" means the gross income payable to a student under a Deed of Covenant by a parent;

"day" includes any part of a day;

[²"day to day care" means–

    (a)   care of not less than 104 nights in total during the 12 month period ending with the relevant week; or

    (b)   where, in the opinion of the [¹²Secretary of State, a period other than 12 months] is more representative of the current arrangements for the care of the child in question, care during that period of not less in total than the number of nights which bears the same ratio to 104 nights as that period bears to 12 months,

and for the purpose of this definition–

    (i)   where a child is a boarder at a boarding school, or is an in-patient in a hospital, the person who, but for those circumstances, would otherwise provide day to day care of the child shall be treated as providing day to day care during the periods in question;

    [³(ii) in relation to an application for child support maintenance, "relevant week" shall have the meaning ascribed to it in head (ii) of sub-paragraph (a) of the definition of "relevant week" in this paragraph;]

    [¹²(iii) in a case where notification is given under regulation 24 of the Maintenance Assessment Procedure Regulations to the relevant persons on different dates, "relevant week" means the period of seven days immediately preceding the date of the latest notification;]]

[⁹. . . .]

[¹³[¹⁴. . .]]

"earnings" has the meaning signed to it by paragraph [¹⁰1, 2A or 3], as the case may be, of Schedule 1;

[⁶"earnings top-up" means the allowance paid by the Secretary of State under the rules specified in the Earnings Top-up Scheme;

"The Earnings Top-up Scheme" means the Earnings Top-up Scheme 1996;]

"effective date" means the date on which a maintenance assessment takes effect for the purposes of the Act;

"eligible housing costs" shall be construed in accordance with Schedule 3;

"employed earner" has the same meaning as in section 2(1)(a) of the Contributions and Benefits Act; [⁹except that it shall include a person gainfully employed in Northern Ireland];

[⁶"family" means–

    (a)   [¹⁶a couple] (including the members of a polygamous marriage);

    (b)   [¹⁶a couple] (including the members of a polygamous marriage) and any child or children living with them for whom at least one member of that couple has day to day care;

    (c)   where a person who is not a member of [¹⁶a couple] has day to day care of a child or children, that person and any such child or children;

and for the purposes of this definition a person shall not be treated as having day to day care of a child who is a member of that person's household where the child in question is being looked after by a local authority within the meaning of section 22 of the Children Act 1989 or, in Scotland, where the child is boarded out with that person by a local authority under the provisions of section 21 of the Social Work (Scotland) Act 1968;]

[⁸[¹⁴. . .]]

"grant" means any kind of educational grant or award and includes any scholarship, exhibition, allowance or bursary but does not include a payment made under section 100 of the Education Act 1944 or section 73 of the Education (Scotland) Act 1980;

"grant contribution" means any amount which a Minister of the Crown or an education authority treats as properly payable by another person when assessing the amount of a student's grant and by which that amount is, as a consequence, reduced;

"home" means–
(a) the dwelling in which a person and any family of his normally live; or
(b) if he or they normally live in more than one home, the principal home of that person and any family of his,

and for the purpose of determining the principal home in which a person normally lives no regard shall be had to residence in [¹⁵a care home or an independent hospital or to the provision of a care home service or an independent health care service] during a period which does not exceed 52 weeks or, where it appears to the [¹²Secretary of State] that the person will return to his principal home after that period has expired, such longer period as [the Secretary of State] considers reasonable to allow for the return of that person to that home;

"housing benefit" has the same meaning as in section 130 of the Contributions and Benefits Act;

[¹⁸"Housing Benefit Regulations" means the Housing Benefit Regulations 2006;]

[¹⁸"Housing Benefit (State Pension Credit) Regulations" means the Housing Benefit (Persons who have attained the qualifying age for state pension credit) Regulations 2006;]

"Income Support Regulations" means the Income Support (General) Regulations 1987;

[¹⁵"independent health care service" has the meaning assigned to it by section 2(5)(a) and (b) of the Regulation of Care (Scotland) Act 2001;

"independent hospital" has the meaning assigned to it by section 2 of the Care Standards Act 2000;]

[²⁰"Independent Living Fund (2006)" means the Trust of that name established by a deed dated 10th April 2006 and made between the Secretary of State for Work and Pensions of the one part and Margaret Rosemary Cooper, Michael Beresford Boyall and Marie Theresa Martin of the other part;]

[¹"Independent Living (1993) Fund" means the charitable trust of that name established by a deed made between the Secretary of State for Social Security of the one part and Robin Glover Wendt and John Fletcher Shepherd of the other part;

"Independent Living (Extension) Fund" means the charitable trust of that name established by a deed made between the Secretary of State for Social Security of the one part and Robin Glover Wendt and John Fletcher Shepherd of the other part;]

[⁴"the Jobseekers Act" means the Jobseekers Act 1995;]

"Maintenance Assessment Procedure Regulations" means the Child Support (Maintenance Assessment Procedure) Regulations 1992;

[¹⁶...]

"non-dependant" means a person who is non-dependant for the purposes of either–
(a) regulation 3 of the Income Support Regulations; or
[¹⁸(b) regulation 3 of the Housing Benefit Regulations or, as the case may be, regulation 3 of the Housing Benefit (State Pension Credit) Regulations;]

or who would be a non-dependant for those purposes if another member of the household in which he is living were entitled to income support or housing benefit as the case may be;

[¹⁵. . .]

"occupational pension scheme" has the same meaning as in [⁹section 1 of the Pension Schemes Act 1993];

"ordinary clothing or footwear" means clothing or footwear for normal daily use, but does not include school uniforms, or clothing or footwear used solely for sporting activities;

"parent with care" means a person who, in respect of the same child or children, is both a parent and a person with care;

"partner" means–

(a) in relation to a member of [¹⁶a couple] who are living together, the other member of that couple;

(b) in relation to a member of a polygamous marriage, any other member of that marriage with whom he lives;

"patient" means a person (other than a person who is serving a sentence of imprisonment or detention in a young offender institution within the meaning of the Criminal Justice Act 1982 as amended by the Criminal Justice Act 1988 who is regarded as receiving free in-patient treatment within the meaning of the Social Security (Hospital In-Patients) Regulations 1975;

[²²"pensionable age" has the meaning given by the rules in paragraph 1 of Schedule 4 to the Pensions Act 1995;]

"person" does not include a local authority;

"personal pension scheme" has the same meaning as in [⁸section 1 of the Pension Schemes Act 1993] and, in the case of as a self-employed earner, includes a scheme approved by the Inland Revenue under Chapter IV of Part XIV of the Income and Corporation Taxes Act 1988;

"polygamous marriage" means any marriage during the subsistence of which a party to it is married to more than one person and in respect of which any ceremony of marriage took place under the law of a country which at the time of that ceremony permitted polygamy;

[¹⁹"Primary Care Trust" means a Primary Care Trust established under section 16A of the National Health Service Act 1977;]

"prisoner" means a person who is detained in custody pending trial or sentence upon conviction or under a sentence imposed by a court other than a person whose detention is under the Mental Health Act 1983 or the [¹⁷Part 5, 6 or 7 or section 136 of the Mental Health (Care and Treatment) (Scotland) Act 2003 or section 52D or 52M of the Criminal Procedure (Scotland) Act 1995];

[⁸"profit related pay" means any payment by an employer calculated by reference to actual or anticipated profits;]

[²²"qualifying age for state pension credit" means–

(a) in the case of a woman, pensionable age; or

(b) in the case of a man, the age which is pensionable age in the case of a woman born on the same day as the man;]

[²"qualifying transfer" has the meaning assigned to it in Schedule 3A;]

"relevant child" means a child of an absent parent or a parent with care who is a member of the same family as that parent;

"relevant Schedule" means Schedule 2 to the Income Support Regulations (income support applicable amounts);

[¹²"relevant week" means–

(a) in relation to an application for child support maintenance–

(i) in the case of the applicant, the period of seven days immediately preceding the date on which the appropriate maintenance assessment application form (being an effective application within the meaning of regulation 2(4) of the Maintenance Assessment Procedure Regulations) is submitted to the Secretary of State;

(ii) in the case of a person to whom a maintenance assessment enquiry form is given or sent as the result of such an application, the period of seven days immediately preceding the date on which that form is given or sent to him or, as the case may be, the date on which it is treated as having been given or sent to him under regulation 1(6)(b) of the Maintenance Assessment Procedure Regulations;

(b) where a decision ("the original decision") is to be–

(i) revised under section 16 of the Act; or

    (ii)   superseded by a decision under section 17 of the Act on the basis that the original decision was made in ignorance of, or was based upon a mistake as to some material fact or was erroneous in point of law,

the period of seven days which was the relevant week for the purposes of the original decision;

  (c)   where a decision ("the original decision") is to be superseded by a decision under section 17 of the Act–

    (i)   on an application made for the purpose on the basis that a material change of circumstances has occurred since the original decision was made, the period of seven days immediately preceding the date on which that application was made;

    (ii)   subject to paragraph (b), in a case where a relevant person is given notice under regulation 24 of the Maintenance Assessment Procedure Regulations, the period of seven days immediately preceding the date of that notification;

except that where, under paragraph 15 of Schedule 1 to the Act, the Secretary of State makes separate maintenance assessments in respect of different periods in a particular case, because he is aware of one or more changes of circumstances which occurred after the date which is applicable to that case under paragraph (a), (b) or (c) the relevant week for the purposes of each separate assessment made to take account of each such change of circumstances, shall be the period of seven days immediately preceding the date on which notification was given to the Secretary of State of the change of circumstances relevant to that separate maintenance assessment;]

[15. . .]

"retirement annuity contract" means an annuity contract for the time being approved by the Board of Inland Revenue as having for its main object the provision of a life annuity in old age or the provision of an annuity for a partner or dependant and in respect of which relief from income tax may be given on any premium;

"self-employed earner" has the same meaning as in section 2(1)(b) of the Contributions and Benefits Act [9except that it shall include a person gainfully employed in Northern Ireland otherwise than in employed earner's employment (whether or not he is also employed in such employment)];

[15"state pension credit" means the social security benefit of that name payable under the State Pension Credit Act 2002;]

"student" means a person, other than person in receipt of a training allowance, who is aged less than 19 and attending a full-time course of advanced education or who is aged 19 or over and attending a full-time course of study at an educational establishment; and for the purposes of this definition–

  (a)   a person who has started on such a course shall be treated as attending it throughout any period of term or vacation within it, until the last day of the course or such earlier date as he abandons it or is dismissed from it;

  (b)   a person on a sandwich course (within the meaning of paragraph 1(1) of Schedule 5 to the [2Education (Mandatory Awards) (No. 2) Regulations 1993] shall be treated as attending a full-time course of advanced education or, as the case may be, of study;

"student loan" means a loan which is made to a student pursuant to arrangements made under section 1 of the Education (Student Loans) Act 1990;

[1. . .]

"training allowance" has the same meaning as in regulation 2 of the Income Support Regulations;

[16...]

"weekly council tax" means the annual amount of the council tax in question payable in respect of the year in which the effective date falls, divided by 52;

[21"the Welfare Reform Act" means the Welfare Reform Act 2007;]

[11"work-based training for young people or, in Scotland, Skillseekers training"] means–

  (a)   arrangements made under section 2 of the Employment and Training Act 1973 or section 2 of the Enterprise and new towns (Scotland) Act 1990; or

(b) arrangements made by the Secretary of State for persons enlisted in Her Majesty's forces for any special term of service specified in regulations made under section 2 of the Armed Forces Act 1966 (power of Defence Council to make regulation as to engagement of persons in regular forces);

for purposes which include the training of persons who, at the beginning of their training, are under the age of 18.

[14"working tax credit" means a working tax credit under section 10 of the Tax Credits Act 2002;]

"year" means a period of 52 weeks;

[1(2A) Where any provision of these Regulations requires the income of a person to be estimated and that or any other provision of these Regulations requires that the amount of such estimated income is to be taken into account for any purposes after deducting from it a sum in respect of income tax or of primary Class 1 contributions under the Contributions and Benefits Act [8or, as the case may be, the Contributions and Benefits (Northern Ireland) Act;] or of contributions paid by that person towards an occupational or personal pension scheme, then [2subject to sub-paragraph (e)]–

(a) the amount to be deducted in respect of income tax shall be calculated by applying to that income the rates of income tax applicable at the [8relevant week] less only the personal relief to which that person is entitled under Chapter I of Part VII of the Income and Corporation Taxes Act 1988 (personal relief); but if the period in respect of which that income is to be estimated is less than a year, the amount of the personal relief deductible under this sub-paragraph shall be calculated on a pro rata basis; [9and the amount of income to which each tax rate applies shall be determined on the basis that the ratio of that amount to the full amount of the income to which each tax rate applies is the same as the ratio of the proportionate part of that personal relief to the full personal relief]

(b) the amount to be deducted in respect of Class 1 contributions under the Contributions and Benefits Act [8or, as the case may be, the Contributions and Benefits (Northern Ireland) Act;] shall be calculated by applying to that income the appropriate primary percentage applicable in the relevant week; and

(c) the amount to be deducted in respect of contributions paid by that person towards an occupational [2. . .] pension scheme shall be one-half of the sums so [2paid; and]

[2(d) the amount to be deducted in respect of contributions towards a personal pension scheme shall be one half of the contributions paid by that person or, where that scheme is intended partly to provide a capital sum to discharge a mortgage secured on that person's home, 37.5 per centum of those contributions;

(e) in relation to any bonus or commission which may be included in that person's income–

(i) the amount to be deducted in respect of income tax shall be calculated by applying to the gross amount of that bonus or commission the rate or rates of income tax applicable in the relevant week;

(ii) the amount to be deducted in respect of primary class 1 contributions under the Contributions and Benefits Act [8or, as the case may be, the Contributions and Benefits (Northern Ireland) Act;] [8. . .] shall be calculated by applying to the gross amount of that bonus or commission the appropriate main primary percentage applicable in the relevant week [3but no deduction shall be made in respect of the portion (if any) of the bonus or commission which, if added to estimated income, would cause such income to exceed the upper earnings limit for Class 1 contributions as provided for in section 5(1)(b) of the Contributions and Benefits Act] [8or, as the case may be, the Contributions and Benefits (Northern Ireland) Act;] and

(iii) the amount to be deducted in respect of contributions paid by that person in respect of the gross amount of that bonus or commission towards an occupational pension scheme shall be one half of any sum so paid.]

(3) In these Regulations, unless the context otherwise requires, a reference–

(a)   to a numbered Part is to the Part of these Regulations bearing that number;
(b)   to a numbered Schedule is to the Schedule to these Regulations bearing that number;
(c)   to a numbered regulation it to the regulation in these Regulations bearing that number;
(d)   in a regulation or Schedule to a numbered paragraph it to the paragraph in that regulation or Schedule bearing that number;
(e)   in a paragraph to a lettered or numbered sub-paragraph is to the sub-paragraph in that paragraph bearing that letter or number.

(4)   [⁷These Regulations are subject to the provisions of Parts VIII and IX of the Departure Direction and Consequential Amendments Regulations and] the regulations in Part II and the provisions of the Schedules to these Regulations are subject to the regulations relating to special cases in Part III.

Amendments

1.   Child Support (Miscellaneous Amendments) Regulations 1993 (SI 1993 No.913) reg 19(2) and (3) (April 5, 1993).
2.   Child Support and Income Support (Amendment) Regulations 1995 (SI 1995 No.1045) reg 41(2) and (3) (April 18, 1995).
3.   Child Support (Miscellaneous Amendments) (No.2) Regulations 1995 (SI 1995 No.3261) reg 40(2) and (3) (January 22, 1996).
4.   Social Security and Child Support (Jobseeker's Allowance) (Consequential Amendments) Regulations 1996 (SI 1996 No.1345), reg 6(2) (October 7, 1996).
5.   Child Benefit, Child Support and Social Security (Miscellaneous Amendments) Regulations 1996 (SI 1996 No.1803) reg 7 (April 7, 1997).
6.   Child Support (Miscellaneous Amendments) Regulations 1996 (SI 1996 No.1945) reg 18(2) and (3) (October 7, 1996).
7.   Child Support Departure Direction and Consequential Amendments Regulations 1996 (SI 1996 No.2907) reg 68(3) (December 2, 1996).
8.   Child Support (Miscellaneous Amendments) (No. 2) Regulations 1996 (SI 1996 No.3196) reg 10(2) and (3) (January 13, 1997).
9.   Child Support (Miscellaneous Amendments) Regulations 1998 (SI 1998 No.58) regs 30 and 42 (January 19, 1998).
10. Child Support (Miscellaneous Amendments) Regulations 1999 (SI 1999 No.977) reg 6(2)(a) (October 4, 1999).
11. Child Support (Miscellaneous Amendments) Regulations 1999 (SI 1999 No.977) reg 6(2)(b) (April 6, 1999).
12. Social Security Act 1998 (Commencement No. 7 and Consequential and Transitional Provisions) Order 1999 (SI 1999 No.1510) art 14(1)(a) – (c) (June 1, 1999).
13. Social Security and Child Support (Tax Credits) Consequential Amendments Regulations 1999 (SI 1999 No.2566) Part III, Sch 2 (October 5, 1999).
14. Child Support (Miscellaneous Amendments) Regulations 2003 (SI 2003 No.328) reg 6(2) (April 6, 2003).
15. Child Support (Miscellaneous Amendments) (No.2) Regulations 2003 (SI 2003 No.2779) reg 4(2) (November 5, 2003).
16. Civil Partnership (Pensions, Social Security and Child Support) (Consequential, etc. Provisions) Order 2005 (SI 2005 No.2877) art 2(4) and Sch 4, para 2(2) (December 5, 2005).
17. Mental Health (Care and Treatment) (Scotland) Act 2003 (Consequential Provisions) Order 2005 (SI 2005 No.2078) arts 1(9) and (10) and 15 and Sch 2 para 15 (October 5, 2005); and Mental Health (Care and Treatment) (Scotland) Act 2003 (Modification of Subordinate Legislation) Order 2005 (SSI 2005 No.445) art 2 and Sch, para 18 (October 5, 2005).
18. Housing Benefit and Council Tax Benefit (Consequential Provisions) Regulations 2006 (SI 2006 No.217) reg 5 and Sch 2, para 4(2) (March 6, 2006).
19. National Health Service Reform and Health Care Professions Act 2002 (Supplementary, Consequential etc. Provisions) Regulations 2002 (SI 2002 No.2469) reg 11 and Sch 8 (October 1, 2002).
20. Independent Living Fund (2006) Order 2007 (SI 2007 No.2538) reg 3(2) (October 1, 2007).
21. Employment and Support Allowance (Consequential Provisions) (No.2) Regulations 2008 (SI 2008 No.1554) reg 58(2) (October 27, 2008).
22. Child Support (Miscellaneous and Consequential Amendments) Regulations 2009 (SI 2009 No.736) reg 3(2) (April 6, 2009).

PART II

CALCULATION OR ESTIMATION OF CHILD SUPPORT MAINTENANCE

Calculation or estimation of amounts

2.–(1) Where any amount [³is to be considered in connection with any calculation made under these Regulations], it shall be calculated or estimated as a weekly amount and, except where the context otherwise requires, any reference to such an amount shall be construed accordingly.

(2) Subject to [¹regulations 11(6) and (7) and 13(2) and [²regulation 8A(5)] of the Maintenance Assessment Procedure Regulations], where any calculation made under [¹the Act or] these Regulations results in a fraction of a penny that fraction shall be treated as a penny if it is either one half or exceeds one half, otherwise it shall be disregarded.

(3) [⁴The Secretary of State] shall calculate the amounts to be taken into account for the purposes of these Regulations by reference, as the case may be, to the dates, weeks, months or other periods specified herein provided that if he becomes aware of a material change of circumstances occurring after such date, week, month or other period but before the effective date, he shall take that change of circumstances into account.

Amendments

1.   Child Support and Income Support (Amendment) Regulations 1995 (SI 1995 No.1045) reg 42 (April 18, 1995).

2.   Child Support (Miscellaneous Amendments) (No 3) Regulations 1995 (SI 1995 No.3265) reg 3 (January 22, 1996).

3.   Child Support (Miscellaneous Amendments) Regulations 1998 (SI 1998 No.58) reg 43 (January 19, 1998).

4.   Social Security Act 1998 (Commencement No.7 and Consequential and Transitional Provisions) Order 1999 (SI 1999 No.1510) art 15 (June 1, 1999).

Calculation of AG

3.–(1) The amounts to be taken into account for the purposes of calculating AG in the formula set out in paragraph 1(2) of Schedule 1 to the Act are–

(a)   with respect to each qualifying child, an amount equal to the amount specified in column (2) of paragraph 2 of the relevant Schedule for a person of the same age (income support personal allowance for child or young person);

[¹(b)   with respect to a person with care of one or more qualifying children-

(i)   where one or more of those children is aged less than 11, an amount equal to the amount specified in column (2) of paragraph 1(1)(e) of the relevant Schedule (income support personal allowance for a single claimant aged not less than 25);

(ii)   where no one of those children are aged less than 11 but one or more of them is aged less than 14, an amount equal to 75 per centum of the amount specified in head (i) above; and

(iii)   where no one of those children are aged less than 14 but one or more of them is aged less than 16, an amount equal to 50 per centum of the amount specified in head (i) above;]

[³(c)   an amount equal to the amount specified in paragraph 3(1)(b) of the relevant Schedule.]

(d)   [². . .]

(2) The amounts referred to in paragraph (1) shall be the amounts applicable at the effective date.

Amendments

1.   Child Support (Miscellaneous Amendments and Transitional Provisions) Regulations 1994 (SI 1994 No.227) reg 4(2) (February 7, 1994).

2.   Child Benefit, Child Support and Social Security (Miscellaneous Amendments) Regulations 1996 (SI 1996 No.1803) reg 8(b) (April 7, 1997).

3.   Child Support (Miscellaneous Amendments) Regulations 1998 (SI 1998 No.58) reg 44 (April 6, 1998).

Basic rate of child benefit
4. For the purposes of paragraph 1(4) of Schedule 1 to the Act "basic rate" means the rate of child benefit which is specified in [1regulation 2(1)(a)(i) or 2(1)(b) of the Child Benefit Rates Regulations (weekly rate for only, elder or eldest child and for other children)] applicable to the child in question at the effective date.

Amendment
1. Child Benefit, Child Support and Social Security (Miscellaneous Amendments) Regulations 1996 (SI 1996 No.1803) reg 9 (April 7, 1997).

Definitions
"the Act": see reg 1(2).
"Child Benefit Rates Regulations": see reg 1(2).
"effective date": see reg1(2).

The general rule
5. For the purposes of paragraph 2(1) of Schedule 1 to the Act–
(a)   the value of C, otherwise than in a case where the other parent is the person with care, is nil; and
(b)   the value of P is 0.5.

Definition
"the Act": see reg 1(2).

The additional element
6.–[1(1)   For the purposes of the formula in paragraph 4(1) of Schedule 1 to the Act, the value of R is–
(a)   where the maintenance assessment in question relates to one qualifying child, 0.15;
(b)   where the maintenance assessment in question relates to two qualifying children, 0.20; and
(c)   where the maintenance assessment in question relates to three or more qualifying children, 0.25.]
(2)   For the purposes of the alternative formula in paragraph 4(3) of Schedule 1 to the act–
(a)   the value of Z is [2 1.5];
(b)   the amount for the purposes of paragraph (b) of the definition of Q is the same as the amount specified in [3regulation 3(1)(c)] (income support family premium) in respect of each qualifying child.

Amendments
1. Child Support (Miscellaneous Amendments and Transitional Provisions) Regulations 1994 (SI 1994 No.227) reg 4(3) (February 7, 1994).
2. Child Support and Income Support (Amendment) Regulations 1995 (SI 1995 No.1045) reg 43 (April 18, 1995).
3. Child Support (Miscellaneous Amendments) Regulations 1998 (SI 1998 No.58) reg 45 (April 6, 1998).

Definition
"the Act": see reg 1(2).

Net income: calculation or estimation of N
7.–(1)   Subject to the following provisions of this regulation, for the purposes of the formula in paragraph 5(1) of Schedule 1 to the act, the amount of N (net income of absent parent) shall be the aggregate of the following amounts–
(a)   the amount, determined in accordance with part I of schedule 1, of any earnings of the absent parent;
(b)   the amount, determined in accordance with part II of Schedule 1, of any benefit payments under the Contributions and Benefits Act [1[4, the Jobseekers Act or the Welfare Reform Act]] paid to or in respect of the absent parent;

(c) the amount, determined in accordance with Part III of Schedule 1, of any other income of the absent parent;

(d) the amount, determined in accordance with Part III of Schedule 1, of any income of a relevant child which is treated as the income of the absent parent;

(e) any amount, determined in accordance with Part V of Schedule 1, which is treated as the income of the absent parent.

(2) Any amounts referred to in Schedule 2 shall be disregarded.

(3) Where an absent parent's income consists–

(a) only of [²work-based training for young people or, in Scotland, Skillseekers training] allowance; or

(b) in the case of a student, only of grant, an amount paid in respect of grant contribution or student loan or any combination thereof; or

(c) only of prisoner's pay,

then for the purposes of determining N such income shall be disregarded.

(4) Where a parent and any other person are beneficially entitled to any income but the shares of their respective entitlements are not ascertainable the [³Secretary of State] shall estimate their respective entitlements having regard to such information as is available but where sufficient information on which to base an estimate is not available the parent and that other person shall be treated as entitled to that income in equal shares.

(5) Where any income normally received at regular intervals has not been received it shall, if it is due to be paid and there are reasonable grounds for believing it will be received, be treated as if it has been received.

Amendments

1. Social Security and Child Support (Jobseeker's Allowance) (Consequential Amendments) Regulations 1996 (SI 1996 No.1345) reg 6(6) and 7(a) (October 7, 1996).

2. Child Support (Miscellaneous Amendments) Regulations 1999 (SI 1999 No.977) reg 6(3) (April 6, 1999).

3. Social Security Act 1998 (Commencement No.7 and Consequential and Transitional Provisions) Order 1999 (SI 1999 No.1510) art 16 (June 1, 1999).

4. Employment and Support Allowance (Consequential Provisions) (No.2) Regulations 2008 (SI 2008 No.1554) reg 58(3) (October 27, 2008).

Definitions

"the Act": see reg 1(2).

"Contributions and Benefits Act": see reg 1(2).

"earnings": see reg 1(2).

"effective date": see reg 1(2).

"grant": see reg 1(2).

"grant contribution": see reg 1(2).

"the Jobseekers Act": see reg 1(2).

"person": see reg 1(2).

"prisoner": see reg 1(2).

"student": see reg 1(2).

"student loan": see reg 1(2).

"training allowance": see reg 1(2).

Net income; calculation or estimation of M

8. For the purposes of paragraph 5(2) of Schedule 1 to the Act, the amount of M (net income of the parent with care) shall be calculated in the same way as N is calculated under regulation 7 but as if references to the absent parent were references to the parent with care.

Definitions

"the Act": see reg 1(2).

"parent with care": see reg 1(2).

Exempt income; calculation or estimation of E

9.–(1) For the purposes of paragraph 5(1) of Schedule 1 to the Act, the amount of E (exempt income of absent parent) shall, subject to paragraphs (3) and (4), be the aggregate of the following amounts–

(a)   an amount equal to the amount specified in column (2) of paragraph 1(1)(e) of the relevant Schedule (income personal allowance for a single claimant aged not less than 25);

(b)   an amount in respect of housing costs determined in accordance with regulations 14 to [⁵16 and] 18;

[²(bb)   where applicable, an amount in respect of a qualifying transfer of property determined in accordance with schedule 3A;]

(c)   [⁷...]

(d)   where, if the parent were a claimant [¹²who had not attained the qualifying age for state pension credit], the conditions in paragraph 11 of the relevant Schedule (income support disability premium) would be satisfied in respect of him, an amount equal to the amount specified in column (2) of paragraph 15(4)(a) of that Schedule (income support disability premium);

(e)   where–
   (i)   if the parent were a claimant, the conditions in paragraph 13 of the relevant Schedule (income support severe disability premium) would be satisfied, an amount equal to the amount specified in column (2) of paragraph 15(5(a) of that Schedule (except that no such amount shall be taken into account in the case of an absent parent in respect of whom [¹⁰a carer's allowance] under section 70 of the Contributions and Benefits Act is payable to some other person);
   (ii)   if the parent were a claimant, the conditions in paragraph 14ZA of the relevant Schedule (income support a carer premium) would be satisfied in respect of him, an amount equal to the amount specified in column (2) of paragraph 15(7) of that Schedule;
   [⁸(iii)   if the parent were a claimant, the conditions in paragraph 13A of the relevant Schedule (income support enhanced disability premium) would be satisfied in respect of him, an amount equal to the amount specified in paragraph 15(8)(b) of that Schedule;]

(f)   where, if the parent were a claimant, the conditions in paragraph 3 of the relevant Schedule (income support family premium) would be satisfied in respect of a relevant child of that parent [⁷...], the amount specified in [⁴sub-paragraph (b) of] that paragraph or, where those conditions would be satisfied only by virtue of the case being one to which paragraph (2) applies, half that amount;

(g)   in respect of each relevant child–
   (i)   an amount equal to the amount of the personal allowance for that child, specified in column (2) of paragraph 2 of the relevant Schedule (income support personal allowance) or, where paragraph (2) applies, half that amount;
   (ii)   if the conditions set out in paragraph 14(b) and (c) of the relevant Schedule (income support disabled child premium) are satisfied in respect of that child, an amount equal to the amount specified in column (2) of paragraph 15(6) of the relevant Schedule or, where paragraph (2) applies, half that amount;
   [⁹(iii)   if the conditions set out in paragraph 13A of the relevant Schedule (income support enhanced disability premium) are satisfied in respect of that child, an amount equal to the amount specified in paragraph 15(8)(a) of that Schedule or, where paragraph (2) applies, half that amount;]

[¹¹(h)   where the absent parent or his partner is resident in a care home or an independent hospital or is being provided with a care home service or an independent health care service, the amount of fees paid in respect of that home, hospital or service, as the case may be, but where it has been determined that the absent parent in question or his partner is entitled to housing benefit in respect of fees for that home, hospital or service, as the case may be, the net amount of such fees after deduction of housing benefit;]

[²(i)   where applicable, an amount in respect of travelling costs determined in accordance with schedule 3B.]

(2)　　This paragraph applies where–
(a)　　the absent parent has a partner;
(b)　　the absent parent and the partner are parents of the same relevant child; and
(c)　　the income of the partner, calculated under regulation 7(1) [¹(but excluding the amount mentioned in sub-paragraph (d) of that regulation)] as if that partner were an absent parent to whom that regulation applied, exceeds the aggregate of–
　　(i)　　the amount specified in column 2 of paragraph 1(1)(e) of the relevant Schedule (income support personal allowance for a single claimant aged not less than 25);
　　(ii)　　half the amount of the personal allowance for that child specified in column (2) of paragraph 2 of the relevant Schedule (income support personal allowance);
　　(iii)　　half the amount of any income support disabled child premium specified in column (2) of paragraph 15(6) of that Schedule in respect of that child; [²and]
　　(iv)　　half the amount of any income support family premium specified in paragraph [⁴3 [⁷(1)](b) of the relevant Schedule] except where such premium is payable irrespective of that child; [². . .].
　　[⁶(v)　　where a departure direction has been given on the grounds that a case falls within regulations 27 of the Departure Direction and Consequential Amendments Regulation (partner's contribution to housing costs), the amount of the housing costs which corresponds to the percentage of the housing costs mentioned in regulation 40(7) of those Regulation.]

(3)　　Where an absent parent does not have day to day care of any relevant child for 7 nights each week but does have day to day care of one or more such children for fewer than 7 nights each week, [⁴any amount] to be taken into account under sub-paragraphs (1)(c) [⁴or (f)] shall be reduced so that they bear the same proportion to the amount referred to in those sub-paragraphs as the average number of nights each week in respect of which such care is provided has to 7.

(4)　　Where an absent parent has day to day care of a relevant child for fewer than 7 nights each week, any amounts to be taken into account under sub-paragraph (1)(g) in respect of such child shall be reduced so that they bear the same proportion to the amounts referred to in that sub-paragraph as the average number of nights each week in respect of which such care is provided has to 7.

(5)　　The amounts referred to in paragraph (1) are the amounts applicable at the effective date.

Amendments
1.　　Child Support (Miscellaneous Amendments) Regulations 1993 (SI 1993 No 913) reg 20 (April 5, 1993).
2.　　Child Support and Income Support (Amendment) Regulations 1995 (SI 1995 No.1045) reg 44(2) and (3) (April 18, 1995).
3.　　Child Support (Miscellaneous Amendments) (No.2) Regulations 1995 (SI 1995 No.3261) reg 42 (January 22, 1996).
4.　　Child Benefit, Child Support and Social Security (Miscellaneous Amendments) Regulations 1996 (SI 1996 No.1803) reg 11(2)-(4) (April 7, 1997).
5.　　Child Support (Miscellaneous Amendments) Regulations 1996 (SI 1996 No.1945) reg 19 (October 7, 1996).
6.　　Child Support Departure Direction and Consequential Amendments Regulations 1996 (SI 1996 No.2907) reg 68(4) (December 2, 1996).
7.　　Child Support (Miscellaneous Amendments) Regulations 1998 (SI 1998 No.58) reg 47(2) and (3) (April 6, 1998).
8.　　Child Support (Miscellaneous Amendments) Regulations 2002 (SI 2002 No.1204) reg 5(a) (April 30, 2002).
9.　　Child Support (Miscellaneous Amendments) Regulations 2002 (SI 2002 No.1204) reg 9(1)(g) (April 30, 2002).
10.　　Child Support (Miscellaneous Amendments) Regulations 2003 (SI 2003 No.328) reg 4(2) (April 1, 2003).
11.　　Child Support (Miscellaneous Amendments) (No.2) Regulations 2003 (SI 2003 No.2779) reg 4(3) (November 5, 2003).

12. Child Support (Miscellaneous and Consequential Amendments) Regulations 2009 (SI 2009 No.736) reg 3(3) (April 6, 2009).

Definitions
"the Act": see reg 1(2).
"care home": see reg 1(2).
"care home service": see reg 1(2).
"claimant": see reg 1(2).
"Contributions and Benefits Act": see reg 1(2).
"day to day care": see reg 1(2).
"Departure Direction and Consequential Amendments Regulations": see reg 1(2).
"effective date": see reg 1(2).
"housing benefit": see reg 1(2).
"Income Support Regulations": see reg 1(2).
"independent health care service": see reg 1(2).
"independent hospital": see reg 1(2).
"partner": see reg 1(2).
"relevant child": see reg 1(2).
"relevant Schedule": see reg 1(2).

Exempt income: calculation or estimation of F

10. For the purposes of paragraph 5(2) of Schedule 1 to the Act, the amount of F (exempt income of parent with care) shall be calculated in the same way as E is calculated under regulation 9 but as if references to the absent parent were references to the parent with care [¹except that–
 (a) sub-paragraph (bb) of paragraph (1) of that regulation shall not apply unless at the time of the making of the qualifying transfer the parent with care would have been the absent parent had the Child Support Act 1991 been in force at the date of the making of the transfer; and
 (b) paragraph (3) and (4) of that regulation shall apply only where the parent with care shares the day to day care of the child mentioned in those paragraphs with one or more other persons.]

Amendment
1. Child Support and Income Support (Amendment) Regulations 1995 (SI 1995 No.1045) reg 45 (April 18, 1995).

Definitions
"the Act": see reg 1(2).
"day to day care": see reg 1(2).
"parent with care": see reg 1(2).

[¹Assessment income: [³ [⁴working tax credit]] paid to or in respect of a parent with care or an absent parent]

10A.–(1) Subject to paragraph (2), where [³[⁴working tax credit]] is paid to or in respect of a parent with care or an absent parent, that parent shall, for the purposes of Schedule 1 to the Act, be taken to have no assessable income.
 (2) Paragraph (1) shall apply to an absent parent only if–
 (a) he is also a parent with care; and
 (b) either–
  (i) a maintenance assessment in respect of a child in relation to whom he is a parent with care is in force; or
  (ii) the [²Secretary of State] is considering an application for such an assessment to be made.]

Amendments
1. Child Support (Miscellaneous Amendments) (No.2) Regulations 1996 (SI 1996 No.3196) reg 11 (January 13, 1997).
2. Social Security Act 1998 (Commencement No.7 and Consequential and Transitional Provisions) Order 1999 (SI 1999 No.1510) art 16 (June 1, 1999).

3.   Social Security and Child Support (Tax Credits) Consequential Amendments Regulations 1999 (SI 1999 No.2566) Parts I and II, Sch 2 (October 5, 1999).

4.   Child Support (Miscellaneous Amendments) Regulations 2003 (SI 2003 No.328) reg 6(4) (April 6, 2003).

Definitions
"the Act": see reg 1(2).
"working credit": see reg 1(2).

[¹**Assessable income: state pension credit paid to or in respect of a parent with care or an absent parent**

10B.   Where state pension credit is paid to or in respect of a parent with care or an absent parent, that parent shall, for the purposes of Schedule 1 to the Act, be taken to have no assessable income.]

Amendment
1.   Child Support (Miscellaneous Amendments) (No.2) Regulations 2003 (SI 2003 No. 2779) reg 4(4) (November 5, 2003).

Definition
"state pension credit": see reg 1(2).

Protected income

11.–(1)   For the purposes of paragraph 6 of Schedule 1 to the Act the protected income level of an absent parent shall, [²subject to paragraphs (3), (4)[⁶, (6) and (6A),]] be the aggregate of the following amounts–

(a)   where–

    (i)   the absent parent does not have a partner, an amount equal to the amount specified in column (2) of paragraph 1(1)(e) of the relevant Schedule (income support personal allowance for a single claimant aged not less than 25 years);

    (ii)   the absent parent has a partner, an amount equal to the amount specified in column (2) of paragraph 1(3)(c) of the relevant Schedule (income support personal allowance for a couple where both members are aged not less than 18 years);

    (iii)   the absent parent is a member of a polygamous marriage, an amount in respect of himself and one of his partners, equal to the amount specified in sub-paragraph (ii) and, in respect of each of his other partners, an amount equal to the difference between the amount specified in sub-paragraph (ii) and sub-paragraph (i);

(b)   an amount in respect of housing costs determined in accordance with regulations 14,15, 16 and 18, or, in a case where the absent parent is a non-dependant member of a household who is treated as having no housing costs by [⁴regulation 15(4)], the non-dependant amount which would be calculated in respect of him under [²paragraphs (1), (2) and (9) of [¹¹regulation 74 of the Housing Benefit Regulations or, as the case may be, regulation 55 of the Housing Benefit (State Pension Credit) Regulations] (non-dependant deductions) if he were a non-dependant in respect of whom a calculation were to be made under those paragraphs (disregarding any other provision of that regulation)];

(c)   [⁸. . .]

(d)   where, if the parent were a claimant, the conditions in paragraph 11 of the relevant Schedule (income support disability premium) would be satisfied, an amount equal to the amount specified in column (2) of the paragraph 15(4) of that Schedule (income support disability premium);

(e)   where, if the parent were a claimant, the conditions in paragraph 13 or 14ZA of the relevant Schedule (income support severe disability and carer premiums) would be satisfied in respect of either or both premiums, an amount equal to the amount or amounts specified in column (2) of paragraph 15(5) or, as the case

may be, (7) of that Schedule in respect of that or those premiums (income support premiums);
(f)   where, if the parent were a claimant, the conditions in paragraph 3 of the relevant Schedule (income support family premium) would be satisfied, the amount specified in [⁵sub-paragraph (b) of] that paragraph;
(g)   in respect of each child who is a member of the family of the absent parent–
        (i)   an amount equal to the amount of the personal allowance for that child, specified in column (2) of paragraph 2 of the relevant Schedule (income support personal allowance);
        (ii)   if the conditions set out in paragraphs 14(b) and (c) of the relevant Schedule (income support disabled child premium) are satisfied in respect of that child, an amount equal to the amounts specified in column (2) of paragraph 15(6) of the relevant Schedule;
(h)   where, if the parent where a claimant, the conditions specified in Part III of the relevant Schedule would be satisfied by the absent parent in question or any member of his family in relation to any premium not otherwise included in this regulation, an amount equal to the amount specified in Part IV of that Schedule (income support premiums) in respect of that premium;
[¹⁰(i) where the absent parent or his partner is resident in a care home or an independent hospital or is being provided with a care home service or an independent health care service, the amount of fees paid in respect of that home, hospital or service, as the case may be, but where it has been determined that the absent parent in question or his partner is entitled to housing benefit in respect of fees for that home, hospital or service, as the case may be, the net amount of such fees after deduction of housing benefit;]
[²(j)   where–
        (i)   the absent parent is, or that absent parent and any partner of his are, the only person or persons resident in, and liable to pay council tax in respect of, the home for which housing costs are included under sub-paragraph (b), the amount of weekly council tax for which he is liable in respect of that home, less any applicable council tax benefit;
        (ii)   where other persons are resident with the absent parent in, and liable to pay council tax in respect of, the home for which housing costs are included under sub-paragraph (b), an amount representing the share of the weekly council tax in respect of that home applicable to the absent parent, determined by dividing the total amount of council tax due in that week by the number of persons liable to pay it, less any council tax benefit applicable to that share, provided that if the absent parent is required to pay and pays more than that share because of default by one or more of those other persons, the amount for the purposes of this regulation shall be the amount of weekly council tax the absent parent pays, less any council tax benefit applicable to such amount;]
(k)   an amount of [¹£30.00];
[²(kk) an amount in respect of travelling costs determined in accordance with Schedule 3B;]
(l)   where the income of–
        (i)   the absent parent in question;
        (ii)   any partner of his; and
        (iii)   any child or children for whom an amount is included under sub-paragraph (g)(i);
exceeds the sum of the amounts to which reference is made in sub-paragraphs [²(a) to (kk)], [¹15 per centum] of the excess.
(2)   For the purposes of sub-paragraph(1) of paragraph (1) "income" shall be calculated–
(a)   in respect of the absent parent in question or any partner of his, in the same manner as N (net income of absent parent) is calculated under regulation 7 except–

      (i)   there shall be taken into account the basic rate of any child benefit and any maintenance which in either case is in payment in respect of any member of the family of the absent parent;

      (ii)   there shall be deducted the amount of any maintenance under a maintenance order which the absent parent or his partner is paying in respect of a child in circumstances where an application for a maintenance assessment could not be made in accordance with the Act in respect of that child; [³. . .]

      [³(iii) to the extent that it falls under sub-paragraph (b), the income of any child in that family shall not be treated as the income of the parent or his partner and Part IV of Schedule 1 shall not apply; [⁴. . .]]

      [⁴(iv) paragraph 27 of Schedule 2 shall apply as though the reference to paragraph 3(2) and (4) of Schedule 3 were omitted;

      (v)   there shall be deducted the amount of any maintenance which is being paid in respect of a child by the absent parent or his partner under an order requiring such payment made by a court outside Great Britain; and]

      [⁹(vi) there shall be taken into account any child tax credit which is payable to the absent parent or his partner; and]

  (b)   in respect of any child in that family, as being the total of [³that child's relevant income(within the meaning of paragraph 23 of Schedule 1), there being disregarded any maintenance in payment to or in respect of him,] but only to the extent that such income does not exceed the amount included under sub-paragraph (g) and paragraph (1) (income support personal allowance for a child and income support disabled child premium) reduced, as the case may be, under paragraph (4).

  (3)   Where an absent parent does not have day to day care of any child (whether or not a relevant child) for 7 nights each week but does have day to day care of one or more such children for fewer than 7 nights each week [⁵any amount], to be taken into account under [⁸sub-paragraph (f)] of paragraph (l) [⁵. . .] income support family premium) shall be reduced so that they bear the same proportion to the amounts referred to in those sub-paragraphs as the average number of nights each week in respect of which such care is provided has to 7.

  (4)   Where an absent parent has day to day care of a child (whether or not a relevant child) for fewer than 7 nights each week any amounts in relation to that child to be taken into account under sub-paragraph (g) of paragraphs (1) (income support personal allowance for child and income support disabled child premium) shall be reduced so that they bear the same proportion to the amounts referred to in that sub-paragraph as the average number of nights in respect of which such care is provided has to 7.

  (5)   The amounts referred to in paragraph (1) shall be the amounts applicable at the effective date.

  [³(6)   If the application of the above provisions of this regulation would result in the protected income level of an absent parent being less than 70 per centum of his net income, as calculated in accordance with regulation 7, those provisions shall not apply in his case and instead his protected income level shall be 70 per centum of his net income as so calculated.

  [⁷(6A) In a case to which paragraph (6) does not apply, if the application of paragraphs (1) to (5) and of regulation 12(1)(a) would result in the amount of child support maintenance payable being greater than 30 per centum of the absent parent's net income calculated in accordance with regulation 7, paragraphs (1) to (5) shall not apply in his case and instead his protected income level shall be 70 per centum of his net income as so calculated.]

  (7)   Where any calculation under paragraph (6) [⁷or (6A)] results in a fraction of a penny, that fraction shall be treated as a penny.]

Amendments

   1.   Child Support (Miscellaneous Amendments and Transitional Provisions) Regulations 1994 (SI 1994 No.227) reg 4(4) and (5) (February 7, 1994).

   2.   Child Support and Income Support (Amendment) Regulations 1995 (SI 1995 No.1045) reg 46(2) (April 18, 1995).

3.   Child Support and Income Support (Amendment) Regulations 1995 (SI 1995 No.1045) reg 46(3)-(6) (April 18, 1995).

4.   Child Support (Miscellaneous Amendments) (No.2) Regulations 1995 (SI 1995 No.3261) reg 43(2) – (5) (January 22, 1996).

5.   Child Benefit, Child Support and Social Security (Miscellaneous Amendments) Regulations 1996 (SI 1996 No.1803) reg 12(2) and (3) (April 7, 1997).

6.   Child Support (Miscellaneous Amendments) Regulations 1996 (SI 1996 No.1945) reg 20(2) (October 7, 1996).

7.   Child Support (Miscellaneous Amendments) Regulations 1996 (SI 1996 No.1945) reg 20(3) and (4) (August 5, 1996).

8.   Child Support (Miscellaneous Amendments) Regulations 1998 (SI 1998 No.58) reg 49(2) and (3) (April 6, 1998).

9.   Child Support (Miscellaneous Amendments) Regulations 2003 (SI 2003 No.328) reg 6(5) (April 6, 2003).

10. Child Support (Miscellaneous Amendments) (No.2) Regulations 2003 (SI 2003 No.2779) reg 4(5) (November 5, 2003).

11. Housing Benefit and Council Tax Benefit (Consequential Provisions) Regulations 2006 (SI 2006 No.217) reg 5 and Sch 2, para 4(3) (March 6, 2006).

Definitions

"the Act": see reg 1(2).
"care home": see reg 1(2).
"care home service": see reg 1(2).
"child tax credit": se reg 1(2).
"claimant": see reg 1(2).
"council tax benefit": see reg 1(2).
"couple": see reg 1(2).
"effective date": see reg 1(2).
"family": see reg 1(2).
"Housing Benefit Regulations": see reg 1(2).
"Housing Benefit (State Pension Credit) Regulations": see reg 1(2).
"Income Support Regulations": see reg 1(2).
"independent health care service": see reg 1(2).
"independent hospital": see reg 1(2).
"non-dependant": see reg 1(2).
"partner": see reg 1(2).
"polygamous marriage": see reg 1(2).
"relevant Schedule": see reg 1(2).

General Note

In reg 11(2)(a)(i), maintenance does not include child support maintenance (*R(CS) 4/02*).

Disposable income

12.–[¹(1)   For the purpose of paragraph 6(4) of Schedule 1 to the Act (protected incomr), the disposable income of an absent parent shall be–

(a)   except in a case to which regulation 11(6) [²or (6A)] applies, the aggregate of his income and any income of any member of his family calculated in like manner as under regulation 11(2); [³. . .]

(b)   [³subject to sub-paragraph (c),] in a case to which regulation 11(6) [²or (6A)] applies, his net income as calculated in accordance with regulation 7 [³and]]

[³(c)   in a case to which regulation 11(6) applies and the absent parent is paying maintenance under an order of a kind mentioned in regulation 11(2)(a)(ii) or (v), his net income as calculated in accordance with regulation 7 less the amount of maintenance he is paying under that order.]

(2)   Subject to paragraph (3), where a maintenance assessment has been made with respect to the absent parent and payment of the amount of that assessment would reduce his disposable income below his protected income level the amount of the assessment shall be reduced by the minimum amount necessary to prevent his disposable income being reduced below his protected income level.

(3)   Where the prescribed minimum amount fixed by regulations under paragraph 7 of Schedule 1 to the Act is applicable (such amount being specified in regulation 13) the

amount payable under the assessment shall not be reduced to less than the prescribed minimum amount.

Amendments
1.   Child Support and Income Support (Amendment) Regulations 1995 (SI 1995 No.1045) reg 47 (April 18, 1995).
2.   Child Support (Miscellaneous Amendments) Regulations 1996 (SI 1996 No.1945) reg 21 (August 5, 1996).
3.   Child Support (Miscellaneous Amendments) (No.2) Regulations 1996 (SI 1996 No.3196) reg 12(2)-(4) (January 13, 1997).

Definitions
   "the Act": see reg 1(2).
   "family": see reg 1(2).

The minimum amount

13.–(1)   Subject to regulation 26, for the purposes of paragraph 7(1) of Schedule 1 to the Act the minimum amount shall be [¹2 multiplied by] 5 per centum of the amount specified in paragraph 1(1)(e) of the relevant Schedule (income support personal allowance for a single claimant aged not less than 25).

   (2)   Where the [¹5 per centum amount] calculated under paragraph (1) results in a sum other than a multiple of 5 pence, it shall be treated as the sum which is the next higher multiple of 5 pence.

Amendment
1.   Child Support (Maintenance Assessments and Special Cases) and Social Security (Claims and Payments) Amendment Regulations 1996 (SI 1996 No.481) reg 2 (April 8, 1996).

Definition
   "the Act": see reg 1(2).

Eligible housing costs

14.   Schedule 3 shall have effect for the purpose of determining the costs which are eligible to be taken into account as housing costs for the purposes of these Regulations.

General Note
There is an allowance for an amount in respect of housing costs in both assessable income and protected income (regs 9(1)(b), 10 and 11(1)(b)). This figure will not necessarily be the same for each type of income, nor will it necessarily be the same as the parent's actual housing costs. In this note that amount is referred to as the allowable housing costs. The tribunal should approach the question of allowable housing costs in the following stages.

First, identify the parent's home, as defined in reg 1(2). The only allowable housing costs are those in respect of that home (reg 15(1)).

Second, identify the housing costs in respect of that home. The costs must be determined at the effective date (reg 16). The approach to this stage depends upon whether the parent has been determined by the local authority to be entitled to housing benefit. If so, the parent's housing costs are the weekly rent for the purposes of that benefit less the housing benefit and the non-dependant deductions discussed below (reg 15(2)). If the parent has not been determined to be entitled to housing benefit, the calculation is more complicated,
(i)   Begin by determining the types of eligible housing costs incurred in respect of the parent's home from those listed in Sch 3, paras 1, 2 and (for assessable income purposes only) 3 (regs 14 and 15(1)).
(ii)   Then decide whether the general conditions of entitlement for those costs to be taken into account have been met (Sch 3, para 4).
(iii) If so, make the following deductions: where those costs are shared with someone other than a member of the parent's family, the share of those costs applicable to the other person (reg 15(3)); apportionment for non-residential accommodation covered by the payments under (i) above (Sch 3, para 5); deductions for ineligible service charges, fuel charges and water and allied environmental services (Sch 3, para 6). The result is the parent's housing costs.
Third, if the parent has housing costs, the tribunal must determine to whom those costs are paid. If the parent is a non-dependant member of a household and pays housing costs only to another member or members of that household, the parent is treated as having no housing costs (reg 15(10)). This only applies for the purposes of

calculating assessable income (regs 9(1)(b) and 10) and does not apply for the purposes of the protected income calculation in respect of which a notional allowance is made for housing costs (reg 11(1)(b)).

Fourth, if the parent has housing costs, these must be converted to a weekly figure under reg 16.

Fifth, the tribunal should determine whether the costs exceed the ceiling imposed by reg 18. If they do, no costs are allowed over the ceiling. The result is the allowable housing costs.

Amount of housing costs

15.–(1) Subject to the provisions of this regulation and regulations [¹16 and 18] a parent's housing costs shall be the aggregate of the eligible housing costs payable in respect of his home.

(2) Where a local authority has determined that a parent is entitled to housing benefit, the amount of his housing costs shall, subject to paragraphs (4) to (9), be the weekly amount treated as rent under [⁴regulations 12 and 80 of the Housing Benefit Regulations or, as the case may be, regulations 12 and 61 of the Housing Benefit (State Pension Credit) Regulations] (rent and calculation of weekly amounts) less the amount of housing benefit.

(3) Where a parent has eligible housing costs and another person who is not a member of his family is also liable to make payments in respect of the home, the amount of the parent's housing costs shall be his share of those costs [³but where that other person does not make payments in circumstances where head (a) of paragraph 4(2) of Schedule 3 applies, the eligible housing costs of that parent shall include the housing costs for which, because of that failure to pay, that parent is treated as responsible under that head.]

(4)–(9) [¹. . .]

[¹[²(4) A parent shall be treated as having no housing costs where he is a non dependant member of a household and is not responsible for meeting housing costs except to another member, or other members, of that household.]

Amendments

1. Child Support and Income Support (Amendment) Regulations 1995 (SI 1995 No.1045) reg 48(2)-(4) (April 18, 1995).

2. Child Support (Miscellaneous Amendments) (No. 2) Regulations 1995 (SI 1995 No.3261) reg 44 (January 22, 1996).

3. Child Support (Miscellaneous Amendments) Regulations 1998 (SI 1998 No.58) reg 50 (January 19, 1998).

4. Housing Benefit and Council Tax Benefit (Consequential Provisions) Regulations 2006 (SI 2006 No.217) reg 5 and Sch 2, para 4(4) (March 6, 2006).

Definitions

"eligible housing costs": see reg 1(2).
"family": see reg 1(2).
"home": see reg 1(2).
"housing benefit": see reg 1(2).
"Housing Benefit Regulations": see reg 1(2).
"Housing Benefit (State Pension Credit) Regulations": see reg 1(2).
"non-dependant": see reg 1(2).

General Note

Paragraph (3)

As a result of this provision only half of the housing costs is to be taken into account as an eligible housing cost where the parent whose home the property is is not solely liable for those costs (*CSCS 8/1995*, para 15 and *CCS 8189/1995*). In the latter decision the commissioner refers throughout to reg 50 of these Regulations. There is no such regulation and the words quoted by the commissioner are those of this paragraph.

If the parent occupying the home has to pay the whole of the costs, the case falls within Sch 3, para 4(2)(a) (*CCS 13698/1996*, para 7).

[¹Weekly amount of housing costs

16.–(1) [²Where housing costs are payable by a parent]–

(a) on a weekly basis, the amount of such housing costs shall subject to paragraph (2), be the weekly rate payable at the effective date;

(b)   on a monthly basis, the amount of such housing costs shall subject to paragraph (2), be the monthly rate payable at the effective date, multiplied by 12 and divided by 52;

(c)   by way of rent payable to a housing association, as defined in section 1(1) of the Housing Associations Act 1985 which is registered in accordance with section 5 of that Act, or to a local authority, on a free week basis, that is to say the basis that he pays an amount by way of rent for a given number of weeks in a 52 week period, with a lesser number of weeks in which there is no liability to pay ("free weeks"), the amount of such housing costs shall be [²the amount payable]–
(i)   in the relevant week if it is not a free week; or
(ii)   in the last week before the relevant week which is not a free week, if the relevant week is a free week;

(d)   on any other basis, the amount of such housing costs shall, subject to paragraph (2), be the rate payable at the effective date, multiplied by the number of payment periods, or the nearest whole number of payment periods (any fraction of one half being rounded up), falling within a period of 365 days and divided by 52.

(2)   Where housing costs consist of payments or a repayment mortgage and the absent parent or parent with care has not provided information or evidence as to the rate of repayment of the capital secured and the interest payable on that mortgage at the effective date and that absent parent or parent with care has provided a statement from the lender, in respect of a period ending not more than 12 months prior to the first day of the relevant week, for the purposes of the calculation of exempt income under regulation 9 and protected income under regulation 11–

(a)   if the amount of capital repaid for the period covered by that statement is shown on it, the rate of repayment of capital owing under that mortgage shall be calculated by reference to that amount; and

(b)   if the amount of capital owing and the interest rate applicable at the end of the period covered by that statement are shown on it, the interest payable on that mortgage shall be calculated by references to that amount and that interest rate.]

Amendments
1.   Child Support (Miscellaneous Amendments) Regulations 1996 (SI 1996 No.1945) reg 22 (August 5, 1996).
2.   Child Support (Miscellaneous Amendments) Regulations 1998 (SI 1998 No.58) reg 51(a) and (b) (January 19, 1998).

17. [¹. . .]

Amendment
1.   Child Support and Income Support (Amendment) Regulations 1995 (SI 1995 No.1045) reg 50 (April 18, 1995).

Definitions
"effective date": see reg 1(2).
"relevant week": see reg 1(2).

General Note
Although this regulation provides that the housing costs shall be those payable at the effective date, some of the provisions which determine the effective date have the effect that the effective date may pre-date the change in the housing costs. For example, a change in housing costs which occurs on the second day of a maintenance period and which is notified to the officer on the following day will result in a fresh assessment of which the effective date is the first day of the maintenance period (reg 31(3) of the Maintenance Assessment Procedure Regulations).
    Regulation 17 was revoked by reg 50 of the Amendment Regulations 1995 from 18 April 1995.

Excessive housing costs
18.–(1) Subject to paragraph (2), the amount of the housing costs of an absent parent which are to be taken into account–

(a) under regulation 9(1)(b) shall not exceed the greater of £80.00 or half the amount of N as calculated or estimated under regulation 7;

(b) under regulation 11(1)(b) shall not exceed the greater of £80.00 or half of the amount calculated in accordance with regulation 11(2).

(2) The restriction imposed by paragraph (1) shall not apply where–

(a) the absent parent in question–

    (i) has been awarded housing benefit (or is awaiting the outcome of a claim to that benefit);

    (ii) has the day to day care of any child; or

    (iii) is a person to whom a disability premium under paragraph 11 of the relevant Schedule applies in respect of himself or his partner or would so apply if he were entitled to income support and [²had not attained the qualifying age for state pension credit];

(b) the absent parent in question, following divorce from [¹dissolution of a civil partnership with,] or the breakdown of his relationship with, his former partner, remains in the home he occupied with his former partner;

(c) the absent parent in question has paid the housing costs under the mortgage, charge or agreement in question for a period in excess of 52 weeks before the date of the first application for child support maintenance in relation to a qualifying child of his and there has been no increase in those costs other than an increase in the interest payable under the mortgage or charge or, as the case may be, in the amount payable under the agreement under which the home is held;

(d) the housing costs in respect of the home in question would not exceed the amount set out in paragraph (1) but for an increase in the interest payable under a mortgage or charge secured on that home or, as the case may be, in the amount payable under any agreement under which it is held; or

(e) the absent parent is responsible for making payments in respect of housing costs which are higher than they would be otherwise by virtue of the unavailability of his share of the equity of the property formerly occupied with his partner and which remains occupied by that former partner.

Amendments

1.   Civil Partnership (Pensions, Social Security and Child Support) (Consequential, etc. Provisions) Order 2005 (SI 2005 No.2877) art 2(4) and Sch 4, para 2(3) (December 5, 2005).

2.   Child Support (Miscellaneous and Consequential Amendments) Regulations 2009 (SI 2009 No 736) reg 3(4) (April 6, 2009).

Definitions

"day to day care": see reg 1(2).

"home": see reg 1(2).

"housing benefit": see reg 1(2).

"partner": see reg 1(2).

"relevant Schedule": see reg 1(2).

General Note

Subparagraph (2)(b)

The partner referred to need not be the person with care of the qualifying child (*CCS 12769/1996*, para 11).

PART III
SPECIAL CASES
Special cases

Both parents are absent

19.–(1) Subject to regulation 27, where the circumstances of a case are that each parent of a qualifying child is an absent parent in relation to that child (neither being a person who is treated as an absent parent by regulation 20(2) that case shall be treated as a special case for the purposes of the Act.

(2)　For the purposes of this case–

(a)　where the application is made in relation to both absent parents, separate assessments shall be made under Schedule 1 to the Act in respect of each so as to determine the amount of child support maintenance payable by each absent parent;

(b)　subject to paragraph (3), where the application is made in relation to both absent parents, the value of C in each case shall be the assessable income of the other absent parent and where the application is made in relation to only one the value of C in the case of the other shall be nil;

(c)　[² . . .]

[¹(d)　where the application is made in relation to one absent parent only, the amount of the maintenance requirement applicable in that case shall be one-half of the amount determined in accordance with paragraph 1(2) of Schedule 1 to the Act or, where regulation 23 applies (person caring for children of more than one absent parent), of the amount determined in accordance with paragraphs (2) to (3) of that regulation.]

(3)　Where, for the purposes of paragraph (2)(b), information regarding the income of the other absent parent has not been submitted to the Secretary of State [⁴ . . .] within the period specified in regulation 6(1) of the Maintenance Assessment Procedure Regulations then until such information is acquired the value of C shall be nil.

(4)　When the information referred to in paragraph (3) is acquired the [⁴Secretary of State] shall make a fresh assessment which shall have effect from the effective date in relation to that other absent [³parent or, from the effective date as determined by paragraph (2) of regulation 30 of the Maintenance Assessment Procedure Regulations, whichever is the later.]

Amendments

1.　Child Support (Miscellaneous Amendments) Regulations 1996 (SI 1996 No.1945) reg 23 and 25(5) (October 7, 1996).
2.　Child Support (Miscellaneous Amendments) Regulations 1998 (SI 1998 No 58) reg 52 (April 6, 1998).
3.　Child Support (Miscellaneous Amendments) Regulations 1999 (SI 1999 No.977) reg 6(4) (April 6, 1999).
4.　Social Security Act 1998 (Commencement No.7 and Consequential and Transitional Provisions) Order 1999 (SI 1999 No. 1510) art 17 (June 1, 1999).

Definitions

"the Act": see reg 1(2).
"effective date": see reg 1(2).
"Maintenance Assessment Procedure Regulations": see reg 1(2).
"person": see reg 1(2).

Persons treated as absent parents

20.–(1)　Where the circumstances of a case are that–

(a)　two or more persons who do not live in the same household each provide day to day care for the same qualifying child; and

(b)　at least one of those persons is a parent of that child,

that case shall be treated as a special case for the purposes of the Act.

(2)　For the purposes of this case a parent who provides day to day care for a child of his in the following circumstances is to be treated as an absent parent for the purposes of the Act and these Regulations–

(a)　a parent who provides such care to a lesser extent that the other parent, person or persons who provide such care for the child in question;

(b)　where the persons mentioned in paragraph (1)(a) include both parents and the circumstances are such that care is provided to the same extent by both but each provides care to a greater or equal extent than any other person who provides such care for that child–

(i)　the parent who is not in receipt of child benefit for the child in question; vor

(ii)　if neither parent is in receipt of child benefit for that child, the parent who, in the opinion of the [¹Secretary of State], will not be the principal provider of day to day care for that child.

(3)   Subject to paragraphs (5) and (6), where a parent is treated as an absent parent under paragraph (2) child support maintenance shall be payable by that parent in respect of the child in question and the amount of the child support maintenance so payable shall be calculated in accordance with the formula set out in paragraph (4).

(4)   The formula for the purposes of paragraph (3) is–

$$T = X - \left\{ (X + Y) \times \frac{J}{7 \times L} \right\}$$

where–

T is the amount of child support maintenance payable;

X is the amount of child support maintenance which would be payable by the parent who is treated as an absent parent, assessed under Schedule 1 to the Act as if paragraphs 6 and 7 of that Schedule did not apply, and, where the other parent is an absent parent, as if the value of C was the assessable income of the other parent;

Y is–

(i)   the amount of child support maintenance assessed under Schedule 1 to the Act payable by the other parent if he is an absent parent or which would be payable if he were an absent parent, and for the purposes of such calculation the value of C shall be the assessable income of the parent treated as an absent parent under paragraph(2); or,

(ii)   if there is no such other parent, shall be nil;

J is the total of the weekly average number of nights for which day to day care is provided by the person who is treated as the absent parent in respect of each child included in the maintenance assessment and shall be calculated to 2 decimal places;

L is the number of children who are included in the maintenance assessment in question.

(5)   Where the value of T calculated under the provisions of paragraph (4) is less than zero, no child support maintenance shall be payable.

(6)   The liability to pay any amount calculated under paragraph (4) shall be subject to the provision made for protected income and minimum payments under paragraphs 6 and 7 of Schedule 1 to the Act.

Amendment
  1.   Social Security Act 1998 (Commencement No.7 and Consequential and Transitional Provisions) Order 1999 (SI 1999 No.1510) art 16 (June 1, 1999).

Definitions
  "the Act": see reg 1(2).
  "day to day care": see reg 1(2).
  "person": see reg 1(2).

One parent is absent and the other is treated as absent

21.–(1)   Where the circumstances of a case are that one parent is an absent parent and the other parent is treated as an absent parent by regulation 20(2), that case shall be treated as a special case for the purposes of the Act.

(2)   For the purpose of assessing the child support maintenance payable by an absent parent where this case applies, each reference in Schedule 1 to the Act to a parent who is a person with care shall be treated as a reference to a person who is treated as an absent parent by regulation 20(2).

Definition
  "the Act": see reg 1(2).

Multiple applications relating to an absent parent

22.–(1)   Where an application for a maintenance assessment has been made in respect of an absent parent and–

    (a)   at least one other application for a maintenance assessment has been made in relation to the same absent parent (or a person who is treated as an absent parent by regulation 20(2) but to different children; or

    (b)   at least one maintenance assessment is in force in relation to the same absent parent or a person who is treated as an absent parent by regulation 20(2) but to different children,

that case shall be treated as a special case for the purposes of the Act],

[2(2)   For the purposes of assessing the amount of child support maintenance payable in respect of each application where [3paragraph (1)(a)] applies [3or in respect of the application made in circumstances where paragraph (1)(b) applies] for references to the assessable income of an absent parent in the Act and in these Regulations[4,and subject to paragraph (2ZA),] there shall be substituted references to the amount calculated by the formula–

$$\left\{ (A + T) \times \frac{B}{D} \right\} - CS$$

where–

    A is the absent parent's assessable income;

    T is the sum of the amounts allowable in the calculation or estimation of his exempt income by virtue of Schedule 3A;

    B is the maintenance requirement calculated in respect of the application in question;

    D is the sum of the maintenance requirements as calculated for the purposes of each assessment relating to the absent parent in question; and

    CS is the amount (if any) allowable by virtue of Schedule 3A in calculating or estimating the absent parent's exempt income in respect of a relevant qualifying transfer of property in respect of the assessment in question.]

[4(2ZA)   Where a case falls within regulation 39(1)(a) of the Departure Direction and Consequential Amendment Regulations, for the purposes of assessing the amount of child support maintenance payable in respect of an application for child support maintenance before a departure direction in respect of the maintenance assessment in question is given, for references to the assessable income of an absent parent in the Act and in these Regulations there shall be substituted references to the amount calculated by the formula–

$$(A + T) \times \frac{B}{D}$$

where A,T,B and D have the same meanings as in paragraph (2).]

[3(2A)   Where paragraph (1)(b) applies, and a maintenance assessment has been made in respect of the application referred to in paragraph (1), each maintenance assessment in force at the time of that assessment shall be reduced using the formula for calculation of assessable income set out in paragraph (2) and each reduction shall take effect on the date specified in regulation 33(7) of the Maintenance Assessment Procedure Regulations.]

[5(2B)   Where–

    (a)   a case is treated as a special case for the purposes of the Act by virtue of paragraph (1);

    (b)   more than one maintenance assessment is in force in respect of the absent parent; and

    [6(c)   any of those assessments falls to be replaced by a fresh assessment to be made by virtue of a revision under section 16 of the Act or a decision under section 17 of the Act superseding an earlier decision,]

the formula set out in paragraph (2) or, as the case may be, paragraph (2ZA) shall be applied to calculate or estimate the amount of child support maintenance payable under that fresh assessment.

    (2C)   Where a maintenance assessment falls within sub-paragraph (b) of paragraph (2B) but [6not within] sub-paragraph (c) of that paragraph, the formula set out in paragraph (2) or, as the case may be, paragraph (2ZA) shall be applied to determine whether that maintenance assessment should be increased or reduced as a result of the making of a fresh assessment under sub-paragraph (c) and any increase or reduction shall take effect from the effective date of that fresh assessment.]

(3)   Where more than one maintenance assessment has been made with respect to the absent parent and payment by him of the aggregate of the amounts of those assessments would reduce his disposable income below his protected income level, the aggregate amount of those assessments shall be reduced (each being reduced by reference to the same proportion as those assessments bear to each other) by the minimum amount necessary to prevent his disposable income being reduced below his protected income level provided that the aggregate amount payable under those assessments shall not be reduced to less than the minimum amount prescribed in regulation 13(1).

[[1](4)   Where the aggregate of the child support maintenance payable by the absent parent is less than the minimum amount prescribed in regulation 13(1), the child support maintenance payable shall be–

(a)   that prescribed minimum amount apportioned between the two or more applications in the same ratio as the maintenance requirements in question bear to each other; or

(b)   where, because of the application of regulation 2(2), such an apportionment produces an aggregate amount which is different from that prescribed minimum amount, that different amount.]

(5)   Payment of each of the maintenance assessments calculated under this regulation shall satisfy the liability of the absent parent (or a person treated as such) to pay child support maintenance.

Amendments

1.   Child Support (Miscellaneous Amendments) Regulations 1993 (SI 1993 No.913) reg 23 (April 5, 1993).

2.   Child Support and Income Support (Amendment) Regulations 1995 (SI 1995 No.1045) reg 51 (April 18, 1995).

3.   Child Support (Miscellaneous Amendments) (No.2) Regulations 1995 (SI 1995 No.3261) reg 45(2)-(4) (January 22, 1996).

4.   Child Support Departure Direction and Consequential Amendments Regulations 1996 (SI 1996 No.2907) reg 68(5) (December 2, 1996).

5.   Child Support (Miscellaneous Amendments) Regulations 1998 (SI 1998 No 58) reg 53 (January 19, 1998).

6.   Social Security Act 1998 (Commencement No.7 and Consequential and Transitional Provisions) Order 1999 (SI 1999 No.1510) art 18 (June 1, 1999).

Definitions

"the Act": see reg 1(2).
"Departure Direction and Consequential Amendments Regulations": see reg 1(2).
"Maintenance Assessment Procedure Regulations": see reg 1(2).
"qualifying transfer": see reg 1(2).

Person caring for children of more than one absent parent

23.–(1)   Where the circumstances of a case are that–

(a)   a person is a person with care in relation to two or more qualifying children; and

(b)   in relation to at least two of those children there are different persons who are absent parents or persons treated as absent parents by regulation 20(2);

that case shall be treated as a special case for the purposes of the Act.

(2)   [[1](Subject to paragraph (2A)] in calculating the maintenance requirements for the purposes of this case, for any amount which (but for this paragraph) would have been included under regulation 3(1)(b), [[2](or (c)] (amounts included in the calculation of AG) there shall be substituted an amount calculated by dividing the amount which would have been so included by the relevant number.

[[1](2A)   In applying the provisions of paragraph (2) to the amount which is to be included in the maintenance requirements under regulation 3(1)(b)–

(a)   first take the amount specified in head (i) of regulation 3(1)(b) and divide it by the relevant number;

(b)   then apply the provisions of regulation 3(1)(b) as if the references to the amount specified in column (2) of paragraph 1(1)(e) of the relevant Schedule were references to the amount which is the product of the calculation required by head (a)above, and as if, in relation to an absent parent, the only qualifying children to be included in the assessment were those qualifying children in relation to whom he is the absent parent.]

(3)   ['In paragraph (2) and (2A)] "the relevant number" means the number equal to the total number of persons who, in relation to those children, are either absent parents or persons treated as absent parents by regulation 20(2) except that where in respect of the same child both parents are persons who are either absent parents or persons who are treated as absent parents under that regulation, they shall count as one person.

(4)   Where the circumstances of a case fall within this regulation and the person with care is the parent of any of the children, for C in paragraph 2(1) of Schedule 1 to the Act (the assessable income of that person) there shall be substituted the amount which would be calculated under regulation 22(2) if the references therein to an absent parent were references to a parent with care.

Amendments
1.   Child Support (Miscellaneous Amendments and Transitional Provisions) Regulations 1994 (SI 1994 No.227) reg 4(6) and (7) (February 7, 1994).
2.   Child Benefit, Child Support and Social Security (Miscellaneous Amendments) Regulations 1996 (SI 1996 No.1803) reg 14 (April 7, 1996).

Definitions
"the Act": see reg 1(2).
"person": see reg 1(2).

Persons with part-time care-not including a person treated as an absent parent
24.–(1)   Where the circumstances of a case are that–
(a)   two or more persons who do not live in the same household each provide day to day care for the same qualifying child; and
(b)   those persons do not include any parent who is treated as an absent parent of that child by regulation 20(2).
that case shall be treated as a special case of the purposes of the Act.
(2)   For the purposes of this case–
(a)   the person whose application for a maintenance assessment is being proceeded with shall, subject to paragraph (b), be entitled or receive all of the child support maintenance payable under the Act in respect of the child in question;
(b)   on request being made to the Secretary of State by–
(i)   that person; or
(ii)   any other person who is providing day to day care for that child and who intends to continue to provide that care,
the Secretary of State may make arrangements of the payment of any child support maintenance payable under the Act to the persons who provide such care in the same ratio as that in which it appears to the Secretary of State, that each is to provide such care for the child in question;
(c)   before making an arrangement under sub-paragraph (b), the Secretary of State shall consider all of the circumstances of the case and in particular the interest of the child, the present arrangements for the day to day care of the child in question and any representations or proposals made by the persons who provide such care of that child.

Definitions
"the Act": see reg 1(2).
"day to day care": see reg 1(2).
"person": see reg 1(2).

Care provided in part by a local authority

25.–(1)   Where the circumstances of a case are that a local authority and a person each provide day to day care for the same qualifying child, that case shall be treated as a special case for the purposes of the Act.

(2)   [¹Subject to paragraph (3), in a case where this regulation applies]–

(a)   child support maintenance shall be calculated in respect of that child as if this regulation did not apply;

(b)   the amount so calculated shall be divided by 7 so as to produce a daily amount;

(c)   in respect of each night for which day to day care for that child is provided by a person other than the local authority, the daily amount relating to that period shall be payable by the absent parent (or, as the case may be, by the person treated as an absent parent under regulation 20(2);

(d)   child support maintenance shall not be payable in respect of any night for which the local authority provides day to day care for that qualifying child.

[¹(3)   In a case where more than one qualifying child is included in a child support maintenance assessment application and where this regulation applies to at least one of those children, child support maintenance shall be calculated by applying the formula–

$$S \times \left\{ \frac{A}{7 \times B} \right\}$$

where–

S   is the total amount of child support maintenance in respect of all qualifying children included in that maintenance assessment application, calculated as if this regulation did not apply;

A   is the aggregate of the number of nights of day to day care for all qualifying children included in that maintenance assessment application provided in each week by a person other than the local authority;

B   is the number of qualifying children in respect of whom the maintenance assessment application has been made.]

Amendment

1.   Child Support and Income Support (Amendment) Regulations 1995 (SI 1995 No.1045) reg 52(2) and (3) (April 18, 1995).

Definitions

"the Act": see reg 1(2).
"day to day care": see reg 1(2).
"person": see reg 1(2).

Cases where child support maintenance is not to be payable

26.–(1)   Where the circumstances of a case are that–

(a)   but for this regulation the minimum amount prescribed in regulation 13(1) would apply; and

(b)   any of the following conditions are satisfied–

(i)   the income of the absent parent includes one or more of the payments or awards specified in Schedule 4 or would include such a payment but for a provision preventing the receipt of that payment by reason of it overlapping with some other benefit payment or would, in the case of the payments referred to in paragraph (a)(i) or (iv) of that Schedule, include such a payment if the relevant contribution conditions for entailment had been satisfied;

(ii)   an amount to which regulation [²11(1)(f)] applies (protected income; income support family premium) is taken into account in calculating or estimating [¹under paragraphs (1) to (5) of regulation 11,] the protected income of the absent parent;

(iii)   the absent parent is a child within the meaning of section 55 of the Act;

(iv)   the absent parent is a prisoner; or

(v) the absent parent is a person in respect of whom N (as calculated or estimated under regulation 7(1) is less than the minimum amount prescribed by regulation 13(1),

the case shall be treated as a special case for the purposes of the Act.

(2) For the purposes of this case—

(a) the requirement in paragraph 7(2) of Schedule 1 to the Act (minimum amount of child support maintenance fixed by an assessment to be the prescribed minimum amount) shall not apply;

(b) the amount of the child support maintenance to be fixed by the assessment shall be nil.

Amendments

1. Child Support and Income Support (Amendment) Regulations 1995 (SI 1995 No.1045) reg 53 (April 18, 1995).
2. Child Support (Miscellaneous Amendments) Regulations 1998 (SI 1998 No. 58) reg 54 (April 6, 1998).

Definitions

"the Act": see reg 1(2).
"person": see reg 1(2).
"prisoner": see reg 1(2).

Child who is a boarder or an in-patient

27.–(1) Where the circumstances of a case are that—

(a) a qualifying child is a boarder at a boarding school or is an in-patient in a hospital; and

(b) by reason of those circumstances, the person who would otherwise provide day to day care is not doing so,

that case shall be treated as a special case of the purposes of the Act.

(2) For the purposes of this case, section 3(3)(b) of the Act shall be modified so [¹that] for the reference to the person who usually provides day to day care for the child there shall be substituted a reference to the person who would usually be providing such care for that child but for the circumstances specified in paragraph (1).

Amendment

1. Child Support (Miscellaneous Amendments) Regulations 1993 (SI 1993 No.913) reg 24 (April 5, 1993).

Definitions

"the Act": see reg 1(2).
"day to day care": see reg 1(2).
"person": see reg 1(2).

[¹Child who is allowed to live with his parent under section 23(5) of the Children Act 1989

27A.–(1) Where the circumstances of a case are that a qualifying child who is in the care of a local authority in England and Wales is allowed by the authority to live with a parent of his under section 23(5) of the Children Act 1989, that case shall be treated as a special case for the purposes of the Act.

(2) For the purposes of this case, section 3(3)(b) of the Act shall be modified so that for the reference to the person who usually provides day to day care for the child there shall be substituted a reference to the parent of a child whom the local authority allow the child to live with under section 23(5) the Children Act 1989.]

Amendment

1. Child Support (Miscellaneous Amendments) Regulations 1993 (SI 1993 No. 913) reg 25 (April 5, 1993).

Definitions

"the Act": see reg 1(2).
"day to day care": see reg 1(2).

Amount payable where absent parent is in receipt of income support or other prescribed benefit

28.–(1)   Where the condition specified in section 43(1)(a) of the Act is satisfied in relation to an absent parent (assessable income to be nil where income support [³, income-based jobseeker's allowance] [⁵, income-related employment and support allowance under Part 1 of the Welfare Reform Act,] or other prescribed benefit is paid), the prescribed conditions for the purposes of section 43(1)(b) of the Act are that–

(a)   the absent parent is aged 18 or over;

(b)   he does not satisfy the conditions in paragraph [⁴³(1)(a) or (b)] of the relevant Schedule (income support family premium) [¹and does not have day to day care of any child (whether or not a relevant child)]; and

(c)   [¹his income does not include] one or more of the payments or awards specified in Schedule 4 (other than by reason of a provision preventing receipt of overlapping benefits or by reason of a failure to satisfy the relevant contribution conditions).

(2)   For the purposes of section 43(2)(a) of the Act, the prescribed amount shall be equal to the minimum amount prescribed in regulation 13(1) for the purposes of paragraph 7(1) of Schedule 1 to the Act.

[¹[²(3)   Subject to paragraph (4), where–

(a)   an absent parent is liable under section 43 of the Act and this regulation to make payments in place of payments of child support maintenance with respect to two or more qualifying children in relation to whom there is more than one parent with care; or

(b)   that absent parent and his partner (within the meaning of regulation 2(1) of the Social Security (Claims and Payments) Regulations 1987) are both liable to make such payments,

the prescribed amount mentioned in paragraph (2) shall be apportioned between the persons with care in the same ratio as the maintenance requirements of the qualifying child or children in relation to each of those persons with care bear to each other.]

(4)   If, in making the apportionment required by paragraph (3), the effect of the application of regulation 2(2) would be such that the aggregate amount payable would be different from the amount prescribed in paragraph (2) the Secretary of State shall adjust the apportionment so as to eliminate that difference; and that adjustment shall be varied from time to time so as to secure that, taking one week with another and so far as is practicable, each person with care receives the amount which she would have received if no adjustment had been made under this paragraph.

(5)   The provisions of Schedule 5 shall have effect in relation to cases to which section 43 of the Act and this regulation apply.]

Amendments

1.   Child Support (Miscellaneous Amendments) Regulations 1993 (SI 1993 No.913) reg 26 (April 5, 1993).

2.   Child Support (Maintenance Assessment and Special Cases) Amendment Regulations 1993 (SI 1993 No.925) reg 2(2) (April 26, 1993).

3.   Social Security and Child Support (Jobseeker's Allowance) (Consequential Amendments) Regulations 1996 (SI 1996 No.1345) reg 6(3) (October 7, 1996).

4.   Child Support (Miscellaneous Amendments) Regulations 1998 (SI 1998 No.58) reg 55 (April 6, 1998).

5.   Employment and Support Allowance (Consequential Provisions) (No.2) Regulations 2008 (SI 2008 No.1554) reg 58(4) (October 27, 2008).

Definitions

"the Act": see reg 1(2).

"day to day care": see reg 1(2).

"relevant Schedule": see reg 1(2).

SCHEDULE 1
CALCULATION OF N AND M

PART I
EARNINGS
Chapter 1
Earnings of an employed earner

1.–(1) Subject to sub-paragraphs (2) and (3), "earnings" means in the case of employment as an employed earner, any remuneration or profit derived from that employment and includes–

(a) any bonus, commission, [²payment in respect of overtime], royalty or fee;

[⁶(aa) any profit-related pay, whether paid in anticipation of, or following, the calculation of profits;]

(b) any holiday pay except any payable more than 4 weeks after termination of the employment;

(c) any payment by way of a retainer;

[⁵(d) any payments made by the parent's employer in respect of any expenses not wholly, exclusively and necessarily incurred in the performance of the duties of the employment, including any payment made by the parent's employer in respect of–

(i) travelling expenses incurred by that parent between his home and place of employment; and

(ii) expenses incurred by that parent under arrangements made of the care of a member of his family owing to that parent's absence from home;]

(e) any award of compensation made under section 68(2) or 71(2)(a) of the Employment Protection (Consolidation) Act 1978 (remedies and compensation for unfair dismissal);

(f) any such sum as is referred to in section 112 of the Contributions and Benefits Act (certain sums to be earnings for social security purposes);

(g) any statutory sick pay under Part I of the Social Security and Housing Benefits Act 1982 or statutory maternity pay under Part V of the Social Security Act 1986;

[¹³(gg) any statutory paternity pay under Part 12ZA of the Contributions and Benefits Act or any statutory adoption pay under Part 12ZB of that Act];]

(h) any payment in lieu of notice and any compensation in respect of the absence or inadequacy of any such notice but only insofar as such payment or compensation represents loss of income;

(i) any payment relating to a period of less than a year which is made in respect of the performance of duties as–

(i) an auxiliary coastguard in respect of cost rescue activities;

(ii) a part-time fireman in a fire brigade maintained in pursuance of the Fire Services Acts 1947 to 1959;

(iii) a person engaged part-time in the manning or launching of a life-boat;

(iv) a member of any territorial or reserve force prescribed in part I of Schedule 3 to the Social Security (Contributions) Regulations 1979;

(j) any payment made by a local authority to a member of that authority in respect of the performance of his duties as a member, to her than any expenses wholly, exclusively and necessarily incurred in the performance of those duties.

(2) Earnings shall not include–

(a) any payment in respect of expenses wholly, exclusively and necessarily incurred in the performance of the duties of the employment [⁷except any such payment which is made in respect of housing costs and those housing costs are included in the calculation of the exempt or protected income of the absent parent under regulation 9(1)(b) or, as the case may be, regulation 11(1)(b);]

(b) any occupational pension;

(c) any payment where–

(i) the employment in respect of which it was made has ceased; and

(ii) a period of the same length as the period by reference to which it was calculated has expired since that cessation but prior to the effective date;

(d) any advance of earnings or any loan made by an employer to an employee;

(e) any amount received from an employer during a period when the employee has withdrawn his services by reason of a trade dispute;

(f) any payment in kind;

(g) where, in any week or other period which falls within the period by reference to which earnings are calculated earnings are received both in respect of a previous employment and in respect of a subsequent employment, the earnings in respect of the previous employment.

[⁶(h) any tax-exempt allowance made by an employer to an employee [⁷except any such allowance which is made in respect of housing costs and those housing costs are included in the calculation of the exempt or protected income of the absent parent under regulation 9(1) or, as the case may be, regulation 11(1)(b)].]

(3) The earnings to be taken into account for the purposes of calculating N and M shall be gross earnings less–

(a) any amount deducted from those earnings by way of–

(i) income tax;

(ii) primary Class I contributions under the Contributions and Benefits Act [²or under the Social Security Contributions and Benefits (Northern Ireland) Act 1992]; and

(b)   one half of any sums paid by the parent towards an occupational [² . . .] pension scheme.

[²(c)   one half of any sums paid by the parent towards a personal pension scheme, or, where that scheme is intended partly to provide a capital sum to discharge a mortgage secured upon the parent's home, 37.5 per centum of any such sums.]

   2.–[²(1)   Subject to sub-paragraphs [⁶(1A)] to (4), the amount of the earnings to be taken into account for the purpose of calculating N and M shall be calculated or estimated by reference to the average earnings at the relevant week having regard to such evidence as is available in relation to that person's earnings during such period as appears appropriate to the [¹⁰Secretary of State] beginning not earlier than eight weeks before the relevant week and ending not later than the date of the assessment and for the purpose of that calculation or estimate he may consider evidence of that person's cumulative earnings during the period beginning with the start of the year of assessment (within the meaning of section 832 of the Income and Corporation Taxes Act 8 in which the relevant week falls and ending with a date no later than the date of the assessment.]

   [⁶(1A)   Subject to sub-paragraph (4), where a person has claimed, or has been paid, [¹¹ [¹²working tax credit or child tax credit]] on any day during the period beginning not earlier than eight weeks before the relevant week and ending not later than the date on which the assessment is made, the [¹⁰Secretary of State] may have regard to the amount of earnings taken into account in determining entitlement to those benefits in order to calculate or estimate the amount of earnings to be taken into account for the purposes of calculating N and M, notwithstanding the fact that entitlement to those benefits may have been determined by reference to earnings attributable to a period other than that specified in sub-paragraph (1).]

   [⁶(2)   Where a person's earnings during the period of 52 weeks ending with the relevant week include–
(a)   a bonus, commission, or payment of profit-related pay made in anticipation of the calculation profits which is paid separately from or in relation to a longer period than, the other earnings with which it is paid; or
(b)   a payment in respect of profit-related pay made following the calculation of the employer's profits, the amount of that bonus, commission or profit- related payment shall be the determined for the purposes of the calculation of earnings by aggregating any such payments received in that period and dividing by 52.]

   (3)   Subject to sub-paragraph (4), the amount of any earnings of a student shall be determined by aggregating the amount received in the year ending with the relevant week and dividing by 52 or, where the person in question has been a student for less than a year, by aggregating the amount received in the period starting with his becoming a student and ending with the relevant week and dividing by the number of complete weeks in that period.

   [⁶(3A)   Where a case is one to which regulation 30A(1) or (3) of the Maintenance Assessment Procedure Regulations applies (effective dates of new maintenance assessments in particular cases), the term "relevant week" shall, for the purpose of this paragraph, mean the 7 days immediately proceeding the date on which the information or evidence is received which enables [¹⁰the Secretary of State] to make a new maintenance assessment calculation in accordance with the provisions of Part I of Schedule 1 to the Act in respect of that case for a period beginning after the effective date applicable to that case.

   (4)   Where a calculation would, but for this sub-paragraph, produce an amount which, in the opinion of the [¹⁰Secretary of State], does not accurately reflect the normal amount of the earnings of the person in question, such earnings, or any part of them, shall be calculated by reference to such other period as may, in the particular case, enable the normal weekly earnings of that person to be determined more accurately and for this purpose the [¹⁰Secretary of State] shall have regard to–
(a)   the earnings received, or due to be received, from any employment in which the person in question is engaged, has been engaged or is due to be engaged;
(b)   the duration and pattern, or the expected duration and pattern, of any employment of that person.

Chapter 2
Earnings of a self-employed earner

   [⁸**2A.**–(1)   Subject to paragraphs [¹⁷...], 2C, 4 and 5A, "earnings" in the case of employment as a self-employed earner shall have the meaning given by the following provisions of this paragraph.

   (2)   "Earnings" means the [¹⁷...] taxable profits from self-employment of that earner [¹⁷...], less the following amounts–
(a)   any income tax relating to the taxable profits from the self-employment determined in accordance with sub-paragraph (3);
(b)   any National Insurance Contributions relating to the taxable profits from the self-employment determined in accordance with sub-paragraph (4);
(c)   one half of any premium paid in respect of a retirement annuity contract or a personal pension scheme or, where that scheme is intended partly to provide a capital sum to discharge a mortgage or charge secured upon the self-employed earner's home, 37.5 per centum of the contributions payable.

   (3)   For the purposes of sub-paragraph (2)(a) the income tax to be deducted from the [¹⁷...] taxable profits shall be determined in accordance with the following provisions–
(a)   subject to head (d), an amount of earnings [¹⁴calculated as if it were equivalent to any personal allowance which would be] applicable to the earner by virtue of the provisions of Chapter 1 of Part VII of the Income and Corporation Taxes Act 1988 (personal reliefs) shall be disregarded;
(b)   subject to head (c), an amount equivalent to income tax shall be calculated in relation to the earnings remaining following the application of head(a) (the "remaining earnings");

(c)   the tax rate applicable at the effective date shall be applied to all the remaining earnings, where necessary increasing or reducing the amount payable to take account of the fact that the earnings relate to a period greater or less than one year;

(d)   the amount to be disregarded by virtue of head (a) shall be calculated by reference to the yearly rate applicable at the effective date, that amount being reduced or increased in the same proportion to that which the period represented by the taxable profits bears to the period of one year.

(4)   For the purposes of sub-paragraph (2)(b) above, the amount to be deducted in respect of National Insurance Contributions shall be the total of–

(a)   the amount of Class 2 contributions (if any) payable under section 11(1) or, as the case may be, (3), of the Contributions and Benefits Act; and

(b)   the amount of Class 4 Contributions (if any) payable under section 15(2) of that Act,

at the rates applicable at the effective date.

[17(5)   For the purposes of this paragraph, "taxable profits" means profits calculated in accordance with Part 2 of the Income Tax (Trading and Other Income) Act 2005.

(6)   A self-employed earner who is a person with care or an absent parent shall provide to the Secretary of State on demand a copy of–

(a)   any tax calculation notice issued to him by Her Majesty's Revenue and Customs; and

(b)   any revised notice issued to him by Her Majesty's Revenue and Customs.]

2B.   [17...]

[172C.   Where the Secretary of State accepts that it is not reasonably practicable for a self-employed earner to provide any of the information specified in paragraph 2A(6), "earnings" in relation to that earner shall be calculated in accordance with paragraph 3.]]

3.–(1)   [8Where paragraph 2C applies and subject] to sub-paragraphs (2) and (3) and to paragraph 4, "earnings" in the case of employment as a self-employed earner means the gross receipts of the employment including, where an allowance in the form of periodic payments is paid under section 2 of the Employment and Training Act 1973 or section 2 of the Enterprise and New Towns (Scotland) Act 1990 in respect of the relevant week for the purpose of assisting him in carrying on his business, the total of those payments made during the period by reference to which his earnings are determined under paragraph 5.

(2)   Earnings shall not include–

(a)   any allowance paid under either of those sections in respect of any part of the period by reference to which his earnings are determined under paragraph 5 if no part of that allowance is paid in respect of the relevant week;

(b)   any income consisting of payments received for the provision of board and lodging accommodation unless such payments from the largest element of the recipient's income.

(3)   [1Subject to sub-paragraph (7),] there shall be deducted from the gross receipts referred to in sub-paragraph (1)–

(a)   [1except in a case to which paragraph 4 applies,] any expenses which are reasonably incurred and are wholly and exclusively defrayed for the purposes of the earner's business in the period by reference to which his earnings are determined under paragraph 5(1) or, where paragraph 5(2) applies, any such expenses relevant to the period there mentioned (whether or not defrayed in that period);

(b)   [1except in a case to which paragraph 4 [2or 5(2)applies,] any value added tax paid in the period by reference to which earnings are determined in excess of value added tax received in that period;

(c)   any amount in respect of income tax determined in accordance with sub-paragraph (5);

(d)   any amount in respect of National Insurance contributions determined in accordance with sub-paragraph (6);

(e)   one half of any premium paid in respect of a retirement annuity contract or a personal pension scheme[2, or, where that scheme is intended partly to provide a capital sum to discharge a mortgage or charge secured upon the parent's home, 37.5 per centum of the contributions payable].

(4)   For the purposes of sub-paragraph (3)(a)–

(a)   such expenses include–

    (i)   repayment of capital on any loan used for the replacement, in the course of business, of equipment or machinery, or the repair of an existing business asset except to the extent that any sum is payable under an insurance policy for its repair;

    (ii)   any income expended in the repair of an existing business asset except to the extent that any sum is payable under an insurance policy for its repair;

    (iii)   any payment of interest on a loan taken out for the purposes of the business;

(b)   such expenses do not include–

    (i)   [17...];

    (ii)   any capital expenditure;

    (iii)   [17...];

    (iv)   [17...];

    (v)   [17...];

    (vi)   any expenses incurred in providing business entertainment;

    (vii)   [17...].

[6(5)   For the purposes of sub-paragraph (3)(c), the amount in respect of income tax shall be determined in accordance with the following provisions–

(a)   subject to head (c), an amount of chargeable earnings [¹⁴calculated as if it were equivalent to any personal allowance which would be] applicable to the earner by virtue of the provisions of Chapter 1 of Part VII of the Income and Corporate Taxes Act 1988 (Personal Relief) shall be disregarded;

(b)   [⁷subject to head (bb),] an amount equivalent to income tax shall be calculated with respect to taxable earnings at the rates applicable at the effective date;

[⁷(bb) where taxable earnings are determined over a period of less or more than one year, the amount of earnings to which each tax rate applies shall be reduced or increased in the same proportion to that which the period represented by the chargeable earnings bears to the period of one year;]

(c)   the amount to be disregarded by virtue of head (a) shall be calculated by reference to the yearly rate applicable at the effective date, that amount being reduced or increased in the same proportion to that which the period represented by chargeable earnings bears to the period of one year;

(d)   in this sub-paragraph, "taxable earnings" means the chargeable earnings of the earner following the disregard of any applicable personal allowance.]

(6)   For the purposes of sub-paragraph (3)(d), the amount to be deducted in respect of National Insurance contributions shall be the total of–

(a)   the amount of Class 2 contributions (if any) payable under section 11(1) or, as the case may be, [²(3)] of the Contributions and Benefits Act; and

(b)   the amount of Class 4 contributions (if any) payable under section 15(2) of that Act,

at the rates applicable [¹to the chargeable earnings] at the effective date.

[²(7)   In the case of a self-employed earner whose employment is carried on in partnership or is that of a share fisherman within the meaning of the Social Security (Mariners' Benefits) Regulations 1975, sub-paragraph (3) shall have effect as though it requires–

(a)   a deduction from the earner's estimated or, where appropriate, actual share of the gross receipts of the partnership or fishing boat, of his share of the sums likely to be deducted or, where appropriate, deducted from those gross receipts under heads (a) and (b) of that sub-paragraph; and

(b)   a deduction from the amount so calculated of the sums mentioned in heads (c) to (e) of that sub-paragraph.]

[¹(8)   In sub-paragraphs (5) and (6) "chargeable earnings" means the gross re-receipts of the employment less any deductions mentioned in sub-paragraph (3)(a) and (b).]

4.   In a case where a person is self-employed as a childminder the amount of earnings referable to that employment shall be one-third of the gross receipts.

5.–(1)   Subject to sub-paragraphs [²(2) to (3)]–

(a)   where a person has been a self-employed earner for 52 weeks or more including the relevant week, the amount of his earnings shall be determined by reference to the average of the earnings which he has received in the 52 weeks ending with the relevant week;

(b)   where the person has been a self-employed earner for a period of less than 52 weeks including the relevant week, the amount of his earnings shall be determined by reference to the average of the earnings which he has received during that period.

(2)   [²Subject to sub-paragraph (2A), where] a person who is a self-employed earner provides in respect of the employment a profit and loss account and, where appropriate, a trading account or a balance sheet or both, and the profit and loss accounts in respect of a period at least 6 months but not exceeding 15 months and that period terminates within the [²24 months] immediately preceding the effective date, the amount of his earnings shall be determined by reference to the average of the earnings over the period to which the profit and loss account relates and such earnings shall include receipts relevant to that period (whether or not received in that period).

[²(2A)   Where the [¹⁰Secretary of State] is satisfied that, in relation to the person referred to in sub-paragraph (2) there is more than one profit and loss account, each in respect of different periods, both or all of which satisfy the conditions mentioned in that sub-paragraph, the provisions of that sub-paragraph shall apply only to the account which relates to the latest such period, unless [¹⁰the Secretary of State] is satisfied that the latest such account is not available for reasons beyond the control of that person, in which case he may have regard to any such other account which satisfies the requirements of that sub-paragraph.]

(3)   Where a calculation would, but for this sub-paragraph, produce an amount which, in the opinion of the [¹⁰Secretary of State] , does not accurately reflect the normal amount of the earnings of the person in question, such earnings, or any part of them, shall be calculated by reference to such other period as may, in the particular case, enable the normal weekly earnings of that person to be determined more accurately and for this purpose the [¹⁰Secretary of State] shall have regard to–

(a)   the earnings received, or due to be received, from any employment in which the person in question is engaged, or has been engaged or is due to be engaged;

(b)   the duration and pattern, or the expected duration and pattern, of any employment of that person.

(4)   In sub-paragraph (2)–

(a)   "balance sheet" means a statement of the financial position of the employment disclosing its assets, liabilities and capital at the end of the period in question;

(b)   "profit and loss account" means a financial statement showing net profit or loss of the employment for the period in question; and

(c)   "trading account" means a financial statement showing the revenue from sales, the cost of those sales and the gross profit arising during the period in question.

[⁶(5)   Subject to sub-paragraph (3), where a person has claimed, or has been paid, [¹¹[¹²working tax credit or child tax credit]] on a day during the period beginning not earlier than eight weeks before the relevant week and ending not later than the date on which the assessment is made, the [¹⁰Secretary of State] may have regard to the amount of earnings taken into account in determining entitlement to those benefits in order to calculate or estimate the amount of earnings to be taken into account for the purposes of calculating N and M, notwithstanding the fact that entitlement to those benefits may have been determined by reference to earnings attributable to a period other than that specified in sub-paragraph (1).]

[⁸(6)   This paragraph applies only where the earnings of a self-employed earner have the meaning given by paragraph 3 of this Schedule.

5A.–(1)   Subject to sub-paragraph (2) of this paragraph, the earnings of a self-employed earner may be determined in accordance with the provisions of paragraph 2A only where the [¹⁷...] taxable profits concerned relate to a period of not less than 6, and not more than 15 months, which terminated not more than 24 months prior to the relevant week;

(2)   Where there is more than one week [¹⁷...] taxable profit figure which would satisfy the conditions set out in sub-paragraph (1), the earnings calculation shall be based upon the figure pertaining to the latest such period;

(3)   [¹⁷...]]

PART II
BENEFIT PAYMENTS

6.–(1)   The benefit payments to be taken into account in calculating or estimating N and M shall be determined in accordance with this Part.

(2)   "Benefit payments" means any benefit payments under the Contributions and Benefits Act [³[¹⁸, the Jobseekers Act or the Welfare Reform Act]] except amounts to be disregarded by virtue of Schedule 2.

(3)   The amount of any benefit payment to be taken into account shall be determined by reference to the rate of that benefit applicable at the effective date.

7.–(1)   Where a benefit payment under the Contributions and Benefits Act includes an adult or child dependency increase–

(a)   if that benefit is payable to a parent, the income of that parent shall be calculated or estimated as if it did not include that amount;

(b)   if that benefit is payable to some other person but includes an amount in respect of the parent, the income of the parent shall be calculated or estimated as if it included that amount.

[³(1A)   For the purposes of sub-paragraph (1), an addition to a contribution-based jobseeker's allowance under [⁹regulation 10(4)] of the Jobseekers's Allowance (Transitional Provisions) Regulations [⁹1996] shall be treated as a dependency increase included with a benefit under the Contributions and Benefits Act.]

(2)   [¹² . . .]

(3)   [¹² . . .]

(4)   [¹² . . .]

(5)   [¹² . . .]

[⁴(6)   Where child benefit in respect of a relevant child is in payment at the rate specified in regulation 2(1)(a)(ii) of the Child Benefit Rates Regulations, the difference between that rate and the basic rate applicable to that child, as defined in regulation 4.]

PART III
OTHER INCOME

8.   The amount of the other income to be taken into account in calculating or estimating N and M shall be the aggregate of the following amounts determined in accordance with this Part.

9.   Any periodic payment of pension or other benefit under an occupational or personal pension scheme or a retirement annuity contract or other such scheme for the provision of income in retirement.

[⁹**9A.**–(1)   Where a war disablement pension includes an adult or child dependency increase–

(a)   if that pension, including the dependency increase, is payable to a parent, the income of that parent shall be calculated or estimated as if it did not include that amount;

(b)   if that pension, including the dependency increase, is payable to some other person but includes an amount in respect of the parent, the income of the parent shall be calculated or estimated as if it included that amount.

(2)   For the purposes of this paragraph, a "war disablement pension" includes [¹⁶a war widow's pension, a war widower's pension and a surviving civil partner's war pension], a payment made to compensate for non-payment of such a pension, and a pension or payment analogous to such a pension or payment paid by the government of a country outside Great Britain.]

10.   Any payment received on account of the provision of board and lodging which does not come within Part I of this Schedule.

11.   Subject to regulation 7(3)(b) and paragraph 12, any payment to a student of–

(a)   grant;

(b)   an amount in respect of grant contribution;

(c)   covenant income except to the extent that it has been taken into account under sub-paragraph (b);

(d)   a student loan.

12.   The income of student shall not include any payment–

(a)　intended to meet tuition fees or examination fees;

(b)　intended to meet additional expenditure incurred by disabled student in respect of his attendance on a course;

(c)　intended to meet additional expenditure connected with term time residential study away from the student's educational establishment;

(d)　on account of the student maintaining a home at a place other than that at which he resides during his course;

(e)　intended to meet the cost of books, and equipment (other than special equipment) or, if not so intended, an amount equal to the amount allowed under [¹²regulation 62(2A)(b) of the Income Support (General) Regulations 1987 towards such costs;]

(f)　intended to meet travel expenses incurred as a result of his attendance on the course.

13.　Any interest, dividend or other income derived from capital.

14.　Any maintenance payments in respect of a parent.

[⁵**14A.**–(1)　Subject to sub-paragraph (2), the amount of any earnings top-up paid to or in respect of the absent parent or the parent with care.

(2)　Subject to sub-paragraphs (3) and (4), where earnings top-up is payable and the amount which is payable has been calculated by reference to the weekly earnings of either the absent parent and another person or the parent with care and another person–

(a)　if during the period which is used to calculate his earnings under paragraph 2 or, as the case may be, paragraph 5, the normal weekly earnings of that parent exceed those of the other person, the amount payable by way of earnings top-up shall be treated as the income of that parent;

(b)　if during that period, the normal weekly earnings of that parent equal those of the other person, half of the amount payable by way of earnings top-up shall be treated as the income of that parent;

(c)　if during that period, the normal weekly earnings of that parent are less than those of that other person, the amount payable by way of earnings top-up shall both be treated as the income of that parent.

(3)　Where any earnings top-up is in payment and, not later than the effective date, the person, or, if more than one, each of the persons by reference to whose engagement and normal engagement in remunerative work that payment has been calculated is no longer the partner of the person to whom the payment is made, the payment in question shall be treated as the income of the parent in question only where that parent is in receipt of it.

(4)　Where earnings top-up is in payment and, not later that the effective date, either or both of the persons by reference to whose engagement and normal engagement in remunerative work that payment has been calculated has ceased to be employed, half of the amount payable by way of earnings top-up shall be treated as the income of the parent in question.]

[¹²**14B.**–(1)　Subject to sub-paragraph (2), payments to a person of working tax credit shall be treated as the income of the parent who has qualified for them by his normal engagement in remunerative work at the rate payable at the effective date.

(2)　Where working tax credit is payable and the amount which is payable has been calculated by reference to the earnings of the absent parent and another person–

(a)　if during the period which is used to calculate his earnings under paragraph 2 or, as the case may be, paragraph 5, the normal weekly earnings of that parent exceed those of the other person, the amount payable by way of working tax credit shall be treated as the income of that parent;

(b)　if during that period the normal weekly earnings of that parent equal those of the other person, half of the amount payable by way of working tax credit shall be treated as the income of that parent; and

(c)　if during that period the normal weekly earnings of that parent are less than those of that other person, the amount payable by way of working tax credit shall not be treated as the income of that parent.]

15.　Any other payments or other amounts received on a periodical basis which are not otherwise taken into account under Part I, II, IV or V of this Schedule [⁷except payments or other amounts which

(a)　are excluded from the definition of "earnings" by virtue of paragraph 1(2);

(b)　are excluded from the definition of "the relevant income of a child" by virtue of paragraph 23; or

(c)　are the share of housing costs attributed by virtue of paragraph (3) of regulation 15 to any former partner of the partner of the parent of the qualifying child in respect of whom the maintenance assessment is made and are paid to that parent.]

16.–(1)　Subject to sub-paragraphs (2) to [¹²(7)] the amount of any income to which this Part applies shall be calculated or estimated–

(a)　where it has been received in respect of the whole of the period of 26 weeks which ends at the end of the relevant week, by dividing such income received in that period by 26;

(b)　where it has been received in respect of part of the period of 26 weeks which ends at the end of the relevant week, by dividing such income received in that period by the number of complete weeks in respect of which such income is received and for this purpose income shall be treated as received in respect of a week if it is received in respect of any day in the week in question.

(2)　The amount of maintenance payments made in respect of a parent–

(a)   where they are payable weekly and have been paid at the same amount in respect of each week in the period of 13 weeks which ends at the end of the relevant week, shall be the amount equal to one of those payments;

(b)   in any other case, shall be the amount calculated by aggregating the total amount of those payments received in the period of 13 weeks which ends at the end of the relevant week and dividing by the number of weeks in that period in respect of which maintenance was due.

(3)   In the case of a student–

(a)   the amount of any grant and any amount paid in respect of grant contribution shall be calculated by apportioning it equally between the weeks in respect of which it is payable;

(b)   the amount of any covenant income shall be calculated by dividing the amount payable in respect of a year by 52 (or, where such amount is payable in respect of a lesser period, by the number of complete weeks in that period) and, subject to sub-paragraph (4), deducting £5.00;

(c)   the amount of any student loan shall be calculated by apportioning the loan equally between the weeks in respect of which it is payable and, subject to sub-paragraph (4), deducting £10.00.

(4)   For the purposes of sub-paragraph (3)–

(a)   not more than £5.00 shall be deducted under sub-paragraph (3)(b);

(b)   not more than £10.00 in total shall be deducted under sub-paragraphs (3)(b) and (c).

(5)   Where in respect of the period of 52 weeks which ends at the end of the relevant week a person is in receipt of interest, dividend or other income which has been reproduced by his capital, the amount of that income shall be calculated by dividing the aggregate of the income so received by 52.

(6)   Where a calculation would, but for this sub-paragraph, produce an amount which, in the opinion of the [¹⁰Secretary of State], does not accurately reflect the normal amount of the other income of the person in question, such income, or any part of it, shall be calculated by&reference to such other period as may, in the particular case, enable the other income of that person to be determined more accurately and for this purpose the [¹⁰Secretary of State] shall have regard to the nature and pattern of receipt of such income.

[¹²(7)   This paragraph shall not apply to payments of working tax credit referred to in paragraph 14B.]

PART IV
INCOME OF CHILD TREATED AS INCOME OF PARENT

17.   The amount of any income of a child which is to be treated as the income of the parent in calculating or estimating N and M shall be the aggregate of the amounts determined in accordance with this Part.

18.   Where a child has income which falls within the following paragraphs of this Part and that child is a member of the family of his parent (whether that child is a qualifying child in relation to that parent or not), the relevant income of that child shall be treated as that of his parent.

19.   Where child support maintenance is being assessed for the support of only one qualifying child, the relevant income of that child shall be treated as that of the parent with care.

20.   Where child support maintenance is being assessed to support more than one qualifying child, the relevant income of each of those children shall be treated as that of the parent with care to the extent that it does not exceed the aggregate of–

(a)   the amount determined under–

     (i)   regulation 3(1)(a) (calculation of AG) in relation to the child in question; and

     (ii)   the total of any other amounts determined under regulation 3(1)(b) [⁴and c] which are applicable in the case in question divided by the number of children for whom child support maintenance is being calculated,

less the basic rate of child benefit (within the meaning for regulation 4) for the child in question; and

(b)   [²one-and-a-half times] the total of the amounts calculated under regulation 3(1)(a) (income support personal allowance for child or young person) in respect of that child and regulation [⁷3(1)(c)] (income support family premium).

21.   Where child support maintenance is not being assessed for the support of the child whose income is being calculated or estimated, the relevant income of that child shall be treated as that of this parent to the extent that it does not exceed the amount determined under regulation 9(1)(g).

22.–[³(1)]   Where a benefit under the Contributions and Benefits Act includes an adult or child dependency increase in respect of a relevant child, the relevant income of that child shall be calculated or estimated as if it included that amount.

[³(1A)   For the purposes of sub-paragraph (1), an addition to a contribution-based jobseeker's allowance under [⁹regulation 10(4)] of the Jobseeker's Allowance (Transitional Provisions) Regulation [⁹1996] shall be treated as a dependency increase included with a benefit under the Contributions and Benefits Act.]

[⁹(1B).–(1)   Where a war disablement pension includes a dependency allowance paid in respect of a relevant child, the relevant income of that child shall be calculated or estimated as if it included that amount.

(2)   For the purposes of this paragraph, a ''war disablement pension'' includes [¹⁶a war widow's pension, a war widower's pension and a surviving civil partner's war pension], a payment made to compensate for non-payment of such a pension, and a pension or payment analogous to such a pension or payment paid by the government to a country outside Great Britain.]

23.   For the purposes of this Part, ''the relevant income of a child'' does not include–

(a)   any earnings of the child in question;

(b)   payments by an absent parent [⁷to] the child for whose maintenance is being assessed;

(c)   where the class of persons who are capable of benefiting from a discretionary trust include the child in question, payments from that trust except in so far as they are made to provide for food, ordinary clothing and footwear, gas, electricity or fuel charges or housing costs; or

(d)   any interest payable on arrears of child support maintenance for that child;

[²(e)   the first £10 of any other income of that child]

24.   The amount of the income of a child which is treated as the income of the parent shall be determined in the same way as if such income were the income of the parent.

PART V
AMOUNTS TREATED AS THE INCOME OF A PARENT

25.   The amounts which fall to be treated as income of the parent in calculating or estimating N and M shall include amounts to be determined in accordance with this Part.

26.   Where [¹⁰the Secretary of State] is satisfied–

(a)   that a person has performed a service either–

     (i)   without receiving any remuneration in respect of it; or

     (ii)   for remuneration which is less than that normally paid for that service;

(b)   that the service in question was for the benefit of–

     (i)   another person who is not a member of the same family as the person in question; or

     (ii)   a body which is neither a charity nor a voluntary organisation;

(c)   that the service in question was performed for a person who, or as the case may be, a body which was able to pay remuneration at the normal rate for the service in question;

(d)   that the principal purpose of the person undertaking the service without receiving any or adequate remuneration is to reduce his assessable income for the purposes of the Act; and

(e)   that any remuneration foregone would have fallen to be taken into account as earnings,

the value of the remuneration foregone shall be estimated by [¹⁰the Secretary of State] and an amount equal to the value so estimated shall be treated as income of the person who performed those services.

27.   Subject to paragraphs 28 to 30, where the [¹⁰Secretary of State] is satisfied that, otherwise than in the circumstances set out in paragraph 26, a person has intentionally deprived himself of–

(a)   any income or capital which would otherwise be a source of income;

(b)   any income or capital which it would be reasonable to expect would be secured by him,

with a view to reducing the amount of his assessable income, his net income shall include the amount estimated by [¹⁰the Secretary of State] as representing the income which that person would have had if he had not deprived himself of or failed to secure that income, or as the case may be, that capital.

28.   No amount shall be treated as income by virtue of paragraph 27 in relation to–

[⁴(a)   if the parent satisfies the conditions for payment of the rate of child benefit specified in regulation 2(1)(a)(ii) of the Child Benefit Rates Regulations, an amount representing the difference between that rate and the basic rate, as defined in regulation 4;]

(b)   if the parent is a person to, or in respect of, whom income support is payable, [³a contribution-based jobseeker's allowance];

(c)   a payment from a discretionary trust or a trust derived from a payment made in consequence of a personal injury.

29.   Where an amount is included in the income of a person under paragraph 27 in respect of income which would become available to him on application, the amount included under that paragraph shall be included from the date on which it could be expected to be acquired.

30.   Where [¹⁰the Secretary of State] determines under paragraph 27 that a person has deprived himself of capital which would otherwise be a source of income, the amount of that capital shall be reduced at intervals of 52 weeks, starting with the week which falls 52 weeks after the first week in respect of which income from it is included in the calculation of the assessment in question, by an amount equal to the amount which the [¹⁰Secretary of State] estimates would represent the income from that source in the immediately preceding period of 52 weeks.

31.   Where a payment is made on behalf of a parent or a relevant child in respect of food, ordinary clothing or footwear, gas, electricity or fuel charges, housing costs or council tax, an amount equal to the amount which the [¹⁰Secretary of State] estimates represents the value of that payment shall be treated as the income of the parent in question except to the extent that such amount is–

(a)   disregarded under paragraph 38 of Schedule 2;

(b)   a payment of school fees paid by or on behalf of someone other than the absent parent.

32.   Where paragraph 26 applies the amount to be treated as the income of the parent shall be determined as if it were earnings from employment as an employed earner and in a case to which paragraph 27 or 31 applies the amount shall be determined as if it were other income to which Part III of this Schedule applies.

Amendments

1.   Child Support (Miscellaneous Amendments) Regulations 1993 (SI 1993 No.913) reg 27(1), (3) and (4) (April 5, 1993).

2.   Child Support and Income Support (Amendment) Regulations 1995 (SI 1995 No.1045) reg 54(2)-(11) (April 18, 1995).

3.   Social Security and Child Support (Jobseeker's Allowance) (Consequential Amendments) Regulations 1996 (SI 1996 No.1345) regs 6(4) and (6) and 7(b) (October 7, 1996).
4.   Child Benefit, Child Support and Social Security (Miscellaneous Amendments) Regulations 1996 (SI 1996 No.1803) reg 17(2)-(4) (April 7, 1997).
5.   Child Support (Miscellaneous Amendments) Regulations 1996 (SI 1996 No.1945) reg 24(2)-(4) (October 7, 1996).
6.   Child Support (Miscellaneous Amendments) (No.2) Regulations 1996 (SI 1996 No.3196) reg 13(2)-(5) (January 13, 1997).
7.   Child Support (Miscellaneous Amendments) Regulations 1998 (SI 1998 No.58) reg 56(2)-(6) (January 19, 1998).
8.   Child Support (Miscellaneous Amendments) Regulations 1999 (SI 1999 No.977) reg 6(5)(a)-(d) (October 4, 1999).
9.   Child Support (Miscellaneous Amendments) Regulations 1999 (SI 1999 No.977) reg 6(5)(e)-(h) (April 6, 1999).
10.   Social Security Act 1998 (Commencement No.7 and Consequential and Transitional Provisions) Order 1999 (SI 1999 No.1510) art 19 (a)-(e) (June 1, 1999).
11.   Social Security and Child Support (Tax Credits) Consequential Amendments Regulations 1999 (SI 1999 No.2566) Parts I and II, Sch 2 (October 5, 1999).
12.   Child Support (Miscellaneous Amendments) Regulations 2003 (SI 2003 No.328) reg 6(6) (April 6, 2003).
13.   Child Support (Miscellaneous Amendments) Regulations 2004 (SI 2004 No.2415) reg 5(2) (September 16, 2004).
14.   Child Support (Miscellaneous Amendments) Regulations 2005 (SI 2005 No.785) reg 4(2) (March 16, 2005).
15.   Child Support (Miscellaneous Amendments) (No.2) Regulations 2003 (SI 2003 No.2779) reg 4(6) (November 5, 2003).
16.   Civil Partnership (Pensions, Social Security and Child Support) (Consequential, etc. Provisions) Order 2005 (SI 2005 No.2877) art 2(4) and Sch 4, para 2(4) (December 5, 2005).
17.   Child Support (Miscellaneous Amendments) Regulations 2007 (SI 2007 No.1979) reg 4 (August 1, 2007).
18.   Employment and Support Allowance (Consequential Provisions) (No.2) Regulations 2008 (SI 2008 No.1554) reg 58(5) (October 27, 2008).

Definitions

"the Act": See reg 1(2).
"child tax credit": see reg 1(2).
"Child Benefit Rates Regulations": see reg 1(2).
"Contributions and Benefits Act": see reg 1(2).
"covenant income": see reg 1(2).
"earnings": see reg 1(2).
"earnings top-up": see reg 1(2).
"effective date": see reg 1(2).
"employed earner": see reg 1(2).
"family": see reg 1(2).
"grant": see reg 1(2).
"grant contribution": see reg 1(2).
"Maintenance Assessment Procedure Regulations": see reg 1(2).
"the Jobseekers Act": see reg 1(2).
"occupational pension scheme": see reg 1(2).
"parent with care": see reg 1(2).
"partner": see reg 1(2).
"person": see reg 1(2).
"personal pension scheme": see reg 1(2).
"profit-related pay": see reg 1(2).
"relevant week": see reg 1(2).
"retirement annuity contract": see reg 1(2).
"self-employed earner": see reg 1(2).
"student": see reg 1(2).
"student loan": see reg 1(2).
"working tax credit": see reg 1(2).
"year": see reg 1(2).

General Note

Paragraph 6

The amount of a benefit payment is the amount actually received, not the amount that should have been paid if entitlement had been correctly determined (*CCS 1039/1997*, paras 12-13). Subparagraph (3) identifies the date on which the amount of the payment to be taken into account is determined. If it is later decided that the amount should not have been paid, that cannot alter the fact that at that date that was the amount in payment (*ibid*, para 14).

Paragraph 9

In *R(CS) 2/00*, the commissioner decided that payments of an injury pension paid to a firefighter following an injury on duty come within this paragraph and are not disregarded under Sch 2, para 5. An appeal against this decision was dismissed by the Court of Appeal in *Wakefield v Secretary of State for Social Security* also reported as *R(CS) 2/00*.

Paragraph 14

Tribunals should make adequate findings of fact to indicate whether maintenance is paid as spousal maintenance to the parent with care or maintenance for the qualifying child (*R2/96 (CSC)*, paras 5 and 13). Clearly child support maintenance payments do not fall within this paragraph as they are defined by s1(2) of the Act as being payments with respect to the child rather than the parent.

In *CCS 13698/1996* (paras 11-12) and *CCS 13923/1996* (para 8) it was held that this paragraph did not apply to maintenance paid by the absent parent to the parent with care or vice versa and that a similar qualification was to be implied elsewhere in the Schedule with no distinction being drawn between one parent paying cash to the other and one parent settling a liability of the other. On this view, this paragraph only covers payments of maintenance by a person who is not a parent of the qualifying child. There was unanimity among the commissioners that these two decisions should not be reported.

Paragraph 15

In the case of rental income, the only amounts that may be deducted from the gross rental income are those authorised by Sch 2, especially para 23 (*R(CS) 3/00*, para 23).

It is suggested that this paragraph does not cover child support maintenance payments received by a parent in respect of any child, whether or not a qualifying child. See the general note to Sch 2 para 44 on p99.

Regular payments made by a person other than a parent which are intended and used for the payment of school fees are subject to a trust or equity and are not to be regarded as income of either parent or of the child (*CCS 15/1994*, paras 6-8).

Paragraphs 17-24

These paragraphs provide for income of a child who is living as member of a parent's family to be treated as income of a parent. First it is necessary to identify the child's income. This is done on normal principles. Where benefit is paid (to whom is not specified) which includes an increase in respect of the child, this is counted as the child's income (para 22). Certain items of income are then disregarded under para 23. The overall result is the relevant income of the child. The amount of this income is then determined as provided in para 24. This amount is then attributed by virtue of para 18 to the parent who is identified under paras 19-21, subject to any limits set therein. In the case of the income of a qualifying child, the income is attributed to the parent with care (paras 19-20). This provision is necessary as, where each parent has day to day care of the child, the child will be a member of the family of each.

It is suggested that any income of a child which derives from the parent with care should be disregarded. If it is not the following anomaly can result. Imagine that a parent with care earns a low wage and pays the qualifying child £15 a week pocket money. £10 of that is disregarded under para 23(e). This leaves £5 which is treated as the income of the parent with care. However, if this £5 is so treated, the parent with care will have that sum double counted in the assessable income calculation.

Paragraph 22

The amendments to this paragraph have been appallingly drafted. Original there were no subparagraphs. Then the original paragraph was numbered as subpara (1) and subpara (1A) added. Why was it not numbered (2)? Then the rest was added. The obvious intention was to add subparas (1B) and (2), but that is not how they were numbered in the amending legislation. A superfluous "22" was included for some reason and there seems no reason why subpara (1B) could not be numbered as (2) and subpara (2) as (3). Be that as it may, the legislation as printed is as set out in the amending legislation.

Paragraph 23

All payments by an absent parent to the child are disregarded under head (b). Previously all payments "in respect of" the child were disregarded. This would include child support maintenance, which by virtue of s1(2) of the Act is defined as being paid with respect to the child. It would also include any other payments in respect of the child such as those which are covered by para 31. If payments covered by para 31 were not excluded by this head, they would be double counted. If the absent parent paid pocket money to a qualifying child, in so far as it was not disregarded under para 23(e), it would be treated as income of the parent with care. Where the person with care was treated as having no assessable income (because the person is not a parent of the child or because the person is in receipt of a relevant benefit under Sch 1, para 5(4) to the Act), the pocket money could not be taken into account under the formula assessment and could only be taken into account in reduction of money owed by the absent parent (*R(CS) 9/98*, para 9).

Paragraphs 25-32

These paragraphs only apply to amounts that would not otherwise be treated as income (*CCS 318/1998*, para 26).

Paragraph 26

Tribunals will in particular need to pay careful attention to the following points:

(i)   The precise nature of the service needs to be identified. Until this has been done it is impossible to decide the normal rate for the service. Merely identifying a job by a title such as 'shop assistant' will often be insufficient since there will be a range of work and of remuneration associated with such broad descriptions.

(ii)   Evidence will be needed of the normal rate for the services identified. This will need to be examined to ensure that it relates to work of the same description as that performed by the person. Again reliance on job titles may mislead.

(iii)   The paragraph presupposes that the services are such that there is a normal rate for them. This gives rise to a number of problems. The first is that there will often not be a rate for a particular job but a range of payments. Actual payment will depend on a number of factors. The service performed will be one, but others will include the locality where the work is undertaken, the state of the job market at the time, the employee's qualifications and experience, and the ability of the employer to pay. The emphasis in this paragraph is on remuneration that has been foregone and that will require all factors relevant to the level of that remuneration to be considered. Second, it may well be that, quite apart from the matters just considered, there is a range of payments for the work with some employers paying better than others. If the payment falls outside that range there will be no difficulty in applying subpara (a)(ii), although the possible application of subpara (c) will then have to be considered. Otherwise an estimate will have to be made of the payment which the employer in question was likely to make. A third problem is that the services may be unique – eg, a person may be assisting in the running of a business by performing a combination of duties which do not correspond to any single job in the job market. In such a case the tribunal must undertake a more hypothetical exercise and attribute an appropriate income to the work. The alternative approach would be to hold that if there is no equivalent job with which to compare the work in question, the paragraph does not apply and no earnings are attributed to the person in respect of it. This approach cannot be right; it amounts to saying that the more unique and therefore in a sense the more valuable the work to an employer, the less likely it is that earnings will be attributed in respect of it.

(iv)   It is essential to establish that the principal purpose of undertaking the service without appropriate remuneration is to reduce the person's assessable income. This is a subjective test. This was discussed by the commissioner in *CCS 3675/2004*. He emphasised that the issue was the purpose of the parent's actions, not their effect (paras 19 and 23). He decided that the test is whether the parent's principal purpose was to reduce income that would otherwise have been taken into account in determining assessable income (para 24). It is not necessary that the parent's purpose must be directed, principally or even at all, to the child support scheme.

Income which falls within this paragraph is treated as other income to which Part III of this Schedule applies (para 32).

Where a person is paid wholly or partly in kind, the value of the payment in kind is disregarded in deciding whether s/he has been paid less than the amount normally paid for the service provided (*CIS 11482/1995*, paras 11-12). Where there has been a payment partly in kind and partly in cash, it is clear from the wording of this paragraph that only the value of the remuneration foregone is to be attributed to the person concerned. In other words, the value of the cash payment is taken into account as actual earnings and the remuneration forgone is added to it. The wording of this paragraph avoids the contortions of interpretation and application that were found necessary in such circumstances on the wording of the income support provision in *CIS 11482/1995*.

In *CCS 4912/1998*, the commissioner interpreted this paragraph broadly and controversially, producing the same effect as if the veil of incorporation had been lifted from a personal service company. The same result can be achieved more satisfactorily by using a departure direction under reg 24 of the Departure Direction Regulations on the basis of diversion of income or under reg 25 of those Regulations on the basis of lifestyle inconsistent with declared income.

Paragraph 27

This paragraph is the companion to para 26. It deals with disposals of, and failures to obtain, income or income-earning capital whereas para 26 deals with services. Paragraph 27 is unhappily worded. At one point it refers to the intentional deprivation of something a person has never had. The wording used later in the paragraph is better in referring to deprivation or failure to secure.

Subparagraph (a) applies where a person has had income or capital but no longer has it. It only deals with deprivation of income or capital. It is for the person to prove that the income or capital has been disposed of (*R(SB) 38/85*, para 18). If this cannot be proved the person must be taken as still in possession of the income or capital. No question of applying this paragraph then arises and the person will be unable to claim any benefit that might otherwise be derived from para 30. If deprivation is proved, it is necessary to investigate whether it was done intentionally with a view to reducing assessable income. The test is a subjective one, although the reasonableness of a person's action will be a relevant factor in assessing any evidence by that person on the reasons for so acting. Usually the tribunal will have to infer the purpose for the deprivation (see the general note to para 26 on inferences of intention). A person is deprived of capital even if it is replaced by something else (*R(SB) 40/85*, para 8). So a person who spends money on the purchase of an item of equal value is still deprived of that money. However, the fact that something is acquired in exchange will be relevant to the question whether the deprivation was effected with a view to reducing the assessable income. Since there is no discretion in this paragraph, it is only through this reasoning that the expenditure of capital on the purchase of non-income producing assets can escape this paragraph. If an income producing resource is disposed of and replaced by a lower income producing resource, it will be possible to apply this paragraph to the difference.

Subparagraph (b) applies where a person has never had the income or capital in question but has failed to secure it in circumstances in which it would be reasonable to expect that it would be secured. Whether securing the income or capital was to be expected is an objective consideration, but it is still necessary to establish an intention to deprive with a view to reducing assessable income. The application of this paragraph will give rise to difficult decisions for tribunals. Some cases of failure to secure income will be relatively straightforward: the person may have failed to cash a cheque (*CSB 598/1989*, para 11), to claim a benefit (subject to para 28) or to put money in an account bearing as high a rate of interest as possible. In other cases detailed consideration of evidence will be needed before a tribunal can decide whether it was reasonable to expect the income to be secured. For example, a dividend may not have been declared by a company in which a person has an interest. It is obvious that a dividend should have been declared if that person had such control over the company as to be able to determine or influence the dividend provided that it would be appropriate to declare a dividend given the financial position and the plans of the company. Evidence on each of these matters will need to be considered. Yet other cases will present difficult decisions on how far a person can be expected to act in securing income – eg, the chances of a person securing a particular job or type of job. Decisions on failure to secure capital will almost always be difficult. Capital here must mean capital which produces income. A person with sufficient cash may be expected to subscribe to a rights issue, but a tribunal cannot be expected to decide which shares a stock market investor could reasonably be expected to purchase. Moreover, the concern with this paragraph is with income which will be derived from the capital that should have been secured. There will, however, often be a risk attached to capital investment and this will need to be taken into account in deciding whether or not it was reasonable to expect a particular investment to be secured. In practice it is unlikely that a tribunal will be willing to second-guess investment decisions even with the benefit of hindsight except in blatant cases.

In contrast to para 26, it is only necessary to establish that the deprivation or failure to secure was "with a view to" reducing assessable income. It is not necessary to show that this was its principal purpose. It may therefore be possible to catch cases under this paragraph which fail to satisfy the principal purpose test for para 26. The Upper Tribunal undertook a detailed analysis of the meaning of "with a view to" in *AC v CMEC* [2009] UKUT 152 (AAC). The judge concluded that the test was whether the parent had the reduction of assessable income as an operative purpose. The same issue has arisen again before a different judge of the Upper Tribunal.

Income attributed under this paragraph is part of the parent's net income and is treated as other income to which Part III of this Schedule applies (para 32). Net income is calculated under regs 7 and 8. It includes income determined in accordance with Part III. It excludes any amount specified in Sch 2 and para 2. It follows that income tax should be deducted from the income attributed. This makes sense, as income tax would be deducted if the income were actually received. See *CCS 185/2005*, para 15.

In *CCS 4912/1998*, the commissioner interpreted this paragraph broadly and controversially, producing the same effect as if the veil of incorporation had been lifted from a personal service company. The same result can be achieved more satisfactorily by using a departure direction under reg 24 of the Departure Direction Regulations on the basis of diversion of income or under reg 25 of those Regulations on the basis of lifestyle inconsistent with declared income.

In *CCS 2678/2007*, the commissioner decided that this paragraph could apply to failures to secure employment or self-employment. Any uncertainty in the availability of work would be relevant to the parent's motivation or purpose.

Paragraph 28(c)

Personal injury in the form of a disease also covers injuries as a result of the disease – eg, an amputation necessary as a result of contracting meningitis and septicaemia (*R(SB) 2/89*, para 15). The key factor is the nature of the injury and not the particular loss for which the income from the trust is compensation. It would therefore cover financial loss as a result of an injury (such as loss of earnings) as much as the loss of amenity or the pain and suffering associated with the injury.

Paragraph 31

This provision only applies where a payment is made on behalf of a parent or child. It does not, therefore, cover cases where an item is bought by one parent as a present for a child or out of a sense of responsibility. It is not sufficient that the payment should be for the benefit of the parent or child. There must be evidence which shows that the purchase was on behalf of the other parent or child. This evidence might take the form of a request that the item be purchased. The most obvious cases where this provision will apply are those where the clear legal responsibility is that of the parent with care (eg, to pay rent or an electricity bill), but payment is made by someone else such as a former partner under a divorce settlement or by a grandparent.

The treatment of payment by one parent of the housing costs in respect of the home occupied by the other but for which both are liable is unclear. According to *CSCS 8/1995* (para 16) and *CCS 8189/1995* (para 9) the amount by which the payment exceeds that person's share of the housing costs falls to be treated as income under this paragraph. However, in *CCS 13698/1996* (paras 11-12) the commissioner decided that payments of maintenance by the absent parent to the parent with care fell outside Sch 1, even though the result is to render the concluding words of head (b) *otiose*. Accordingly, payments by the absent parent of the parent with care's share of the housing costs are not to be taken into account as the parent with care's income. On this view the commissioner did not have to decide whether the payments should be treated as for the joint benefit of the parent with care and the child (*ibid*, para 10). *CCS 13923/1996* (para 8) is to the same effect as *CCS 13698/1996* (paras 11-12). There was unanimity among the commissioners that these two decisions should not be reported. On housing costs see further reg 15(3) and the general note thereto.

This paragraph first lists items of expenditure on which may be attributed to a parent, and then exempts from its scope certain payments. One of these is school fees. As this is an exemption for an item which would otherwise fall within this paragraph, the reference to school fees cannot include tuition fees, which would not fall within any of the items listed earlier. The school fees which are not to be treated as the parent's income must be those related to accommodation and board rather than tuition. The exemption does not apply when the fees are paid by the absent parent, although according to *CCS 13698/1996* (para 12) the reference to the absent parent is *otiose*.

A payment is made "on behalf of" a parent or a child if the person making payment undertakes liability as agent of the parent or child or discharges a liability of the parent or child as their agent (*CCS 1318/1997* para 16 approved in *CCS 318/1998* para 27).

SCHEDULE 2
AMOUNTS TO BE DISREGARDED WHEN CALCULATING OR ESTIMATING N and M

1. The amounts referred to in this Schedule are to be disregarded when calculating or estimating N and M (parent's net income).

2. An amount in respect of income tax applicable to the income in question where not otherwise allowed for under these Regulations.

3. Where a payment is made in a currency other than sterling, an amount equal to any banking charge or commission payable in converting that payment to sterling.

4. Any amount payable in a country outside the United Kingdom where there is a prohibition against the transfer to the United Kingdom of that amount.

5. Any compensation for personal injury and any payments from a trust fund set up for that purpose.

6. Any advance of earnings or any loan made by an employer to an employee.

7. Any payment by way of, or reduction or discharge of liability resulting from entitlement to, housing benefit or council tax benefit..

8. Any disability living allowance, mobility supplement or any payment intended to compensate for the non-payment of any such allowance or supplement.

9. Any payment which is–

(a) an attendance allowance under section 64 of the Contributions and Benefits Act;

(b) an increase of disablement pension under section 104 or 105 of that Act (increases where constant attendance needed or for exceptionally severe disablement);

(c) a payment made under regulations made in exercise of the power conferred by Schedule 8 to that Act (payments for pre- 1948 cases);

(d) an increase of an allowance payable in respect of constant attendance under that Schedule;

(e) payable by virtue of articles 14,15,16, 43 or 44 of the Personal Injuries (Civilians) Scheme 1983 (allowances for constant attendance and exceptionally severe disablement and severe disablement occupational allowance) or any analogous payment; or

(f) a payment based on the need for attendance which is paid as part of a war disablement pension.

10. Any payment under section 148 of the Contributions and Benefits Act (pensioners' Christmas bonus).

11. Any social fund payment within the meaning of Part VIII of the Contributions and Benefits Act.

12. Any payment made by the Secretary of State to compensate for the loss (in whole or in part) of entitlement to housing benefit.

13. Any payment made by the Secretary of State to compensate for loss of housing benefit supplement under regulation 19 of the Supplementary Benefit (Requirements) Regulations 1983.

14. Any payment made by the Secretary of State to compensate a person who was entitlement to supplementary benefit in respect of a period ending immediately before 11th April 1988 but who did not become entitlement to income support in respect of a period beginning with that day.

15. Any concessionary payment made to compensate for the non-payment of income support, [[13] state pension credit] [[5]income-based jobseeker's allowance,] disability living allowance, or any payment to which paragraph 9 applies.

[¹⁶15A. A payment made by the Secretary of State under section 2 of the Employment and Training Act 1973 by way of In-Work Credit, Better Off In-Work Credit or Return to Work Credit.]

16. Any payments of child benefit to the extent that they do not exceed the basic rate of that benefit as defined in regulation 4.

17. Any payment made under regulations 9 to 11 or 13 of the Welfare Food Regulations 1988 (payments made in ;ace of milk tokens or the supply of vitamins).

18. subject to paragraph 20 and to the extent that it does not exceed £10.00–

(a)   war disablement pension or war widow's pension [¹³or war widower's pension] or a payment made to compensate for non-payment of such a pension;

(b)   a pension paid by the government of a country outside Great Britain and which either–
   (i)   is analogous to a war disablement pension; or
   (ii)   is analogous to a war widow's pension [¹³or war widower's pension].

[¹²18A.   Subject to paragraph 20, and to the extent that it does not exceed £10.00, a payment made in respect of a parent under a scheme mentioned in section 1(2) of the Armed Forces (Pensions and Compensation) Act 2004 (compensation schemes for armed and reserve forces).]

19.–(1)   Except where sub-paragraph (2) applies and subject to sub-paragraph (3) and paragraphs 20,38 and 47, [⁴up to £20.00] of any charitable or voluntary payment made, or due to be made, at regular intervals.

(2)   Subject to sub-paragraph (3) and paragraphs 38 and 47, any charitable or voluntary payment made or due to be made at regular intervals which is intended and used for an item other than food, ordinary clothing or footwear, gas, electricity or fuel charges, housing costs of any member of the family or the payment of council tax.

(3)   Sub-paragraphs (1) and (2) shall not apply to a payment which is made by a person for the maintenance of any member of his family or of his former partner or of his children.

(4)   For the purposes of sub-paragraph (1) where a number of charitable or voluntary payments fall to be taken into account they shall be treated as though they were one such payment.

20.–(1)   Where, but for this paragraph, more than [⁴£20.00] would be disregarded under paragraphs [¹²18 to 19(1)] in respect of the same week, only [⁴£20.00] in aggregate shall be disregarded and where an amount falls to be deducted from the income of a student under paragraph 16(3)(b) or (c) of Schedule 1, that amount shall count as part of the [⁴£20.00] disregard allowed under this paragraph.

(2)   Where any payment which is due to be paid in one week is paid in another week, sub-paragraph (1) and paragraphs [¹²18 to 19(1)] shall have effect as if that payment were received in the week in which it was due.

21.   In the case of a person participating in arrangements for training made under section 2 of the Employment and Training Act 1973 or section 2 of the Enterprise and New Towns (Scotland) Act 1990 (functions in relation to training for employment etc.) or attending a course at an employment rehabilitation centre established under section 12 of the 1973 Act–

(a)   any travelling expenses reimbursed to the person;

(b)   any living away from home allowance under section 2(2)(d) of the 1973 Act or section 2(4)(c) of the 1990 act;

(c)   any training premium,

but this paragraph, except in so far as it relates to a payment mentioned in sub-paragraph (a), (b), or (c), does not apply to any part of any allowance under section 22(d) of the 1973 Act or section 2(4)(c) of the 1990 Act.

22.   Where a parent occupies a dwelling as his home and that dwelling is also occupied by a person, other than a non-dependant or a person who is provided with board and lodging accommodation, and that person is contractually liable to make payments in respect of his occupation of the dwelling to the parent, the amount or, as the case may be, the amounts specified in [⁹paragraph 19 of Schedule 9 to the Income Support (General) Regulations 1987 which would have applied if he had been in receipt of income support.]

23.   Where a parent, who is not a self-employed earner, is in receipt of rent or any other money in respect of the use and occupation of property other than his home, that rent or other payment to the extent of any sums which that parent is liable to pay by way of–

[¹(a)   payments which are to be taken into account as eligible housing costs under sub-paragraphs (b), (c), (d) and (t) of paragraph 1 of schedule 3 (eligible housing costs for the purposes of determining exempt income and protected income) and paragraph 3 of that Schedule (exempt income; additional provisions relating to eligible housing costs);]

(b)   council tax payable in respect of that property;

(c)   water and sewerage charges payable in respect of that property.

24.   [²For each week in which a parent provides] board and lodging accommodation in his home otherwise than as a self-employed earner–

(a)   £20.00 of any payment for that accommodation made by[², on behalf or in respect of] the person to whom that accommodation is provided; and

(b)   where any such payment excess £20.00, 50 per centum of the excess.

25.   Any payment made to a person in respect of an adopted child who is a member of his family that is made in accordance with any regulations made under section 57A or pursuant to section 57A(6) of the Adoption Act 1976 (permitted allowances) [¹²or paragraph 3 of Schedule 4 to the Adoption and Children Act 2002] or, as the case may be, [⁸section 51A] of the Adoption (Scotland) Act 1978 (schemes for the payment of allowances to adopters)–

(a)   where the child is not a child in respect of whom child support maintenance is being assessed, to the extent that it exceeds [¹the aggregate of the amounts to be taken into account in the calculation of E under regulation 9(1)(g)], reduced, as the case may be, under regulation 9(4);

(b)   in any other case, to the extent that it does not exceed the amount of the income of a child which is treated as that of his parent by virtue of Part IV [⁷of Schedule 1.]

[¹²**25A.**   Any payment made to a person in accordance with regulations made pursuant to section 14F of the Children Act 1989 (special guardianship support services) in respect of a child who is a member of his family.]

26.   Where a local authority makes a payment in respect of the accommodation and maintenance of a child in pursuance of paragraph 15 of Schedule 1 to the Children Act 1989 (local authority contribution to child's maintenance) to the extent that it exceeds the amount referred to in [¹regulation 9(1)(g)] (reduced, as the case may be, under regulation 9(4)).

27.   Any payment received under a policy of insurance taken out to insure against the risk of being unable to maintain repayments on a loan taken out to acquire an interest in, or to meet the cost of repairs or improvements to, the parent's home and used to meet such repayments, to the extent that the payment received under that policy [²exceeds] [³the total of the amount of the payments set out in paragraphs 1(b), 3(2) and (4) of Schedule 3 as modified, where applicable, by regulation 18.]

28.   In the calculation of the income of the parent with care, any maintenance payments made by the absent parent in respect of his qualifying child.

29.   Any payment made by a local authority to a person who is caring for a child under section 23(2)(a) of the Children Act 1989 (provision of accommodation and maintenance by a local authority for children whom the authority is looking after) or, as the case may be, section 21 of the Social Work (Scotland) Act 1968 or by a voluntary organisation under section 59(1)(a) of the Children Act authority under regulation 9 of the Boarding Out and Fostering of Children (Scotland) Regulations 1985 (provision of accommodation and maintenance for children in care).

30.   Any payment made by a health authority[¹⁵, Primary Care Trust], local authority or voluntary organization in respect of a person who is not normally a member of the household but is temporarily in the care of a member of it.

31.   Any payment made by a local authority under section 17 or 24 of the Children Act 1989 or, as the case may be, section 12, 24 or 26 of the Social Work (Scotland) Act 1968 (local authorities' duty to promote welfare of children and powers to grant financial assistance to persons looked after, or in, or formerly in, their care).

32.   Any resettlement benefit which is paid to the parent by virtue of regulation 3 of the Social Security (Hospital In-Patients) Amendment (No. 2) Regulations 1987 (transitional provisions).

33.–(1)   Any payment or repayment made–

(a)   as respects England and Wales, under regulation 3,5, or 8 of the National Health Service (Travelling Expenses and Remission of Charges) Regulations 1988 (travelling expenses and health service supplies);

(b)   as respects Scotland, under regulation 3, 5 or 8 of the National Health Service (Travelling Expenses and Remission of Charges) (Scotland) Regulation 1988 (travelling expenses and health service supplies).

(2)   Any payment or repayment made by the Secretary of State for Health, the Secretary of State for Scotland or the Secretary of State for Wales which is analogous to a payment or repayment mentioned in sub-paragraph (1).

34.   Any payment made (other than a training allowance), whether by the Secretary of State or any other person, under the Disabled Persons Employment Act 1944 or in accordance with arrangements made under section 2 of the Employment and training act 1973 to assist disabled persons to obtain or retain employment despite their disability.

35.   Any contribution to the expenses of maintaining a household which is made by a non-dependant member of that household.

36.   Any sum in respect of a course of study attended by a child payable by virtue of regulations and under section 81 of the Education Act 1944 (assistance by means of scholarship or otherwise), or by virtue of section 2(1) of the Education Act 1962 (awards for courses of further education) or section 49 of the Education (Scotland) Act 1980 (power to assist persons to take advantage of educational facilities).

[¹¹**36A.**   Any sum in respect of financial assistance given, or given under arrangements made, by the Secretary of State (in relation to England) or the National Assembly for Wales (in relation to Wales) under section 14 of the Education Act 2002 (power of Secretary of State and National Assembly for Wales to give financial assistance for purposes related to education), to a child.]

37.   Where a person receives income under an annuity purchased with a loan which satisfies the following conditions–

(a)   that loan was made as part of a scheme under which not less than 90 per centum of the proceeds of the loan were applied to the purchase by the person to whom it was made of an annuity ending with his life or with the life of the survivor of two or more persons (in this paragraph referred to as "the annuitants" who include the person to whom the loan was made;

(b)   that the interest on the loan is payable by the person to whom it was made or by one of the annuitants;

(c)   that at the time the loan was made the person to whom it was made or each of the annuitants had attained the age of 65;

(d)   that the loan was secured on a dwelling in Great Britain and the person to whom the loan was made or one of the annuitants owns an estate or interest in that dwelling; and

(e)   that the person to whom the loan was made or one of the annuitants occupies the dwelling on which it was secured as his home at the time the interest is paid, the amount, calculated on a weekly basis equal to–

    (i)   where, or insofar as, section 26 of the Finance Act 1982 (deduction of tax for certain loan interest) applies to the payments of the interest on the loan, the interest which is payable after the deduction of a sum equal to income tax on such payments at the basis rate for the year of assessment in which the payment of interest becomes due;

    (ii)   in any other case the interest which is payable on the loan without deduction of such a sum.

38.   Any payment of the description specified in paragraph 39 of Schedule 9 to the Income Support Regulations (disregard of payments made under certain trusts and disregard of certain other payments) and any income derived from the investment of such payments.

39.   Any payment made to a juror or witness in respect of attendance at court other than compensation for loss of earnings or for loss of a benefit payable under the Contributions and Benefits Act [⁵or the Jobseekers Act].

40.   Any special war widow's payment made under–

(a)   the Naval and Marine Pay and Pensions (Special War Widows Payment) Order 1990 made under section 3 of the Naval and Marine Pay and Pensions Act 1865;

(b)   the Royal Warrant dated 19th February 1990 amending the Schedule to the Army Pensions warrant 1977;

(c)   the Queen's Order dated 26th February 1990 made under section 2 of the Air Force (Constitution) Act 1917;

(d)   the Home Guard War Widows Special Payments Regulations 1990 made under section 151 of the Reserve Forces Act 1980;

(e)   the Orders dated 19th February 1990 amending Orders made on 12th December 1980 concerning the Ulster Defence Regiment made in each case under section 140 of the Reserve Forces Act 1980,

and any analogous payment by the Secretary of State for Defence to any person who is not a person entitled under the provisions mentioned in sub-paragraphs (a) to (e).

41.   Any payment to a person as holder of the Victoria Cross or the George Cross or any analogous payment.

42.   Any payment made either by the Secretary of State for the Home Department or by the Security of State for Scotland under a scheme established to assist relatives and other persons to visit persons in custody.

43.   Any amount by way of a refund of income tax deducted from profits or emoluments chargeable to income tax under Schedule D or Schedule E.

44.   Maintenance payments (whether paid under the Act or otherwise) insofar as they are not treated as income under Part III or IV [⁷of Schedule 1.]

45.   Where following a divorce[¹⁴, dissolution of a civil partnership] or separation–

(a)   capital is divided between the parent and the person who was his partner before the divorce[14, dissolution of the civil partnership] or separation; and

(b)   that capital is intended to be used to acquire a new home for that parent or to acquire furnishing for a home of his,

income derived from the investment of that capital for one year following the date on which that capital became available to the parent.

[¹**46.**   Except in the case of a self-employed earner, payments in kind.]

47.   Any payment made by the Joseph Rowntree Memorial Trust from money provided to it by the Secretary of State for Health for the purpose of maintaining a family fund for the benefit of severely handicapped children.

48.   Any payment of expenses to a person who is–

(a)   engaged by a charitable or voluntary body; or

(b)   a volunteer,

if he otherwise derives no remuneration or profit from the body or person paying those expenses.

[¹**48A.**   Any guardian's allowance under Part III of the Contributions and Benefits Act.

48B.   Any payment in respect of duties mentioned in paragraph 1(1)(i) of Chapter I of Part I of Schedule 1 relating to a period of one year or more.]

[⁶**48C.**   Any payment to a person under section 1 of the Community Care (Direct Payments) Act 1996 or section 12B of the Social Work (Scotland) Act 1968(c) in respect of his securing community care services, as defined in section 46 of the National Health Services and Community Care Act 1990.]

[⁹**48D.**   Any payment of child tax credit.]

[¹⁰[¹³**48E.**   Any payment made by a local authority, or by the National Assembly for Wales, to a person relating to a service which is provided to develop or sustain the capacity of that person to live independently in his accommodation.]]

[¹³**48F.**   Any supplementary pension under article 29(1A) of the Naval, Military and Air Forces etc. (Disablement and Death) Service Pensions Order 1983 (pensions to [¹⁴widows, widowers and surviving civil partners]) or under article 27(3) of the Personal Injuries (Civilians) Scheme 1983 (pensions to [¹⁴widows, widowers and surviving civil partners]).]

49. In this Schedule–

"concessionary payment" means a payment made under arrangements made by the Secretary of State with the consent of the Treasury which is charged either to the National Insurance Fund or to a Departmental Expenditure Vote to which payments of benefit under the Contributions and Benefits Act [⁵or the Jobseekers Act] are charged;

"health authority" means a health authority established under the National Health Service Act 1977 or the National Health Service (Scotland) Act 1978;

"mobility supplement" has the same meaning as in regulation 2(1) of the Income Support Regulations;

"war disablement pension" and "war widow" have the same meanings as in section 150(2) of the Contributions and Benefits Act.

Amendments

1. Child Support (Miscellaneous Amendments) Regulations 1993 (SI 1993 No.913) regs 28-32 (April 5, 1993).
2. Child Support and Income Support (Amendment) Regulations 1995 (SI 1995 No.1045) reg 55(2)-(4) (April 18, 1995).
3. Child Support (Miscellaneous Amendments) (No.2) Regulations 1995 (SI 1995 No.3261) reg 46 (January 22, 1996).
4. Child Support (Maintenance Assessments and Special Cases) and Social Security (Claims and Payments) Amendment Regulations 1996 (SI 1996 No.481) reg 3 (April 8, 1996, but see reg 4 of SI 1996 No.481 for transitional provisions).
5. Social Security and Child Support (Jobseeker's Allowance) (Consequential Amendments) Regulations 1996 (SI 1996 No.1345) regs 6(5), (6) and (7)(c) (October 7, 1996).
6. Child Support (Miscellaneous Amendments) (No.2) Regulations 1996 (SI 1996 No.3196) reg 14 (January 13, 1997).
7. Child Support (Miscellaneous Amendments) Regulations 1998 (SI 1998 No.58) reg 57 (January 19, 1998).
8. Child Support (Miscellaneous Amendments) Regulations 1999 (SI 1999 No.977) reg 6(6) (April 6, 1999).
9. Child Support (Miscellaneous Amendments) Regulations 2003 (SI 2003 No.328) reg 6(7)(a) and (b) (April 6, 2003).
10. Child Support (Miscellaneous Amendments) Regulations 2003 (SI 2003 No.328) reg 6(7)(c) (April 1, 2003).
11. Child Support (Miscellaneous Amendments) Regulations 2004 (SI 2004 No.2415) reg 5(3) (September 16, 2004).
12. Child Support (Miscellaneous Amendments) Regulations 2005 (SI 2005 No.785) reg 4(3) (March 16, 2005).
13. Child Support (Miscellaneous Amendments) (No.2) Regulations 2003 (SI 2003 No.2779) reg 4(7) (November 5, 2003).
14. Civil Partnership (Pensions, Social Security and Child Support) (Consequential, etc. Provisions) Order 2005 (SI 2005 No.2877) art 2(4) and Sch 4, para 2(5) (December 5, 2005).
15. National Health Service Reform and Health Care Professions Act 2002 (Supplementary, Consequential etc. Provisions) Regulations 2002 (SI 2002 No.2469) reg 9 and Sch 6 (October 1, 2002).
16. Child Support (Miscellaneous and Consequential Amendments) Regulations 2009 (SI 2009 No.736) reg 3(5) (April 6, 2009).

Definitions

"child tax credit": see reg 1(2).
"Contributions and Benefits Act": see reg 1(2).
"council tax benefit": see reg 1(2).
"earnings": see reg 1(2).
"family": see reg 1(2).
"home": see reg 1(2).
"housing benefit": see reg 1(2).
"the Jobseekers Act": see reg 1(2).
"non-dependant": see reg 1(2).
"ordinary clothing or footwear": see reg 1(2).
"parent with care": see reg 1(2).
"partner": see reg 1(2).
"person": see reg 1(2).
"self-employed earner": see reg 1(2).
"state pension credit": see reg 1(2).

"student": see reg 1(2).
"training allowance": see reg 1(2).

General Note
Paragraph 5
This paragraph applies to compensation for "personal injury". A personal injury may be physical or mental. In the latter case there must be a recognisable psychiatric illness (*McLoughlin v O'Brian* [1983] 1 AC 410). It may also take the form of a disease (*R(SB) 2/89*, para 11) and will include any injuries sustained as a result of the disease – eg, an amputation following meningitis and septicaemia (*ibid*, para 15).

The compensation must be paid for the personal injury and not merely because of it. Strictly, compensation is not paid for an injury, but for the consequences of the injury (*Baker v Willoughby* [1969] 3 All ER 1528 at 1532, per Lord Reid). This is true not only of a civil claim for damages, but also a claim for disablement benefit under which entitlement depends on the degree of the resulting disablement. The paragraph cannot, therefore, be read literally.

In *R(CS) 2/00* (para 16), the commissioner held that "compensation for personal injury" only covers payment to an injured party by the person who was liable in tort to make reparation for the injury or who accepted such liability. Any other interpretation would render the reference to a trust fund superfluous as cases where a trust fund was set up would be covered by the earlier words of the paragraph. On this reasoning, the paragraph covers all compensation paid on a civil claim for damage, including compensation for the loss of earnings as a result of the injury. It is arguable that, in the context of child support and having regard to the nature of the type of exclusion covered by this Schedule, compensation should not include compensation for loss of future income, as compensation which replaces income that would otherwise have been received is out of step with the character of the contents of the Schedule. On this reasoning, payments of disablement benefit will not count as compensation for the purposes of this paragraph. This also would be out of step with the character of the contents of the Schedule. An appeal against the commissioner's decision was dismissed by the Court of Appeal in *Wakefield v Secretary of State for Social Security*, also reported as *R(CS) 2/00*.

Paragraph 6
This paragraph is in the same terms as Sch 1 para 1(2)(d).

Paragraph 19
Whether a payment is voluntary is judged by looking at the payer and not the payee. Consequently a payment by British Coal to a miner's widow in lieu of concessionary coal is not a voluntary payment (*R v Doncaster BC ex p Boulton* [1992] 25 HLR 195, QBD and *R(IS) 4/94*). It is irrelevant whether or not the payment in question was legally enforceable (*ibid*). Where payments are made under an annuity which was purchased with money given for the purpose, they are not voluntary since they are made under the terms of the annuity which is a form of contract (*CIS 702/1991*, para 15).

Paragraph 23
This paragraph is not comprehensive of the disregards for parents that fall within it. In particular it does not displace the disregard in para 2 (*CCS 185/2005*, para 16). However, it is not possible to apply the reasoning in *Parsons v Hogg* [1985] 2 All ER 897, as this would override the express terms of the provision (*CCS 1992/2008*, para 11).

Paragraph 44
The question arises of whether or not child support maintenance payments received by a parent, whether or not in respect of a qualifying child, are to be disregarded under this paragraph. Maintenance payments in respect of a parent are covered by Sch 1 para 14, but there is no express reference to child support maintenance payments in Pt III or IV of Sch 1. However, Sch 1 para 15 covers any other payments or amounts received on a periodical basis. This wording is wide enough to cover payments of child support maintenance, but the never ending circles of calculations involved in doing so point to these payments not falling within the words of para 15. Take, as an example, the case of a mother with care of a child whose child support maintenance is being calculated on review. The child support maintenance ultimately payable would have to be taken into account before it was fixed, a plain impossibility. There would be even greater complexities if the mother had care of two children by different fathers and received child support maintenance payments in respect of each. The only way to avoid these circles is by interpreting para 15 as not covering payments of child support maintenance.

Paragraph 45
Capital earmarked for the purpose or acquiring a new home falls within this paragraph for as long as it remains earmarked, although the parent could have used it for another purpose (*CCS 4923/1995*, para 5).

Paragraph 49
Concessionary payments are only made to compensate for the effects of defective legislation and do not include ex gratia payments for the loss of statutory entitlement – eg, was a result of maladministration (*CIS 2285/1999*).

SCHEDULE 3
ELIGIBLE HOUSING COSTS

Eligible housing costs for the purposes of determining exempt income and protected income

    1.   Subject to the following provisions of this Schedule, [⁶the following amounts payable] in respect of the provision of a home shall be eligible to be taken into account as housing costs for the purposes of these Regulations—

    (a)   [⁶amounts payable by way of rent;]

    (b)   [⁶amounts payable by way of mortgage interest;]

    (c)   [⁶amounts payable by way of interest] under a hire purchase agreement to buy a home;

    (d)   [⁶amounts payable by way of interest] on loans for repairs and improvements to the home [¹, including interest on a loan for any service charge imposed to meet the cost of such repairs and improvements;]

    (e)   [⁶amounts payable] by way of ground rent or in Scotland, payments by way of feu duty;

    (f)   [⁶amounts payable] payments under a co-ownership scheme;

    (g)   [⁶amounts payable] in respect of, or in consequence of, the use and occupation of the home;

    (h)   where the home is a tent, [⁶amounts payable] payments in respect of the tent and the site on which it stands;

    (i)   [⁶amounts payable] in respect of a licence or permission to occupy the home (whether or not board is provided);

    (j)   [⁶amounts payable] by way of mesne profits or, in Scotland, violent profits;

    (k)   [⁶amounts payable by way of] service charges, the payment of which is a condition on which the right to occupy the home depends;

    (l)   [⁶amounts payable] under or relating to a tenancy or licence of a Crown tenant;

    (m)   mooring charges payable for a houseboat;

    (n)   where the home is a caravan or a mobile home, [⁶amounts payable] in respect of the site on which it stands;

    (o)   any contribution payable by a parent resident in an almshouse provided by a housing association which is either a charity of which particulars are entered in the register of charities established under section 4 of the Charities Act 1960 (register of charities) or an exempt charity within the meaning of that Act, which is a contribution towards the cost of maintaining that association's almshouses and essential services in them;

    (p)   [⁶amounts payable] under a rental purchase agreement, that is to say an agreement for the purchase of a home under which the whole or part of the purchase price is to be paid in more than one instalment and the completion of the purchase is deferred until the whole or a specified part of the purchase price has been paid;

    (q)   where, in Scotland, the home is situated on or pertains to a croft within the meaning of section 3(1) of the Crofters (Scotland) Act 1955, the [⁶amounts payable] in respect of the croft land;

    (r)   where the home is provided by an employer (whether under a condition or term in a contract of service or otherwise), [⁶amounts payable] to that employer in respect of the home, including [⁶any amount deductible by the employer]

    (s)   [¹ . . .]

    (t)   [⁶payments in respect of a loan taken out to pay off another loan but only to the extent that it was incurred in respect of amounts eligible to be taken into account as housing costs by virtue of other provisions of this Schedule.]

Loans for repairs and improvements to the home

    2.   [³Subject to paragraph 2A (loans for repairs and improvements in transitional cases), for the purposes of] paragraph 1(d) "repairs and improvements" means major repairs necessary to maintain the fabric of the home and any of the following measures undertaken with a view to improving its fitness for occupation—

    (a)   installation of a fixed bath, shower, wash basin or lavatory, and necessary associated plumbing;

    (b)   damp proofing measures;

    (c)   provision or improvement of ventilation and natural lighting;

    (d)   provision of electric lightening and sockets;

    (e)   provision or improvement of drainage facilities;

    (f)   improvement of the structural condition of the home;

    (g)   improvements to the facilities for the storing, preparation and cooking of food;

    (h)   provision of heating, including central heating;

    (i)   provision of storage facilities for fuel and refuse;

    (j)   improvements to the insulation of the home;

    (k)   other improvements which the [⁷Secretary of State] considers reasonable in the circumstances.

[³Loans for repairs and improvements in transitional cases

    2A.   In the case of a loan entered into before the first date upon which a maintenance application or enquiry form is given or sent or treated as given or sent to the relevant person, for the purposes of paragraph 1(d) "repairs and improvements" means repairs and improvements of any description whatsoever.]

Exempt income: additional provisions relating to eligible housing costs
    3.–(1)   The additional provisions made by this paragraph shall have effect only for the purpose of calculating or estimating exempt income.
    (2)   Subject to sub-paragraph(6), where the home of an absent parent or, as the case may be, a parent with care, is subject to a mortgage or charge and that parent [⁶is liable to make periodical payments] to reduce the capital secured by that mortgage or charge of an amount provided for in accordance with the terms thereof, [⁶those amounts payable] shall be eligible to be taken into account as the housing costs of that parent.
    [⁴(2A)   Where an absent parent or as the case may be a parent with care has entered into a loan for repairs or improvements of a kind referred to in paragraph 1(d) and that parent [⁶is liable to make periodical payments] of an amount provided for in accordance with the terms of that loan to reduce the amount of that loan, [⁶those amounts payable shall be eligible to be taken into account as housing costs of that parent.]]
    (3)   Subject to sub-paragraph (6), where the home of an absent parent or, as the case may be, a parent with care, is held under an agreement and [⁶certain amounts payable] under that agreement are included as housing costs by virtue of paragraph 1 of this Schedule, [⁶any other amounts payable] in accordance with that agreement by the parent in order either–
    (a)   to reduce his liability under that agreement; or
    (b)   to acquire the home to which it relates,
shall also be eligible to be taken into account as housing costs.
    (4)   Where a policy of insurance has been obtained and retained for the purpose of discharging a mortgage or charge on the home of the parent in question, the amount of the [⁶premiums payable] under that policy shall be eligible to be taken into account as a housing cost [³including for the avoidance of doubt such a policy of insurance whose purpose is to secure the payment of monies due under the mortgage or charge in the event of the unemployment, sickness or disability of the insured.]
    [⁵(4A)   Where–
    (a)   an absent parent or parent with care has obtained a loan which constitutes an eligible housing cost falling within sub-paragraph (d) or (t) of paragraph 1; and
    (b)   a policy of insurance has been obtained and retained, the purpose of which is solely to secure the payment of monies due under that loan in the event of the unemployment, sickness or disability of the insured person,
the amount of the premiums payable under that policy shall be eligible to be taken into account as a housing cost.]
    [²(5)   Where a policy of insurance has been obtained and retained for the purpose of discharging a mortgage or charge on the home of the parent in question and also for the purpose of accruing profits on the maturity of the policy, there shall be eligible to be taken into account as a housing cost–
    (a)   where the sum secured by the mortgage or charge does not exceed £60,000 the whole of the [⁶premiums payable] under that policy; and
    (b)   where the sum secured by the mortgage or charge exceeds £60,000, the part of the [⁶premiums payable] under that policy which are necessarily incurred for the purpose of discharging the mortgage or charge or, where that part cannot be ascertained, 0.0277 per centum of the amount secured by the mortgage or charge.]
    [³(5A)   Where a plan within the meaning of regulation 4 of the Personal Equity Plans Regulations 1989 has been obtained and retained for the purpose of discharging a mortgage or charge on the home of the parent in question and also for the purpose of accruing profits upon the realisation of the plan, there shall be eligible to be taken into account as a housing cost–
    (a)   where the sum secured by the mortgage or charge does not exceed £60,000, the whole of the premiums payable in respect of the plan; and
    (b)   where the sum secured by the mortgage or charge exceeds £60,000, that part of the premiums payable in respect of the plan which is necessarily incurred for the purpose of discharging the mortgage or charge or, where that part cannot be ascertained, 0.0277 per centum of the amount secured by the mortgage or charge.
    (5B)   Where a personal pension plan [⁵derived from a personal pension scheme] has been obtained and retained for the purpose of discharging a mortgage or charge on the home of the parent in question and also for the purpose of securing the payment of pension to him, there shall be eligible to be taken into account as a housing cost 25 per centum of the contributions payable in respect of that personal pension plan.]
    (6)   For the purposes of sub-paragraphs (2) and (3), housing costs shall not include–
    (a)   [³any payments in excess of those required] to be made under or in respect of a mortgage, charge or agreement to which either of those sub-paragraphs related;
    (b)   [⁶amounts payable] under any second or subsequent mortgage on the home to the extent that [³they would not be eligible] to be taken into account as housing costs;
    (c)   premiums payable in respect of any policy of insurance against loss caused by the destruction of or damage to any building or land.

Conditions relating to eligible housing costs
    4.–(1)   Subject to the following provisions of this paragraph the housing costs referred to in this Schedule shall be included as housing costs only where–

(a)   [⁵they are necessarily incurred for the purpose of purchasing, renting or otherwise securing possession of the home for the parent and his family, or for the purpose of carrying out repairs and improvements to that home,]

(b)   the parent or, if he is one of a family, he or a member of his family, is responsible for those costs; and

(c)   the liability to meet those costs is to a person other than a member of the same household.

[⁵(1A)   For the purposes of sub-paragraph (1)(a) "repairs and improvements" shall have the meaning given in paragraph 2 of this Schedule.]

(2)   For the purposes of sub-paragraph (1)(b) a parent shall be treated as responsible for housing costs where–

(a)   because the person liable to meet those costs is not doing so, he has to meet those costs in order to continue to live in the home and either he was formerly the partner of the person liable, or he is some other person whom it is reasonable to treat as liable to meet those costs; or

(b)   he pays a share of those costs in a case where–
    (i)   he is living in a household with other persons;
    (ii)   those other persons include persons who are not close relatives of his or his partner;
    (iii)   a person who is not such a close relative is responsible for those costs under the preceding provisions of this paragraph or has an equivalent responsibility for housing expenditure; and
    (iv)   it is reasonable in the circumstances to treat him as sharing that responsibility.

[⁵(3)   Subject to sub-paragraph (4), payments on a loan shall constitute an eligible housing cost only if that loan has been obtained for the purposes specified in sub-paragraph (1)(a).

(4)   Where a loan has been obtained only partly for the purposes specified in sub-paragraph (1)(a), the eligible housing cost shall be limited to that part of the payment attributable to those purposes.]

Accommodation also used for other purposes

5.   Where amounts are payable in respect of accommodation which consists partly of residential accommodation and partly of other accommodation, only such proportion thereof as is attributable to residential accommodation shall be eligible to be taken into account as housing costs.

Ineligible service and fuel charges

6.   Housing costs shall not include–

[⁴[⁹(a)   where the costs are inclusive of ineligible service charges within the meaning of paragraph 1(a)(i) of Schedule 1 to the Housing Benefit Regulations or, as the case may be, paragraph 1(a)(i) of Schedule 1 to the Housing Benefit (State Pension Credit) Regulations (ineligible service charges), the amounts specified as ineligible in paragraph 2 of the appropriate Schedule 1;

(b)   where the costs are inclusive of any of the items mentioned in paragraph 6(2) of Schedule 1 to the Housing Benefit Regulations or, as the case may be, paragraph 6(2) of Schedule 1 to the Housing Benefit (State Pension Credit) Regulations (payment in respect of fuel charges), the deductions prescribed in that paragraph unless the parent provides evidence on which the actual or approximate amount of the service charge for fuel may be estimated, in which case the estimated amount;]

(c)   charges for water, sewerage or allied environmental services and where the amount of such charges is not separately identified, such part of the charges in question as is attributable to those services; [⁴and

(d)   where the costs are inclusive of charges, other than those which are not to be included by virtue of sub-paragraphs (a) to (c), that part of those charges which exceeds the greater of the following amounts–
    (i)   the total of the charges other than those which are ineligible service charges within the meaning of paragraph 1 of Schedule 1 to the Housing Benefit Regulations (housing costs);
    (ii)   25 per centum of the total amount of eligible housing costs,

and for the purposes of this sub-paragraph, where the amount of those charges is not separately identifiable, that amount shall be such amount as is reasonably attributable to those charges.]

Interpretation

7.   In this schedule except where the context otherwise requires–

"close relative" means a parent, parent-in-law, son, son-in-law, daughter, daughter-in-law, step-parents, step-son, step-daughter, brother, sister, [⁸or if any of the preceding persons is one member of a couple, the other member of that couple];

"co-ownership scheme" means a scheme under which the dwelling is let by a housing association and the tenant, or his personal representative, will, under the terms of the tenancy agreement or of the agreement under which he became a member of the association, be entitled, on his ceasing to be a member and subject to any conditions stated in either agreement, to a sum calculated by reference directly or indirectly to the value of the dwelling;

"housing association" has the meaning assigned to it by section 1(1) of the Housing Association Act 1985.

Amendments

1.   Child Support (Miscellaneous Amendments) Regulations 1993 (SI 1993 No.913) reg 33 (April 5, 1993).

2. Child Support (Miscellaneous Amendments and Transitional Provisions) Regulations 1994 (SI 1994 No.227) reg 4(8) (February 7, 1994).
3. Child Support and Income Support (Amendment) Regulations 1995 (SI 1995 No.1045) regs 56(3)-(6), 57 and Sch 1 (April 18, 1995).
4. Child Support (Miscellaneous Amendments) (No.2) Regulations 1995 (SI 1995 No.3261) reg 47(2) and (3) (January 22, 1996).
5. Child Support (Miscellaneous Amendments) (No.2) Regulations 1996 (SI 1996 No.3196) reg 15(3) and (4) (January 13, 1997).
6. Child Support (Miscellaneous Amendments) Regulations 1998 (SI 1998 No.58) regs 58(2) and (3) (January 19, 1998).
7. Social Security Act 1998 (Commencement No.7 and Consequential and Transitional Provisions) Order 1999 (SI 1999 No.1510) art 20 (June 1, 1999).
8. Civil Partnership (Pensions, Social Security and Child Support) (Consequential, etc. Provisions) Order 2005 (SI 2005 No.2877) art 2(4) and Sch 4 para 2(6) (December 5, 2005).
9. Housing Benefit and Council Tax Benefit (Consequential Provisions) Regulations 2006 (SI 2006 No.217) reg 5 and Sch 2 para 4(5) (March 6, 2006).

Definitions
"family": see reg 1(2).
"home": see reg 1(2).
"Housing Benefit Regulations": see reg 1(2).
"Housing Benefit (State Pension Credit) Regulations": see reg 1(2).
"parent with care": see reg 1(2).
"partner": see reg 1(2).
"person": see reg 1(2).
"personal pension scheme": see reg 1(2).

General Note
The provisions dealing with housing costs are mandatory and contain no element of discretion. Accordingly s2 of the Act has no application to them (*CCS 9/1995*, para 8).

Paragraph 1
This paragraph lays down the eligible housing costs for all purposes except the calculation of exempt income where the provisions are supplemented by para 3. Where repayment of a loan or credit is concerned, only interest payments are included and not capital payments. Housing costs are not defined. They bear their normal meaning of costs associated with the provision of housing for an individual or a family (Common Appendix to *R(IS) 3/91* and *R(IS) 4/91*, para 10). This is subject to para 4. The housing costs allowable are those which are reasonably necessary for providing a home or repairs or improvements to it, and do not include other costs which happen to be secured upon it (*CCS 12/1994*, para 35), even if those costs were incurred in order to avoid loss of the home (*ibid*, para 39). They do, however, include loans to a partner to purchase the other partner's former interest in the property from the partner's trustee in bankruptcy (*R(IS) 6/94*). As a result of the Amendment Regulations, payments analogous to those listed are not within the scope of the paragraph.

In *R(CS) 6/98* (para 12), the commissioner declined to express a view on whether the "home" in question was the home at the time in respect of which maintenance is being assessed or the home at the time the expenditure was incurred, although he did say that the former might be the case.

For the significance of the reference to the provision of a home, see the general note to para 4.

The language of "costs" and "payments" makes it clear that housing costs only include actual expenditure and not cases where there is liability but no payment – eg, in a deferred repayment mortgage (*CIS 636/1992*, para 8).

There is no power for decision makers or tribunals to make allowance for voluntary payments by an absent parent towards housing costs of the former matrimonial home now occupied by the parent with care and the qualifying child (*CCS 12/95*, para 5; *R(CS) 9/98*, para 8). The giving of credit for such payments is relevant only to recovery of child support maintenance and not to its assessment: see the Child Support (Management of Payments and Arrears) Regulations 2009 on p45.

Subparagraph (b)
An Islamic Trust Funding Arrangement to facilitate the acquisition of a home, under which the property is conveyed into the name of the parent to be held on trust in unequal shares for that parent and the funding provider with the former required to buy shares from the latter by way of payments which are called mesne profits but calculated by reference to interest rates, is not to be equated with a mortgage under which interest payments are made (*CIS 14483/1996*, para 10). Since the commissioner looked at the legal form of the arrangement rather than its economic substance, it is likely that in child support law the arrangement would fall within subpara (j).

In *R(CS) 3/05*, the commissioner decided that for a current account mortgage the eligible housing costs are limited to the minimum amounts that have to be paid under the terms of the loans. Additional payments that were made in order to reduce the outstanding balance and thereby save interest did not count.

Subparagraph (d)

If this head is to be satisfied there must be a loan. It is not sufficient that a debt (eg, to cover private street works) is deferred and paid in instalments with interest (*R(SB) 3/87*, para 7). It is undecided whether loans taken out in respect of work already undertaken are within this head (*CIS 264/1993*, para 13). Repairs and improvements are defined in paras 2 and 2A.

Tribunals have to consider three matters: (i) the basis upon which the loan was made; (ii) the nature of the works for which the money was borrowed; (iii) the use to which the money was put. In the case of a loan from a commercial lender, its basis is to be found either (a) in a term of the contract of loan requiring that the money be used for a specified purpose or (b) in the representation by the absent parent to the lender of the reason why the money was needed. The basis on which the loan was entered into is likely to be stated in general terms that are not sufficiently detailed and precise to show whether the other conditions are satisfied. So, it is necessary to identify the nature of the work for which the money was borrowed in order to check if the conditions in paras 2 or 2A are satisfied. Interest on money which is borrowed for repairs or improvements, but put to other use, is not a payment in respect of the home for the purposes of the opening words of para 1. See *CCS 349/1997*, paras 9-11. The person's motive in carrying out the repairs or improvements is irrelevant (*ibid*, para 12).

Subparagraph (f)

This provision does not apply where possession proceedings have been brought by a lender against the borrower, since in due course the whole of the lender's interest may pass to the borrower, but at no stage will there be joint ownership between lender and borrower (*CIS 392/1994*, para 9).

Subparagraph (g)

The common law meaning of "use and occupation" is a payment for the use and occupation of land which is made where a person has been given permission to occupy the land of another without any binding terms being agreed about payment, and the words "in respect of, or in consequence of" are restrictive (*R v Bristol CC ex p Jacobs* (1999) 32 HLR 841).

The commissioners decided that the extent of the provision is uncertain (*R(CS) 3/96*, para 23). It does not cover capital repayments as they are the subject of special provision in para 3 which would be anomalous and unnecessary if such repayments fell within this subparagraph. The following do not fall within this provision: premiums on contents and property insurance, because they are also covered by para 3 and anomalies would arise if this subparagraph were interpreted so as to cover them (*R(CS) 3/96*, paras 20-23 and *R 1/94 (CSC)*); payments in respect of the purchase of a home (*R(CS) 6/98*, para 12); repayments on a loan to restock a home with items taken by the other partner on separation (*CSC 2/1996*, para 5); water rates (*CSC 3/1996*, para 5); council tax (*R(CS) 11/98*, paras 9-10). Payments in respect of road charges and interest paid on them are charges in respect of a home (*R(SB) 3/87*, para 8).

Subparagraph (j)

The decision in *CIS 14483/1996* dealing with an Islamic Trust Funding Arrangement is explained in the general note to subpara (b) above. On the basis of the commissioner's reasoning it is likely that such an arrangement will fall within this subparagraph.

Subparagraph (k)

Service charges are not defined. Their meaning was discussed by the Tribunal of Commissioners whose decision appears in the Common Appendix to *R(IS) 3/91* and *R(IS) 4/91* (paras 11 and 15). The words are to be interpreted liberally and mean charges made for services provided in connection with housing. They must be charges which involve the determination and arrangement of a service, which would otherwise be for the occupier to decide on and arrange, in a manner binding on the occupier and which cannot be withdrawn from at leisure. They must bind all those with the same interest in the property or they must run with the land so as to bind successors in occupancy. Buildings insurance is not a service charge (*Dunne v Department of Health and Social Security*, unreported, Court of Appeal in Northern Ireland, January 22 1992 and *CSIS 4/90*, para 8), but counselling and other support services can be (*R v North Cornwall District Council ex p Singer, The Times*, January 12, 1994). The service charges which are covered are limited by para 6.

A service charge may be fixed, in which case the amount changes only when the rent is changed, or variable, in which case the amount varies as the costs to which the charge relates varies. A service charge may be difficult to identify as the landlord may merely quote a figure for "rent" without specifying any amount as relating, for example, to water rates.

The essence of a service charge is that it consists of an arrangement for determining whether a particular service, such as redecoration, is required and, if so, for providing the service or arranging for it to be provided. The arrangement must not only be binding, but binding on all those with the same interest in the property. See the Common Appendix to *R(IS) 3/91* and *R(IS) 4/91* (para 15). This draws a clear and logical distinction between charges which are payable as an incident of the owner's estate or interest in the property and those which arise in some other way such as under a personal contract with the tenant or owner (*R(IS) 19/93*, para 12).

Payments required to be made under the terms of a lease for repairs, redecoration, renewal or insurance are service charges and are connected with the provision of adequate accommodation (Common Appendix, para 18, and *R(IS) 4/92*, paras 12-15). Payment of premiums for insurance required under the terms of mortgage is not a service charge since the obligation arises not from the borrower's interest or estate in the property but from the mortgage. In other words, it arises from the financial arrangements for purchase and not out of the ownership of the property itself (*R(IS) 19/93*, para 14). Likewise, insurance premiums effected between an owner-occupier and an insurance company are not a service charge (*CIS 17/1988*, approved in *R(IS) 4/92*, para 15, and *R(IS) 19/93*, para 15), although they are connected with the provision of adequate accommodation (*R(IS) 4/92*, para 15, and *R(IS) 19/93*, para 15). Payments of administration and other charges related to arrears of mortgage payments are not service charges connected to the adequacy of the accommodation (*CIS 392/1994*, para 7).

Paragraph 2

This paragraph defines repairs and improvements for the purposes of para 1(d).

Repair covers both the remedying of defects and steps taken to prevent these, such as the painting of a house to preserve the woodwork (*CSB 420/1985*, paras 11-12). However, where the alleged repair is of the preventive kind, evidence and findings of fact will be needed on whether the work may properly be considered to have been undertaken as a repair or only for cosmetic reasons (*ibid*, para 12). It would, for example, if the painting of a house were being considered, be necessary to inquire into the state of the paint work at the time and whether the change was merely to change the colour. Repairs must be "necessary to maintain the fabric of the home", a strict test.

They must also be "major". Whether a repair is or is not major is a question of fact (*CSB 265/1987*, para 10). It is a comparative term whose meaning is bound to be somewhat fluid and imprecise, but it will always be relevant to take into account the cost as well as the nature of and the time taken for the work (*ibid*, paras 10 and 12). Chimney-sweeping cannot be a repair (*ibid*, para 7). Where the home consists of a flat or some other part of the building, repairs to some other part of the building than the flat itself are not repairs to the fabric of the home (*CIS 616/1992*, para 16).

The proper approach to improvements was exemplified by the commissioner in *CSCS 3/1996* (para 4) as follows. First facts have to be found as to the previous state of the home so that it can be seen that the work led to an improvement. Then it has to be shown that the improvement was properly undertaken in order to improve the fitness for occupation of the home. The facts, in other words, must show that there was some existing unfitness to be remedied.

Improvements need not be major but they must fall within one of the categories listed and they must be undertaken with a view to improving the fitness of the home for occupation. The reasonableness of the improvements is not a factor except under (k) but this will be a relevant consideration in assessing the credibility of the evidence on this issue. Moreover the work must be undertaken with a view not just to improving the home but to improving its fitness for occupation. The paragraph assumes that there should be a minimum standard of accommodation and allows the cost of bringing the home up to that standard to be taken into account as eligible housing costs. So the test is whether the work is carried out with a view to bringing the home up to a standard above the minimum in a particular respect. This provision is not a licence to install a replacement or additional bathroom or further electric sockets where the current provision is adequate. Care is also needed with self-build homes to ensure that this paragraph is not used to cover the costs of completion rather than of the improvement of a home.

The improvements must be improvements to the home (in other words, to the dwelling – reg 1(2)), although they need not be to the fabric of the home (*CIS 264/1993*, paras 15 and 16).

Subparagraph (a)

Unlike its social security counterpart, this sub-paragraph does not cover sinks.

Subparagraph (k)

The improvements must be made with a view to improving the home's fitness for occupation, which is wider than fitness for habitation and would cover access to the premises (*R(SB) 3/87*, para 10). The improvement must not be viewed from either a subjective or an objective viewpoint, but overall in the broadest possible terms. The tribunal should balance the advantage of the improvement to the person carrying it out against the consequences viewed objectively. An extension to accommodate a large, young family, for example, would be reasonable, despite the fact that it was not reflected in any comparable increase in the value of the property, whereas a similar extension built when most of the family were about to leave home would not be (*CIS 453/1993*, para 8).

Paragraph 2A

"Improvements" bears its ordinary meaning (*CCS 349/1997*, para 10.1).

Paragraph 3

The terms of this paragraph are useful not only in their own right but also for the light they shed on the scope of some of the subparagraphs in paragraph 1. It makes special provision for the purposes of calculating exempt income by extending the eligible housing costs under para 1 to include capital repayments and endowment policy premiums in so far as they cover the capital repayments. Where the policy is designed to produce a profit as well as to cover the capital (eg, in a with profits endowment or a pension mortgage), the part of the premiums necessarily incurred for the purpose of discharging a mortgage or charge should be identifiable by expert evidence. Where this is not possible or the evidence is not available, 0.0277 per cent of the sum secured is used as the eligible housing cost. This figure is sufficient to ensure that the capital would be covered assuming an annual rate of return of 8 per cent over 25 years. Payments of arrears or voluntary additional payments of capital are not covered, nor is the cost of insurance against loss of or damage to the building or land.

This paragraph, like para 1, is limited to costs incurred for the provision of a home or for repairs or improvements to it (*CCS 12/1994*, para 43).

This paragraph is not restricted to policies that are obtained at a time when the mortgage to be secured has already been obtained (*CCS 1321/1997*, para 13).

In *CCS 2750/1995* (para 18), the commissioner held that subpara (4) applied to term assurances while subpara (5) applied to endowment policies. He held that both types of policy, if taken out and retained for the purpose of discharging the loan, were allowable, although the reason for the retention of both policies would require investigation in order to be sure that they were being retained for the specified purpose. With respect to the commissioner, it is doubtful whether his analysis of the relationship of these two subparagraphs is correct. It is suggested that subpara (4) is the general provision which catches any type of assurance or insurance, while subpara (5) provides for a limit on the amount where there is a with-profits element in the arrangement. This does not, however, detract from the need to investigate any apparent over-provision in the finance arrangements. Without expressing a concluded opinion on the point, the commissioner in *CCS 2750/1995* (para 29) said that where only a proportion of a loan is eligible as housing costs, the allowable portion will determine whether the case falls under head (a) or (b).

Subparagraph (2)

This covers an equitable mortgage by deposit of title deeds or certificate (*CCS 9/1995*, para 12). It covers payments which are not fixed at the outset but are subsequently provided for by variation or novation (*ibid*, para 17).

Subparagraphs (4) and (5)

There is no need for the policy to be tied to the mortgage or charge as part of an endowment mortgage. An endowment policy taken out for the purpose of discharging early a repayment mortgage (eg, an arrangement made by a person in poor health in order to avoid the high life premiums involved in an endowment mortgage) is within the wording of these paragraphs with the result that both the premiums on the policy and the capital repayments under the mortgage are eligible housing costs for the purpose of exempt income.

The purpose of the policy must be the discharge of the mortgage or charge. It is not sufficient for the purpose to be to reduce the outstanding capital, as it is only when the whole of the balance of the loan is repaid that the mortgage or charge will be discharged.

In the case of a mortgage which is part repayment and part endowment, the endowment element is within these paragraphs as it is intended that the policy will discharge the outstanding balance at the date of maturity.

The amendment to subpara (4) is made "for the avoidance of doubt" which shows that it is retrospective in its effect. However, in its terms it only applies to policies which secure payment of monies due under the mortgage or charge. The words "monies due" are in contrast to "discharging the mortgage or charge" and suggest that the amendment applies to periodical payments only. Policies which provide for repayment of the capital were considered in *R(CS) 10/98*. This case concerned an assessment for a period before the amendment came into force. The policy concerned was one which secured the payment of all or part of the mortgage capital in the event of death or serious illness. The commissioner held, at para 18, that this fell within the subparagraph as it stood at the relevant time. He did not mention the amendment, nor did he consider whether or not it was necessary, as is suggested above, for the policy to provide for the payment of all, rather than merely part, of the sum secured.

Subparagraph (5B)

The words "personal pension plan" are not defined. The words "personal pension scheme" are used elsewhere in these Regulations, so the choice of different wording must be significant. Technically, a personal pension plan could not be made under the pre-1988 legislation. However, it would be anomalous if this subparagraph were interpreted to exclude these earlier arrangements. Accordingly, it is suggested that the words should be interpreted generally and not limited to any technical meaning.

The plan must have been obtained and retained for the purpose of discharging a mortgage or charge. That purpose need not have been an absolute one, as it is the nature of things that a person might well wish to have as large a pension as possible and intend to resort to the plan only if some other source of finance was not available.

Subparagraph (6)(a)

This provision may not cover the type of mortgage considered in *CIS 141/1993* where the mortgagor had the option at each interest rate increase of continuing with the existing level of payments, with the capital being increased and the term of the mortgage extended. In such a case there are never arrears owing under the terms of the mortgage.

Paragraph 4(1)

This subparagraph lays down three conditions all of which must be satisfied in order for the housing costs to be eligible for child support purposes. First, the costs must be necessarily incurred for the purchasing, renting or otherwise securing the possession of the home or carrying out repairs and improvements to it. The requirement of necessity must be interpreted and applied sensibly with appropriate regard to the realities of property acquisition and of the mortgage market (*Pabari v Secretary of State for Work and Pensions* [2005] 1 All ER 287). The costs must relate to the parent's own home; costs which are met, for example, in respect of the home of a relative or a divorced spouse are not covered. In *CCS 2750/1995* (para 14), the commissioner held that the former version of this head was concerned solely with limiting eligible housing costs to the home of the parent concerned. Clearly in its present form it has a wider function of additionally emphasising the essential purpose of the expenditure. Second, the parent or a member of the parent's family must be responsible for them. It is clear from para 4(1)(c) and (2) that what matters is legal responsibility rather than a voluntary assumption of payment. However, in two cases persons are treated as responsible for costs which they are not legally liable to meet: see subpara (2). What matters is legal liability and not whether the person liable is paying the costs. It will not be unusual, for example, for spouses or partners to be jointly and severally liable on a mortgage but for the payments to be met by only one of them. Third, the liability must be to someone who is not a member of the same household. This goes some way to prevent collusion between members of a household. It may be possible for parties to arrange their affairs so that there are separate households, and tribunals will need to be astute to distinguish genuine arrangements which do result in separate households, even if those arrangements are made in order to fall within subpara (1), and shams.

In order to amount to an eligible housing cost the payment must be made in respect of the provision of the home under para 1 above and must additionally fall within the terms of head (a) of this subparagraph. The terms used in para 1 and head (a) are narrower than "acquiring an interest in the dwelling" which is the equivalent phrase in income support law. The meaning of "provision of a home" was discussed in *R(CS) 12/98* (paras 9-14). According to that decision it covers the initial acquisition of the person's interest in the home and matters which serve to preserve the home, such as repairs and improvements to it. Whether or not it covers the acquisition of a higher or further interest in the home (eg, the purchase by a lessee of the freehold or the purchase of one joint owner of the other's share) is a matter of degree. For example, in the case of the purchase of the freehold, it will be relevant to consider how long the lease has to run, and in the case of the purchase of a joint owner's interest, it will be relevant to consider how secure the person's occupancy is in view of the possibility of the other owner obtaining an order for sale. This interpretation is reinforced by head (a) which requires that the costs be "necessarily incurred" and uses the phrase "otherwise securing possession of the home" in head (a). However, with respect, it is doubtful whether this interpretation gives sufficient weight to the complexities of the analysis which it requires of the child support officers who will have to implement it. In this respect it is in contrast to the approach taken in *R(CS) 14/98* (para 16) where the commissioner declined to distinguish between living with and staying with, commenting that "it is inconceivable that the Secretary of State intended that such fine distinctions should be drawn when they would, in many cases, be highly contentious. No one could describe this legislation as simple, but it does seem designed to produce fairly clear-cut answers to most cases so that a relatively junior child support officer is able to apply the law."

Where a person is on a low income but has a partner with a higher income which can support the family's relatively high housing costs, the person is treated as responsible for those costs, thereby significantly reducing or even eliminating her/his assessable income, although the costs are met in practice by the partner. This is subject to the possibility of a departure direction.

Paragraph 4(2)

This subparagraph provides for two cases in which persons who are paying housing costs for which they are not liable are treated as if they were responsible for those costs. The first is where the person who is liable is not paying and the parent is making payments in order to continue to live in the home. It must be necessary for the parent to meet the costs in order to continue to live in the home. Failure must therefore put the home at risk. So failure to pay a loan which is not secured on the home will not be sufficient. In practice, even if the loan is secured on the home, eviction for non-payment is a difficult and lengthy process. However, tribunals are likely to regard all cases in which the risk of eviction may arise in the event of non-payment as falling within this head. The typical case covered will be where the parent has been deserted by a former partner who is liable for housing costs but is refusing to pay them. If this is the case then the parent is treated as responsible for the costs. The parent may also be treated as responsible in other cases – eg, if a grandparent was meeting the costs. In these other cases, however, it must be reasonable to treat the parent as liable; no issue of reasonableness arises if the person liable was a former partner. The second case covered is where the parent is sharing housing costs with others who also live in the accommodation of whom at least one is not a close relative is liable or treated as liable for those costs, provided that it is reasonable to treat the parent as sharing the responsibility for the costs. The wording speaks of others in the plural, but by virtue of s6(c) Interpretation Act 1978 this will include the singular. Findings of fact on each element of each case will be necessary and decisions on reasonableness will need to be justified in the reasons for decision.

Subparagraph (2)(a) will apply where a parent is occupying the former joint home in respect of which there is shared liability for the housing costs, but is having to meet the whole of those costs the former partner's share of those costs is not being paid (*CCS 13698/1996*, para 7).

Paragraph 5

This allows costs to be apportioned in cases where premises are used for a dual purpose. However, it only covers cases where there is separate accommodation which is put to each use, such as where living accommodation is connected to retail premises or where a business is run from a distinct and separate part of accommodation. It does not cover cases where a business is run from a part of a person's home which is also used for other purposes, such as a business run from a desk in the corner of the living room.

Paragraph 6

Paragraph 1(a)(i) of each Schedule renders charges for meals (including the preparation of meals or the provision of unprepared food) ineligible as a service charge. Paragraph 6(2) of each Schedule covers charges for heating, hot water, lighting and cooking.

Paragraph 7
In the definition of "close relative", the "step" and "in-law" relationships include appropriate references to civil partners. See s246 Civil Partnership Act 2004 and Schedule para 48 Civil Partnership Act 2004 (Relationships Arising Through Civil Partnership) Order 2005, in force from 5 December 2005.

[¹SCHEDULE 3A
AMOUNT TO BE ALLOWED IN RESPECT OF TRANSFERS OF PROPERTY

Interpretation
  1.–(1)   In this Schedule–
"property" means–
  (a)   a legal estate or an equitable interest in land; or
  (b)   a sum of money which is derived from or represents capital, whether in cash or in the form of a deposit with–
   (i)   the Bank of England;
   (ii)   an authorised institution or an exempted person with the meaning of the Banking act 1987;
   (iii)   a building society incorporated or deemed to be incorporated under the Building Societies Act 1986;
  (c)   any business asset as defined in sub-paragraph (2) (whether in the form of money or an interest in land or otherwise);
  (d)   any policy of insurance which has been obtained and retained for the purposes of providing a capital sum to discharge a mortgage or charge secured upon an estate or interest in land which is also the subject of the transfer (in this Schedule referred to as an endowment policy);
"qualifying transfer" means a transfer of property–
  (a)   which was made in pursuance of a court order made, or a written maintenance agreement executed, before 5th April 1993;
  (b)   which was made between the absent parent and either the parent with care or a relevant child [³or both whether jointly or otherwise including, in Scotland, in common property];
  (c)   which was made at a time when the absent parent and the parent with care were living separate and apart;
  [³(d)   the effect of which is that (subject to any mortgage or charge) the parent with care or relevant child is solely beneficially entitled to the property of which the property transferred forms the whole or part, or the business asset, or the parent with care is beneficially entitled to that property or that asset together with the relevant child or absent parent or both, jointly or otherwise or, in Scotland, in common property, or the relevant child is so entitled together with the absent parent;]
  [³(e)   which was not made for the purpose only of compensating the parent with care either for the loss of a right to apply for, or receive, periodical payments or a capital sum in respect of herself, or for any reduction in the amount of such payments or sum;]
"compensating transfer" means a transfer of property which would be a qualifying transfer (disregarding the requirement of paragraph (e) of the definition of
"qualifying transfer") if it were made by the absent parent, but which is made by the parent with care in favour of the absent parent [³or] relevant child [³or both whether jointly or otherwise including, in Scotland, in common property];
"relevant date" means the date of the making of the court order or the execution of the written maintenance agreement in pursuance of which the qualifying transfer was made.
  (2)   For the purposes of sub-paragraph (1) "business asset" means an asset, whether in the form of money or an interest in land or otherwise which, prior to the date of transfer was used in the course of a trade or business carried on–
  (a)   by the absent parent as a sole trader;
  (b)   by the absent parent in partnership, whether with the parent with care or not;
  (c)   by a close company within the meaning of sections 414 and 415 of the Income and Corporation Taxes Act 1988 in which the absent parent was a participator at the date of the transfer.
  (3)   Where the condition specified in regulation 10(a) is satisfied this Schedule shall apply as if references–
  (a)   to the parent with care were references to the absent parent; and
  (b)   to the absent parent were references to the parent with care.

Evidence to be produced in connection with the allowances for transfers of property
  2.–(1)   Where the absent parent produces to the Secretary of State–
  (a)   contemporaneous evidence in writing of the making of a court order or of the execution of a written maintenance agreement, which requires the relevant person to make qualifying transfer of property;
  (b)   evidence in writing and whether contemporaneous or not as to–
   (i)   the fact of the transfer;
   (ii)   the value of the property transferred at the relevant date;

    (iii)   the amount of any mortgage or charge outstanding at the relevant date,

an amount in respect of the relevant value of the transfer determined in accordance with the following provisions of this Schedule shall be allowed in calculating or estimating the exempt income of the absent parent.

(2)   Where the evidence specified in sub-paragraph (1) is not produced within a reasonable time after the Secretary of State has been notified of the wish of the absent parent that [⁴the Secretary of State] consider the question, [⁴he] shall determine the question on the basis that the relevant value of the transfer is nil.

Consideration of evidence produced by other parent

[⁴3.–(1)   Where an absent parent has notified the Secretary of State that he wishes him to consider whether an amount should be allowed in respect of the relevant value of a qualifying transfer, the Secretary of State shall–

    (a)   give notice to the other parent of that application; and

    (b)   have regard in determining the application to any representations made by the other parent which are received within the period specified in sub-paragraph (2).

(2)   The period specified in this sub-paragraph is one month from the date on which the notice referred to in sub-paragraph (1)(a) above was sent or such longer period as the Secretary of State is satisfied is reasonable in the circumstances of the case.]

Computation of qualifying value–business assets and land

4.–(1)   Subject to paragraph 6, where the property [³transferred] by the absent parent is, or includes, an estate or interest in land, or a business asset, the qualifying value of that estate, interest or asset shall be determined in accordance with the formula–[³

$$QV = \frac{(VP - MCP)}{2} - (VAP - MCR) - VCR$$

where–

QV is the qualifying value,

VP is the value at the relevant date of the business asset or the property of which the estate or interest forms the whole or part, and for the purposes of this calculation it is assumed that the estate, interest or asset held on the relevant date by the absent parent or by the absent parent and the parent with care is held by them jointly in equal shares or, in Scotland, in common property; MCP is the amount of any mortgage or charge outstanding immediately prior to the relevant date on the business asset or on the property of which the estate or interest forms the whole or part;

VAP is the value calculated at the relevant date of the business asset or of the property of which the estate or interest forms the whole or part beneficially owned by the absent parent immediately following the transfer (if any);

MCR is, where immediately after the transfer the absent parent is responsible for discharging a mortgage or charge on the business asset or on the property of which the estate or interest forms the whole or part, the amount calculated at the relevant date which is a proportion of any such mortgage or charge outstanding immediately following the transfer, being the same percentage as VAP bears to that property as a whole; and

VCR is the value of any charge in favour of the absent parent on the business asset or on the property of which the estate or interest forms the whole or part, being the amount specified in the court order or written maintenance agreement in relation to the charge, or the amount of a proportion of the value of the business asset or the property on the relevant date specified in the court order or written maintenance agreement.]

(2)   For the purposes of sub-paragraph (1) the value of an estate or interest in land is to be determined upon the basis that the parent with care and any relevant child, if in occupation of the land, would quit on completion of the sale.

Computation of qualifying value – cash, deposits and endowment policies

5.   Subject to paragraph 6, where the property which is the subject of the qualifying transfer is, or includes–

    (i)   a sum of money whether in cash or in the form of a deposit with the Bank of England, an authorised institution or exempted person within the meaning of the Banking Act 1987, or a building society incorporated or deemed to be incorporated under the Building Societies Act 1986, derived from or representing capital; or

    (ii)   an endowment policy,

the amount of the qualifying value shall be determined by applying the formula–

$$QV = \frac{VT}{2}$$

where–

    (a)   QV is the qualifying value; and

    (b)   VT is the amount of cash, the balance of the account or the surrender value of the endowment policy on the relevant date [³and for the purposes of this calculation it is assumed that the cash, balance or policy held on the relevant date by the absent parent and the parent with care is held by them jointly in equal shares or, in Scotland, in common property.]

Transfers wholly in lieu of periodical payments for relevant child

6. Where the evidence produced in relation to a transfer to, or in respect of, a relevant child, shows expressly that the whole of that transfer was made exclusively in lieu of periodical payments in respect of that child–

(a) in a case to which paragraph 4 applies, [³the qualifying value shall be treated as being twice the qualifying value calculated in accordance with that paragraph]; and

(b) in a case to which paragraph 5 applies, the qualifying value shall be [³treated as being twice the qualifying value calculated in accordance with that paragraph.]

Multiple transfers to related persons

7.–(1) Where there has been more than one qualifying transfer from the absent parent–

(a) to the same parent with care;

(b) to or for the benefit of the same relevant child;

(c) to or for the benefit of two or more relevant children with respect to all of whom the same persons are respectively the parent with care and the absent parent;

or any combination thereof, the relevant value by reference to which the allowance is to be calculated in accordance with paragraph 10 shall be the aggregate of the qualifying transfers calculated individually in accordance with the preceding paragraphs of this Schedule, less the value of any compensating transfer or where there has been more than one, the aggregate of the values of the compensating transfers so calculated.

(2) Except as provided by sub-paragraph (1), the values of transfers shall not be aggregated for the purposes of this Schedule.

Computation of the value of compensating transfers

8. [²Subject to paragraph 8A, the value of] a compensating transfer shall be determined in accordance with paragraph 4 to 7 above, but as if any reference in those paragraphs–

(a) to the absent parent were a reference to the parent with care;

(b) to the parent with care were a reference to the absent parent; and

(c) to a qualifying transfer were a reference to a compensating transfer.

[²**8A.**–(1) This paragraph applies where–

(a) the property which is the subject of a compensating transfer is or includes cash or deposits as defined in paragraph 5(i);

(b) that property was acquired by the parent with care after the relevant date;

(c) the absent parent has no legal interest in that property;

(d) if that property is or includes cash obtained by a mortgage or charge, that mortgage or charge was executed by the parent with care after the relevant date and was of property to the whole of which she is legally entitled; and

(e) the effect of the compensating transfer is that the parent with care or a relevant child is beneficially entitled (subject to any mortgage or charge) to the whole of the absent parent's legal estate in the land which is the subject of the qualifying transfer.]

(2) Where sub-paragraph (1) applies, the qualifying value of the compensating transfer shall be the amount of the cash or deposits transferred pursuant to the court order or written maintenance agreement referred to in head (a) of the definition of "qualifying transfer" in paragraph 1(1).

Computation of relevant value of a qualifying transfer

9. The relevant value of a qualifying transfer shall be calculated by deducting from the qualifying value of the qualifying transfer the qualifying value of any compensating transfer between the same persons as are parties to the qualifying transfer.

Amount to be allowed in respect of a qualifying transfer

10. For the purposes of regulation 9(1)(bb), the amount to be allowed in the computation of E, or in case where regulation 10(a) applies, F, shall be–

(a) where the relevant value calculated in accordance with paragraph 9 is less than £5,000, nil;

(b) where the relevant value calculated in accordance with paragraph 9 is at least £5,000, but less than £10,000, £20.00 per week;

(c) where the relevant value calculated in accordance with paragraph 9 is at least £10,000, but less than £25,000, £40.00 per week;

(d) where the relevant value calculated in accordance with paragraph 9 is not less than £25,000, £60.00 per week.

11. this schedule in its application to Scotland shall have effect as if–

(a) in paragraph 1 for the words "legal estate or equitable interest in land" [³and in head (e) of paragraph 8A(1), for the words "legal estate in the land"] there were substituted the words "an interest in land within the meaning of section 2(6) of the Conveyancing and Feudal Reform (Scotland) Act 1970";

(b) in paragraph 4 the word "estate," and the words "estate or" in each place where they respectively occur were omitted.

[³(c) in paragraphs 1, 2, 4 and 8A for the word "mortgage" there were substituted the words "heritable security"]]

Amendments

1. Child Support and Income Support (Amendment) Regulations 1995 (SI 1995 No.1045) reg 57 and Sch 2 (April 18, 1995).
2. Child Support (Miscellaneous Amendments) (No.2) Regulations 1995 (SI 1995 No.3261) reg 48(1) and (2) (December 18, 1995)
3. Child Support (Miscellaneous Amendments) Regulations 1999 (SI 1999 No.977) reg 6(7) (April 6, 1999).
4. Social Security Act 1998 (Commencement No.7 and Consequential and Transitional Provisions) Order 1999 (SI 1999 No.1510) art 21(a) and (b) (June 1, 1999).

General Note

This Schedule makes provision for clean break settlements under court orders or written agreements made before the coming into force of the child support scheme. It provides for an allowance to be made in the absent parent's exempt income calculation based on a sliding scale which is fixed as follows. In the case of settlements expressly made solely in substitution for maintenance payments for a relevant child, the whole of the capital value is taken into account. In other cases, only half the capital value is used. Where the asset is an interest in land or a business asset which is mortgaged or charged, only the difference between the value of the asset and the outstanding principal secured is taken into account. Transfers from a parent with care to the absent parent are offset. The relevant value is that at the date of the order or agreement.

Paragraph 1

"property" The scope of the definition of property is limited. It does not include, for example, shares. Nor does it include cases where one party has conferred a benefit on the other by assuming responsibility for debts, such as mortgage debts.

"qualifying transfer" A qualifying transfer is one made between the absent parent and either the parent with care or a child. Accordingly, if the person with care is not a parent of the child (eg, a grandparent or a subsequent partner of one of the parents), the provisions of this Schedule can only apply if the settlement was between the absent parent and the child.

"court order" and *"written maintenance agreement"* See the general note to s18 of the 1995 Act. It is arguable that in this context "written maintenance agreement" is not limited to agreements which fall within s9(1) of the Act, as this would introduce an irrelevant and unnecessary limitation on the agreements that are covered by this Schedule.

In construing an order or agreement it is permissible to have regard to evidence contained in another document, such as a side letter, which is intended to contain terms of the arrangement (*CCS 16518/1996*, para 7). In the case of a consent order, it is appropriate to interpret the undertakings and the orders of the court as a single whole, because the settlement was negotiated as a package (*CCS 316/1998*, para 19).

"executed" This word is ambiguous. It is used in relation to agreements to mean either made or performed. It is suggested that the more natural meaning of the word is the former (*Terrapin International Ltd v Inland Revenue Commissioners* [1976] 2 All ER 461). Moreover, interpreting "executed" to mean the performance rather than the making of a written agreement would produce the anomaly that the relevant date for a transfer under a court order would be the date that order was made, whereas if the transfer were pursuant to a written agreement, the relevant date would be the date of the transfer.

"asset" It is important to identify clearly the asset being transferred.

"expressly for the purpose only of compensating" In deciding whether or not the specified purpose is expressed, the order or agreement is to be read as a whole (*CCS 16518/1996*, para 12(3) and *CCS 316/1998*, para 19).

The following are irrelevant: (i) subjective evidence of intention or motive; (ii) speculation or inference; (iii) calculations of who may have derived some direct or indirect benefit; (iv) any incidental benefit to a child, such as going on living at the family home after the transfer; (v) any mere statement of intention not affecting the actual interest taken or the terms on which the property is held, such as the standard certificate to postpone a legal aid charge, that the house is to be used by the parent with care as a home for herself or her dependants. See *R(CS) 9/99*, para 15. The preservation of even a right to a nominal sum by way of maintenance for the other party prevents the transfer being a qualifying one (*CCS 16518/1996*, paras 9 and 15).

"loss" This includes the partial loss of a right (*CCS 1554/1997*, para 6 and *R(CS) 9/99*, para 22).

"any right to apply" There are conflicting decisions by commissioners on whether the reference to the loss of any right to apply for periodical payments or a capital sum means the loss of all right to apply (*CCS 16518/1996*, para 12(1)) or the loss of a right to apply (*R(CS) 9/99*, para 19). The question was left open in *CCS 1554/1997* (para 6).

An Edinburgh-based commissioner decided that para 1(1)(e) can never be satisfied when the transfer is made in implementation of a Court decree (*CSCS 1/1998* and *CSCS 2/1998*). The commissioner left open the position in the case of a written agreement (*ibid*, para 13).

Paragraph 5

It is suggested that "money ... derived from ... capital" includes interest which has accrued to that money by the relevant date, namely, the date of the court order or the execution of the written maintenance agreement. This will catch, for example, interest earned on money which is raised from the sale, during the parties' divorce, of the former matrimonial home, but held on deposit in a bank account pending final resolution of the financial settlement.

[¹SCHEDULE 3B
AMOUNT TO BE ALLOWED IN RESPECT OF TRAVELLING COSTS

Interpretation

1.   In this Schedule–

"day" means, in relation to a person who attends at a work place for one period of work which commences before midnight of one day and concludes the following day, the first of those days;

"journey" means a single journey, and "pair of journeys" means two journeys in opposing directions, between the same two places;

"relevant employment" means an employed earner's employment in which the relevant person is employed and in the course of which he is required to attend at a work place, and "relevant employer" means the employer of the relevant person in that employment;

"relevant person" means–

(a)   in the application of the provisions of this Schedule to regulation 9, the absent parent or the parent with care; and

(b)   in the application of the provisions of this Schedule to regulation 11, the absent parent;

[⁴"straight-line distance" means the straight-line distance measured in kilometres and calculated to 2 decimal places, and, where that distance is not a whole number of kilometres, rounded to the nearest whole number of kilometres, a distance which exceeds a whole number of kilometres by 0.50 of a kilometre being rounded up;]

"travelling costs" means the cost of–

(a)   purchasing either fuel or a ticket for the purposes of travel;

(b)   contributing to the costs borne by a person other than a relevant employer in providing transport; or

(c)   paying another to provide transport,

which are incurred by the relevant person in travelling between the relevant person's home and his work place, and where he has more than one relevant employment between any of his work places in those employment's;

"work place" means the relevant person's normal place of employment in a relevant employment, and "deemed work place" means a place which has been selected by the [³Secretary of State] pursuant either to paragraph 8(2) or 15(2) for the purpose of calculating the amount to be allowed in respect of the relevant person's traveling costs.

Computation of amount allowable in respect of travelling costs

2.   For the purpose of regulation 9 and regulation 11 an amount in respect of the travelling costs of the relevant person shall be determined in accordance with the following provisions of this Schedule if the relevant person–

(a)   has travelling costs; and

(b)   provides the information required to enable the amount of the allowance to be determined.

Computation in cases where there is one relevant employment and one work place in that employment

3.   Subject to paragraphs 21 to 23, where the relevant person has one relevant employment and is normally required to attend at only one work place in the course of that employment the amount to be allowed in respect of travelling costs shall be determined in accordance with paragraphs 4 to 7 below.

4.   there shall be calculated or, if that is impracticable, estimated–

(a)   the straight-line distance between the relevant person's home and his work place;

(b)   the number of journeys between the relevant person's home and his work place which he makes during a period comprising a whole number of weeks which appears to the [³Secretary of State] to be representative of his normal pattern of work, there being disregarded any pair of journeys between his work place and his home and where the first journey is from his work place to his home and where the time which elapses between the start of the first journey and the conclusion of the second is not more than two hours.

5.   the results of the calculation or estimate produced by sub-paragraph (a) of paragraph 4 shall be multiplied by the result of the calculation or estimate required by sub-paragraph (b) of that paragraph.

6.   The product of the multiplication required by paragraph 5 shall be divided by the number of weeks in the period.

7.   Where the result of the division required by paragraph 6 is less than or equal to [⁴240], the amount to be allowed in respect of the relevant person's travelling costs shall be nil, and where it is greater than [⁴240] the weekly allowance to be made in respect of the relevant person's travelling costs shall be [⁴6 pence] multiplied by the number by which that number exceeds [⁴240].

Computation in cases where there is more than one work place but only one relevant employment

8.–(1)   Subject to sub-paragraph (2) and paragraphs 21 to 23 below, where the relevant person has one relevant employment but attends at more than one work place the amount to be allowed in respect of travelling costs for the purposes of regulations 9 and 11 shall be determined in accordance with paragraphs 9 to [⁴14].

(2)   Where it appears that the relevant person works at more than one work place but his pattern of work is not sufficiently regular to enable the calculation of the amount to be allowed in respect of his travelling costs to be made readily, the [³Secretary of State] may–
  (a)   select a place which is either one of the relevant person's work places or some other place which is connected with the relevant employment; and
  (b)   apply the provisions of paragraphs 4 to 7 above to actuate the amount of the allowance to be made in respect of travelling costs upon the basis that the relevant person makes one journey form his home to the deemed work place and one journey from the deemed work place to his home on each day on which he attends at a work place in connection with relevant employment,
and the provisions of paragraphs 9 to [⁴14] shall not apply.

(3)   For the purposes of sub-paragraph (2)(b) there shall be disregarded any day upon which the relevant person attends at a work place and in order to travel to or from that work place he undertakes a journey in respect of which–
  (a)   the travelling costs are borne wholly or in part by the relevant employer; or
  (b)   the relevant employer provides transport for any part of the journey for the use of the relevant person,
and where he attends at more than one work place on the same day that day shall be disregarded only if the condition specified in this sub-paragraph is satisfied in respect of all the work places at which he attends on that day.

9.   There shall be calculated, or if that is impracticable, estimated–
  (a)   the straight-line distances between the relevant person's home and each work place; and
  (b)   the straight-line distances between each of the relevant person's work places, other than those between which the does not ordinarily travel.

10.   Subject to paragraph 11, there shall be calculated for each pair of places referred to in paragraph 9 the number of journeys which the relevant person makes between them during a period comprising a whole number of weeks which appears to the [³Secretary of State] to be representative of the normal working pattern of the relevant person.

11.   For the purposes of the calculation required by paragraph 10 there shall be disregarded–
  (a)   any pair of journeys between the same work place and the relevant person's home where the first journey is from his work place to his home and the time which elapses between the start of the first journey and the conclusion of the second is not more than two hours; and
  (b)   any journey in respect of which–
    (i)   the travelling costs are borne wholly or in part by the relevant employer; or
    (ii)   the relevant employer provides transport for any part of the journey for the use of the relevant person.

12.   The result of the calculation of the number of journeys made between each pair of places required by paragraph 10 shall be multiplied by the result of the calculation or estimate of the straight-line distance between them required by paragraph 9.

13.   All the products of the multiplication's required by paragraph 12 shall be added together and the resulting sum divided by the number of weeks in the period.

14.   Where the result of the division required by paragraph 13 is less than or equal to [⁴240], the amount to be allowed in respect of travelling costs shall be nil, and where it is greater than [⁴240], the weekly allowance to be made in respect of the relevant person's traveling costs shall be [⁴6 pence]multiplied by the number by which that number excess [⁴240].

Computation in cases where there is more than one relevant employment
  15.–(1)   Subject to sub-paragraph (2) and paragraphs 21 to 23, where the relevant person has more than one relevant employment the amount to be allowed in respect of travelling costs for the purposes of regulations 9 and 11 shall be determined in accordance with paragraphs 16 to 20.

(2)   Where it appears that in respect of any of his relevant employment's, whilst the relevant person works at more than one work place, his pattern of work is not sufficiently regular to enable the actuation of the amount to be allowed in respect of his traveling costs to be made readily, the [³Secretary of State]–
  (a)   may select a place which is either one of the relevant person's work places in that relevant employment or some other place which is connected with that relevant employment;
  (b)   may calculate the weekly average distance travelled in the course of his journeys made in connection with the relevant employment upon the basis that–
    (i)   the relevant person makes one journey from his home, or form another work place or deemed work place in another relevant employment, to the deemed work place and one journey from the deemed work place to his home, or to another work place or deemed work place in another relevant employment, on each day on which he attends at a work place in connection with the relevant employment in relation to which the deemed work place has been selected, and
    (ii)   the distance he travels between those places is the straight-line distance between them; and
  (c)   shall disregard any journeys made between work places in the relevant employment in respect of which a deemed work place has been selected.

(3)   For the purposes of sub-paragraph (2)(b) there shall be disregarded any day upon which the relevant person attends at a work place and in order to travel to or from that work place he undertakes a journey in respect of which–
(a)   the travelling costs are borne wholly or in part by the relevant employer; or
(b)   the relevant employer provides transport for any part of the journey for the use of the relevant person,
and where in the course of the particular relevant employment he attends at more than one work place on the same day, that day shall be disregarded only if the condition specified in this paragraph is satisfied in respect of all the work places at which he attends on that day in the course of that employment.

16.   there shall be calculated, or if that is impracticable, estimated–
(a)   the straight-line distances between the relevant person's home and each work place; and
(b)   the straight-line distances between each of the relevant person's work places, except–
    (i)   those between which he does not ordinarily travel, and
    (ii)   those for which a calculation of the distance from the relevant person's home is not required by virtue of paragraph 15(c).

[²**17.**   Subject to paragraph 17A, there shall be calculated, or if that is impracticable estimated, for each pair of places referred to in paragraph 16 between which straight-line distances are required to be calculated or estimated, the number of journeys which the relevant person makes between them during a period comprising a whole number of weeks which appears to the [³Secretary of State] to be representative of the normal working pattern of the relevant person.

17A.   For the purposes of the calculation required by paragraph 17, there shall be disregarded-
(a)   any pair of journeys between the same work place and his home where the first journey is from his work place to his home and the time which elapses between the start of the first journey and the conclusion of the second is not more than two hours; and
(b)   any journey in respect of which–
    (i)   the travelling costs are borne wholly or in part by the relevant employer; or
    (ii)   the relevant employer provides transport for any part of the journey for the use of the relevant person.]

18.   The result of the calculation or estimate of the number of journeys made between each pair of places required by paragraph 17 shall be multiplied by the result of the calculation or estimate of the straight-line distance between them required by paragraph 16.

19.   All the products of the multiplication's required by paragraph 18, shall be added together and the resulting sum divided by the number of weeks in the period.

20.   Where the result of the division required by paragraph 19, plus where appropriate the result of the calculation required by paragraph 15 in respect of a relevant employment in which a deemed work place has been selected, is less than or equal to [⁴240] the amount to be allowed in respect of travelling costs shall be nil, and where it is greater than [⁴240] the weekly allowance to be made in respect of the relevant person's travelling costs shall be [⁴6 pence] multiplied by the number by which that number exceeds [⁴240].

Relevant employments in respect of which no amount is to be allowed

21.–(1)   No allowance shall be made in respect of travelling costs in respect of journeys between the relevant person's home and his work place or between his work place and his home in a particular relevant employment if the condition set out in paragraph 22 or 23 is satisfied in respect of that employment.

(2)   The condition mentioned in paragraph 22, or as the case may be 23, is satisfied in relation to a case where the relevant person has more than one work place in a relevant employment only where the employer provides assistance of the kind mentioned in that paragraph in respect of all of the work places to or from which the relevant person travels in the course of that employment, but those journeys in respect of which that assistance is provided shall be disregarded in computing the total distance traveled by the relevant person in the course of the relevant employment.

22.   The condition is that the relevant employer provides transport of any description in connection with the employment which is available to the relevant person for any part of the journey between his home and his work place or between his work place and his home.

23.   The condition is that the relevant employer bears any part of the travelling costs arising from the relevant person travelling between his home and his work place or between his work place and his home in connection with that employment, and for the purposes of this paragraph he does not bear any part of that cost where he does no more than–
(a)   make a payment to the relevant person which would fall to be taken into account in determining the amount of the relevant person's net income;
(b)   make a loan to the relevant person;
(c)   pay to the relevant person an increased amount of remuneration,
to enable the relevant person to meet those costs himself.]

Amendments
1.   Child Support and Income Support (Amendment) Regulations 1995 (SI 1995 No.1045) reg 57 and Sch 2 (April 18, 1995).
2.   Child Support (Miscellaneous Amendments) (No.2) Regulations 1995 (SI 1995 No.3261) reg 49 (January 22, 1996).

3.	Social Security Act 1998 (Commencement No.7 and Consequential and Transitional Provisions) Order 1999 (SI 1999 No.1510) art 22 (June 1, 1999).
4.	Child Support (Miscellaneous Amendments) Regulations 2004 (SI 2004 No.2415) reg 5(4) (September 16, 2004).

General Note

This Schedule provides for allowance to be made in a parent's exempt income and in an absent parent's protected income in respect of costs of travelling between home and work. To qualify the parent must actually incur travelling costs. No sum is allowed, for example, if the parent walks or cycles to work or is taken by a relative or friend free of charge. If a parent does have travelling costs, an allowance is made. It is calculated or estimated by reference to the straight-line distance between home and work place and is based on the travel in a normal week. Straight-line measurement is the method which, by virtue of s8 Interpretation Act 1978, would be applied unless the contrary intention appears. The express reference to this method of measurement avoids any argument that there was a contrary intention. Return journeys from work to home and back to work (eg, for a meal or between shifts) are ignored if the return home lasts for two hours or less. The existence of physical obstructions, such as mountain ranges and river estuaries, is ignored as is the actual distance by road or rail. Where a parent has more than one employer or more than one work place, the decision maker may deem one of them or some other connected place to be the place of work for the purpose of the calculation or estimate. No travelling costs are allowed if the employer provides transport for all or part of the journey or contributes toward the travelling costs, but no contribution is deemed to occur if the employer's sole contribution towards the costs of travel comprises a payment which would be taken into account in calculating net income, a loan or increased pay.

The calculation of distances is made by a computer program based on postcodes. If this issue arises on appeal, the tribunal will need to be satisfied on appropriate evidence of the following matters.
(i)	The decision maker will have to prove the accuracy of the computer program.
(ii)	The postcodes of the parent's home and place of work will need to be established.
(iii)	It will have to be shown that the correct codes were put into the program, and the output from the program on the basis of that input will have to be shown. The tribunal will also need to bear in mind the following factors which may affect the relevance of the outcome of the program to the case under appeal.
(iv)	The postcode may, especially in a rural location, cover a fairly large area.
(v)	A postcode is only provided for buildings to which mail is delivered. Some employers will have mail delivered to a central location or to a Post Office Box number with the result that a person's particular place of work may not have a postcode and may be some distance away from the building to which the postcode applies.
Finally, the tribunal will need to bear in mind two further factors.
(vi)	There is no basis in the legislation for the calculation of distance by reference to postcodes, so the tribunal may calculate the relevant distance by any means that will produce a sufficiently accurate result.
(vii)	The tribunal will only need to concern itself with arguments over the accuracy of the decision maker's calculation if the degree of error is likely to affect the ultimate decision.

SCHEDULE 4
CASES WHERE CHILD SUPPORT MAINTENANCE IS NOT TO BE PAYABLE

The payments and awards specified for the purposes of regulation 26(1)(b)(i) are–
(a)	the following payments under the Contribution and Benefits Act–
	[²(i)	incapacity benefit under section 30A;
	(ii)	long-term incapacity benefit for widows under section 40;
	(iii)	long-term incapacity benefit for widowers under section 41;]
	(iv)	maternity allowance under section 35;
	(v)	[² . . .];
	(vi)	attendance allowance under section 64;
	(vii)	severe disablement allowance under section 68;
	(viii)	[⁴carer's allowance] under section 70;
	(ix)	disability living allowance under section 71;
	(x)	disablement benefit under section 103;
	(xi)	[⁵ . . .]
	(xii)	statutory sick pay within the meaning of section 151;
	(xiii)	statutory maternity pay within the meaning of section 164;
(b)	awards in respect of disablement made under (or under provisions analogous to)–
	(i)	the War Pensions (Coastguards) Scheme 1944 (S.I. 1944 No. 500);
	(ii)	the War Pensions (Naval Auxiliary Personnel) Scheme 1964 (S.I. 1964 No. 1985);
	(iii)	the Pensions (Polish Forces) Scheme 1964 (S.I. 1964 No. 2007);
	(iv)	the War Pensions (Mercantile Marine) Scheme 1964 (S.I. 1964 No. 2058);
	(v)	the Royal Warrant of 21st December 1964 (service in the Home Guard before 1945) (Cmnd. 2563);

> (vi)   the Order by Her Majesty of 22nd December 1964 concerning pensions and other grants in respect of disablement or death due to service in the Home Guard after 27th April 1952 (Cmnd. 2564);
>
> (vii)   the Order by Her Majesty (Ulster Defence Regiment) of 4th January 1971 (Cmnd. 4567);
>
> (viii) the Personal Injuries (Civilians) Scheme 1983 (S.I. 1983 No. 686);
>
> (ix)   the Naval, Military and Air Forces Etc. (Disablement and Death) Service Pensions Order 1983 (S.I. 1983 No. 883); [6...]
>
> [6(x)   the Armed Forces (Pensions and Compensation) Act 2004; and]
>
> (c)   payments from [1[7the Independent Living (1993) Fund, the Independent Living (Extension) Fund or the Independent Living Fund (2006)]].

Amendments

1.   Child Support (Miscellaneous Amendments) Regulations 1993 (SI 1993 No. 913) reg 34 (April 5, 1993).

2.   Child Support and Income Support (Amendment) Regulations 1995 (SI 1995 No.1045) reg 58 (April 13, 1995).

3.   Social Security and Child Support (Tax Credits) Consequential Amendments Regulations 1999 (SI 1999 No.2566) reg 2(2) and Sch 2, Part II (October 5, 1999).

4.   Child Support (Miscellaneous Amendments) Regulations 2003 (SI 2003 No.328) reg 6(8)(a) (April 1, 2003).

5.   Child Support (Miscellaneous Amendments) Regulations 2003 (SI 2003 No.328) reg 6(8)(b) (April 6, 2003).

6.   Child Support (Miscellaneous Amendments) Regulations 2005 (SI 2005 No.785) reg 4(4) (March 16, 2005).

7.   Independent Living Fund (2006) Order 2007 (SI 2007 No.2538) reg 3(3) (October 1, 2007).

Definitions

"Contributions and Benefits Act": see reg 1(2).
"Independent Living (1993) Fund": see reg 1(2).
"Independent Living (Extension) Fund": see reg 1(2).

[1SCHEDULE 5
PROVISIONS APPLYING TO CASES TO WHICH SECTION 43 OF THE ACT AND REGULATION 28 APPLY

[2 . . .]

9.   The provisions of paragraphs (1) and (2) of regulation 5 of the Child Support (Collection and Enforcement) Regulations 1992 shall apply to the transmission of payments in place of payments of child support maintenance under section 43 of the Act and regulation 28 as they apply to the transmission of payments of child support maintenance.

Amendments

1.   Child Support (Miscellaneous Amendments) Regulations 1993 (SI 1993 No.913) reg 26(3) (April 5, 1993).

2.   Social Security Act 1998 (Commencement No.7 and Consequential and Transitional Provisions) Order 1999 (SI 1999 No.1510) art 23 (June 1, 1999).

Definition

"the Act": see reg 1(2).